Time Saving
AIR FRYER
COOKBOOK
For BEGINNERS

*Quick, Easy & Healthy
Recipes for Busy People*

TABLE OF CONTENTS

INTRODUCTION — 5

RECIPE INDEX

- 1 - Moon Pie
- 2 - Brownies For Two
- 3 - Banana Chips With Chocolate Glaze
- 4 - Cinnamon Canned Biscuit Donuts
- 5 - Dark Chocolate Cake
- 6 - Grilled Banana Boats
- 7 - Shortbread Fingers
- 8 - Lemon Iced Donut Balls
- 9 - Mini Crustless Peanut Butter Cheesecake
- 10 - Chocolate Lava Cakes
- 11 - Delicious Vanilla Custard
- 12 - Apple Pie Crumble
- 13 - Pumpkin Pie-spiced Pork Rinds
- 14 - Party S'mores
- 15 - Monkey Bread
- 16 - Crunchy Roasted Potatoes
- 17 - Peanut Cookies
- 18 - Nutella And Banana Pastries
- 19 - Baked Apple
- 20 - Cinnamon Roasted Pumpkin
- 21 - Cinnamon Apple Chips
- 22 - Lemon Tempeh
- 23 - Cream Cheese Shortbread Cookies
- 24 - Cool Mini Zucchini's
- 25 - Keto Butter Balls
- 26 - Roasted Asparagus
- 27 - Roasted Brussels Sprouts With Bacon
- 28 - Ginger Turmeric Chicken Thighs
- 29 - Delicious Spiced Apples
- 30 - Cheesy Garlic Bread
- 31 - Almond Green Beans
- 32 - Chipotle Drumsticks
- 33 - Chocolate Doughnut Holes
- 34 - Baked Jalapeño And Cheese Cauliflower Mash
- 35 - Easy Green Bean Casserole
- 36 - Garlic Parmesan Drumsticks
- 37 - Fried Oreos
- 38 - Spicy Roasted Potatoes
- 39 - Buttered Garlic Broccolini
- 40 - Barbecue Chicken Drumsticks
- 41 - Cocoa Bombs
- 42 - Crunchy Green Beans
- 43 - Potato Wedges
- 44 - Chicken Wrapped In Bacon
- 45 - Easy Mug Brownie
- 46 - Garlic Knots
- 47 - Sweet Potato Fries
- 48 - Chipotle Aioli Wings
- 49 - Strawberry Cups
- 50 - "faux-tato" Hash
- 51 - Parmesan Garlic Fries
- 52 - Crispy Italian Chicken Thighs
- 53 - Coconut Macaroons
- 54 - Balsamic Green Beans With Bacon
- 55 - Roasted Fennel Salad
- 56 - Gingered Chicken Drumsticks
- 57 - Marshmallow Pastries
- 58 - Foil Packet Lemon Butter Asparagus
- 59 - Colorful Vegetable Medley
- 60 - Smoked Halibut And Eggs In Brioche
- 61 - Toasted Coconut Flakes
- 62 - Fingerling Potatoes
- 63 - Cottage And Mayonnaise Stuffed Peppers
- 64 - Almond Flour Battered Wings
- 65 - Nutty Fudge Muffins
- 66 - Roasted Heirloom Carrots With Orange And Thyme
- 67 - Black Bean And Rice Burrito Filling
- 68 - Green Bean Sautée
- 69 - Grits Again
- 70 - Garlic Parmesan-roasted Cauliflower
- 71 - Roasted Cauliflower
- 72 - Skewered Corn In Air Fryer
- 73 - Cauliflower
- 74 - Polenta
- 75 - Zucchini Topped With Coconut Cream 'n Bacon
- 76 - White Wheat Walnut Bread
- 77 - Taco Okra
- 78 - Rosemary Roasted Potatoes With Lemon
- 79 - Cinnamon Sugar Tortilla Chips
- 80 - Whole-grain Cornbread
- 81 - Bacon-wrapped Asparagus
- 82 - Swiss Chard Mix
- 83 - Spice-rubbed Pork Loin
- 84 - Italian Bruschetta With Mushrooms & Cheese
- 85 - Crispy Green Beans
- 86 - Sweet Butternut Squash
- 87 - Crispy Pierogi With Kielbasa And Onions
- 88 - Honey Tater Tots With Bacon

89 - Perfect Asparagus	90 - Savory Roasted Carrots	91 - Crispy 'n Salted Chicken Meatballs	92 - Smokehouse-style Beef Ribs
93 - Buttery Mushrooms	94 - Bacon-balsamic Brussels Sprouts	95 - Chicken Sausage In Dijon Sauce	96 - Bacon-Wrapped Chicken Breasts
97 - Brussels Sprouts	98 - Southwest-style Corn Cobs	99 - Buffalo Chicken Sandwiches	100 - Effortless Chicken Drumsticks
101 - Spicy Fried Green Beans	102 - Perfect Broccoli	103 - Creamy Onion Chicken	104 - Gambas al Ajillo (Garlic Shrimp)
105 - Roasted Belgian Endive With Pistachios And Lemon	106 - Zucchini Gratin	107 - Buttermilk Brined Turkey Breast	108 - Omelet Bread Cups
109 - Glazed Carrots	110 - Alfredo Eggplant Stacks	111 - Bacon-wrapped Chicken	112 - Zucchini Muffins
113 - Parmesan Asparagus	114 - White Cheddar And Mushroom Soufflés	115 - Teriyaki Chicken Legs	116 - Kiwi Muffins with Pecans
117 - Roasted Broccoli Salad	118 - Lemon Caper Cauliflower Steaks	119 - Chicken Gruyere	120 - Crispy Alfredo Chicken Wings
121 - Roasted Broccoli	122 - Crouton-breaded Pork Chops	123 - Chicken Parmesan Casserole	124 - Crunchy Ranch Chicken Wings
125 - Corn Muffins	126 - Spinach And Provolone Steak Rolls	127 - Fish Sticks	128 - Crispy Chicken Nuggets
129 - Asparagus	130 - Cheddar Bacon Ranch Pinwheels	131 - Almond Topped Trout	132 - Corn-Crusted Chicken Tenders
133 - Roasted Brussels Sprouts	134 - Breaded Air Fryer Pork Chops	135 - Lime Flaming Halibut	136 - Air Fried Asparagus with Romesco Sauce
137 - Pesto Vegetable Kebabs	138 - Rib Eye Steak	139 - Broccoli With Cauliflower	140 - Parmesan Artichoke Hearts
141 - Sesame Seeds Bok Choy	142 - Perfect Grill Chicken Breast	143 - Crustless Spinach And Cheese Frittata	144 - Crunchy Cauliflower Bites
145 - Spinach Pesto Flatbread	146 - Jumbo Buffalo Chicken Meatballs	147 - Chives Omelet	148 - Crispy Yellow Squash Chips
149 - Italian Seasoned Easy Pasta Chips	150 - Pecan-crusted Chicken Tenders	151 - Goat Cheese, Beet, And Kale Frittata	152 - Kielbasa & Mushroom Pierogi
153 - Pesto Vegetable Skewers	154 - Rosemary Partridge	155 - Tomatoes Frittata	156 - Crispy Pepperoni Pizza
157 - Vegetable Nuggets	158 - Yummy Shredded Chicken	159 - Crispy Spiced Chickpeas	160 - Bacon-Wrapped Dates
161 - Savory Herb Cloud Eggs	162 - Parmesan Chicken Tenders	163 - Cheddar Cheese Lumpia Rolls	164 - South Asian Pork Momos
165 - Almond Asparagus	166 - Basic Chicken Breasts	167 - Lamb Chops	168 - Crispy Hasselback Potatoes
169 - Curried Eggplant	170 - Chicken Adobo	171 - Crispy Pork Belly	172 - Sweet Potato Boats
173 - Basil Tomatoes	174 - Garlic Ginger Chicken	175 - Mustard Herb Pork Tenderloin	176 - Roasted Hot Chickpeas
177 - Sweet Pepper Nachos	178 - Cajun-breaded Chicken Bites	179 - Friday Night Cheeseburgers	180 - Roasted Pumpkin Seeds with Cardamom
181 - Crispy Cabbage Steaks	182 - Air Fried Chicken Tenderloin	183 - Balsamic Brussels Sprouts	184 - "Roasted Pumpkin Seeds with Cardamom"
185 - Mediterranean Pan Pizza	186 - 15-minute Chicken	187 - Zucchini-Parmesan Chips	188 - "Traditional Swedish Meatballs"

189 - Pesto Spinach Flatbread	190 - Blackened Chicken Tenders	191 - Onion Rings	192 - "Serbian Pork Skewers with Yogurt Sauce"
193 - Stuffed Portobellos	194 - Pulled Turkey Quesadillas	195 - Herb & Cheese Stuffed Mushrooms	196 - "Veggies & Pork Pinchos"
197 - Falafels	198 - Chicken Cordon Bleu	199 - Classic Zucchini Fries	200 - "Spicy Tricolor Pork Kebabs"
201 - Stuffed Mushrooms	202 - Pretzel-crusted Chicken	203 - Perfect Air Fryer Eggs	204 - "Pork Chops with Mustard-Apricot Glaze"
205 - Toasted Ravioli	206 - Italian Roasted Chicken Thighs	207 - Sweet Garlicky Chicken Wings	208 - "Southeast-Asian Pork Chops"
209 - Bacon With Shallot And Greens	210 - Barbecue Chicken Enchiladas	211 - Turkey Scotch Eggs	212 - "Spicy-Sweet Pork Chops"
213 - " Beef Al Carbon (street Taco Meat)"	214 - Air Fried Cheese Chicken	215 - Air Fried Pork Popcorn Bites	216 - "Juicy Double Cut Pork Chops"
217 - Lamb Koftas Meatballs	218 - Lemon And Thyme Sea Bass	219 - Crispy Fish Finger Sticks	220 - "Bavarian-Style Crispy Pork Schnitzel"
221 - Ground Beef	222 - Maple Butter Salmon	223 - Three Meat Cheesy Omelet	224 - "Beef Koftas in Tomato Sauce"
225 - Baked Chicken Nachos	226 - Thyme Scallops	227 - Japanese-Style Omelet	228 - "Beef Meatballs with Cranberry Sauce"
229 - Quick Chicken For Filling	230 - "Timeless Garlic-lemon Scallops"	231 - Ham & Cheddar Omelet	232 - "South American Arepas with Cilantro Sauce"
233 - Chicken Chunks	234 - Restaurant-style Flounder Cutlets	235 - Spanish Chorizo Frittata	236 - "Healthy Burgers"
237 - Chicken Nuggets	238 - "Italian Baked Cod"	239 - Air Fried Shirred Eggs	240 - "Homemade Hot Beef Satay"
241 - Tilapia Fish Fillets	242 - Fish Taco Bowl	243 - Prosciutto, Mozzarella & Eggs in a Cup	244 - "Garlic Steak with Mexican Salsa"
245 - Blackened Red Snapper	246 - Cod Nuggets	247 - Cheese & Ham Breakfast Egg Cups	248 - "Gorgonzola Rib Eye Steak"
249 - Swordfish With Capers And Tomatoes	250 - Bacon-wrapped Cajun Scallops	251 - Air Fried Sourdough Sandwiches	252 - "Chimichurri New York Steak"
253 - Crispy Parmesan Lobster Tails	254 - Mediterranean-style Cod	255 - Sausage & Egg Casserole	256 - "Parsley Crumbed Beef Strips"
257 - Simple Sesame Squid On The Grill	258 - "Catalan Sardines With Romesco Sauce"	259 - Grilled Tofu Sandwich with Cabbage	260 - Air Fried Beef with Veggies & Oyster Sauce
261 - Crab-stuffed Avocado Boats	262 - Potato-crusted Cod	263 - Air Fried Italian Calzone	264 - "Lamb Meatballs with Roasted Veggie Bake"
265 - Cajun Lobster Tails	266 - Salmon Patties	267 - Italian Sausage Patties	
269 - Herbed Haddock	270 - Italian Shrimp	271 - Blueberry Oat Bars	268 - "Herby Roast Beef"
273 - Spicy Prawns	274 - Air Fried Cod With Basil Vinaigrette	275 - Roasted Asparagus with Serrano Ham	272 - "Beef Liver with Onions"
			276 - "African Minty Lamb Kofta"
277 - Crunchy And Buttery Cod With Ritz Cracker Crust	278 - Crab Cakes	279 - Korean Chili Chicken Wings	280 - "Lamb Chops with Lemony Couscous"
281 - Lobster Tails	282 - Snow Crab Legs	283 - Air-Fried Chicken Thighs	284 - "Easy Lamb Chop Bites"

285 - "Outrageous Crispy Fried Salmon Skin"	286 - Spinach And Artichoke-stuffed Peppers	287 - Chicken & Oat Croquettes	288 - "Lamb Taquitos"
289 - Easy Lobster Tail With Salted Butetr	290 - Crispy Apple Fries With Caramel Sauce	291 - Mexican-Style Air Fryer Nachos	292 - "One-Tray Parmesan Chicken Wings"
293 - Lemon-roasted Salmon Fillets	294 - Lemony Green Beans	295 - Salmon Mini Tarts	296 - "Spanish-Style Crusted Chicken Fingers"
297 - Shrimp Burgers	298 - "Tortilla Pizza Margherita"	299 - Rich Cod Fingers	300 - "Quinoa Chicken Nuggets"
301 - Lime Bay Scallops	302 - Caramelized Carrots	303 - Black Bean & Corn Flatbreads	304 - "San Antonio Taco Chicken Strips"
305 - Lemon Pepper-breaded Tilapia	306 - "Broccoli Salad"	307 - Italian Pork Sausage Pizza	308 - "Crunchy Coconut Chicken Dippers"
309 - "Sea Scallops"	310 - Avocado Rolls	311 - Delicious Chicken Tortillas	312 - Popcorn Chicken Tenders
313 - Shrimp Al Pesto	314 - Effortless Mac 'n' Cheese	315 - Spanish Chorizo with Brussels Sprouts	316 - "Cajun Chicken Tenders"
317 - Tuna Cakes	318 - Garden Fresh Green Beans	319 - Plum & Pancetta Bombs	320 - "Almond-Fried Crispy Chicken"
321 - Garlic And Dill Salmon	322 - Cauliflower Steak With Thick Sauce	323 - Paprika Baked Parsnips	324 - Jerusalem Matzah & Chicken Schnitzels
325 - Bacon-wrapped Scallops	326 - Cheddar Soufflés	327 - Cheesy Mushrooms	328 - "Sweet Curried Chicken Cutlets"
329 - Lemon Butter-dill Salmon	330 - Parsley Egg Scramble With Cottage Cheese	331 - Walnut & Cheese Filled Mushrooms	332 - "Lemony Chicken Breast"
333 - Zesty Mahi Mahi	334 - Parsley Omelet	335 - Chili Edamame	336 - "Chicken Parmigiana with Fresh Rosemary"
337 - Tilapia Teriyaki	338 - Denver Eggs	339 - Easy Parmesan Sandwich	340 - "Spinach Loaded Chicken Breasts"
341 - 5-minute Shrimp	342 - Tuna And Arugula Salad	343 - Spicy Cheese Lings	344 - "Chicken Breasts "En Papillote""
345 - Miso Fish	346 - Bunless Breakfast Turkey Burgers	347 - "Italian Pork Scallopini"	348 - "Ham & Cheese Chicken Breasts"
349 - Shrimp "scampi"	350 - Banana-nut Muffins	351 - "Spicy Sweet Beef with Veggie Topping"	352 - "Restaurant-Style Chicken with Yogurt Sauce"
353 - "Crunchy Coconut Shrimp"	354 - Sausage-crusted Egg Cups	355 - "Thai Roasted Beef"	356 - "Tasty Kiev-Style Chicken"
357 - Bell Peppers Cups	358 - Cheesy Bell Pepper Eggs	359 - "Bloody Mary Beef Steak with Avocado"	360 - "Rosemary & Oyster Chicken Breasts"
361 - Healthy Apple-licious Chips	362 - Roasted Peanuts	363 - "Wiener Beef Schnitzel"	364 - "Chicken Thighs with Herby Tomatoes"
365 - Caprese Eggplant Stacks	366 - Spinach Dip	367 - "Sweet & Sour Lamb Strips"	368 - "Chicken Thighs with Parmesan Crust"
369 - "Breadcrumbs Stuffed Mushrooms"	370 - Savory Ranch Chicken Bites	371 - "Crispy Breaded Chicken Bites"	372 - "Classic Buttermilk Chicken Thighs"
373 - Sweet And Sour Brussel Sprouts	374 - Roasted Chickpeas	375 - "Spiced Chicken Tacos"	376 - Thai Chicken Satay

377 - Strawberry Toast	378 - Beef Taco-stuffed Meatballs	379 - "Rice Krispies Chicken Goujons"	380 - "Chicken Asian Lollipop"
381 - Baked Eggs	382 - Wrapped Smokies In Bacon	383 - "Crispy Chicken Tenders with Hot Aioli"	384 - "Chipotle Buttered Turkey"
385 - "Sweet Potato-cinnamon Toast"	386 - Buffalo Cauliflower Wings	387 - Chicken Fillets with Sweet Chili Adobo	388 - "Crab Fritters with Sweet Chili Sauce"
389 - Hole In One	390 - Asian Five-spice Wings	391 - "Greek Chicken Gyros"	392 - Cod Cornflake Nuggets with Avocado Dip
393 - Pizza Eggs	394 - Bacon-wrapped Jalapeño Poppers	395 - Swiss-Style Breaded Chicken	396 - "Gourmet Black Cod with Fennel & Pecans"
397 - Ham And Egg Toast Cups	398 - Bacon-y Cauliflower Skewers	399 - "Chicken Breasts with Avocado-Mango Salsa"	400 - "Pistachio-Crusted Salmon Fillets"
401 - Zucchini And Spring Onions Cakes	402 - Halloumi Fries	403 - "French-Style Sweet Chicken Breasts"	404 - "Salmon Fillets with Broccoli"
405 - Maple-bacon Doughnuts	406 - Italian Dip	407 - "French-Style Chicken Thighs"	408 - "Smoked Trout Frittata"
409 - Cinnamon Granola	410 - Delicious Cheeseburgers	411 - "Air Fried Chicken Bowl with Black Beans"	412 - "Baked Trout en Papillote with Herbs"
413 - Sweet And Spicy Breakfast Sausage	414 - Stuffed Peppers	415 - Creamy Onion Chicken	416 - "Golden Batter Fried Catfish Fillets"
417 - Seasoned Herbed Sourdough Croutons	418 - Bacon And Blue Cheese Burgers	419 - "Cheesy Marinara Chicken"	420 - "Ale-Battered Fish with Tartar Sauce"
421 - Bagels	422 - Bacon Blue Cheese Burger	423 - Garlicky Chicken Cubes On A Green Bed	424 - "Air Fried Tilapia Bites"
425 - Spinach Spread	426 - Jumbo Italian Meatballs	427 - "Thyme Fried Chicken Legs"	428 - "Sesame Halibut Fillets"
429 - Easy Egg Bites	430 - Pesto Coated Rack Of Lamb	431 - "Thyme Turkey Nuggets"	432 - "Peach Salsa & Beer Halibut Tacos"
433 - Bacon & Hot Dogs Omelet	434 - Bjorn's Beef Steak	435 - Old Bay Crab Sticks with Garlic Mayo	436 - "Brussels Sprouts with Garlic Aioli"
437 - Peppered Maple Bacon Knots	438 - Bacon And Cheese-stuffed Pork Chops	439 - "Sesame Prawns with Firecracker Sauce "	440 - "Zucchini Fries with Tabasco Dip"
441 - Scrambled Eggs	442 - Air Fried Thyme Garlic Lamb Chops	443 - "Ale-Battered Scampi with Tartare Sauce"	444 - "Parmesan Zucchini Boats"
445 - Creamy Parsley Soufflé	446 - Parmesan-crusted Pork Chops	447 - "Louisiana-Style Shrimp"	448 - "Aunt's Roasted Carrots with Cilantro Sauce"
449 - Bacon Eggs	450 - Avocado Egg Rolls	451 - "Spicy Shrimp with Coconut-Avocado Dip"	452 - "Tasty Balsamic Beets"
453 - Tuscan Toast	454 - Hot Air Fried Green Tomatoes	455 - "Rosemary Cashew Shrimp" 459 - Herbed Garlic Lobster	456 - "Chili Corn on the Cob" 460 - "Parmesan Broccoli Bites"
457 - Country Gravy	458 - Mediterranean Bruschetta	463 - "Cod Fillets with Ginger-Cilantro Sauce"	464 - Indian Aloo Tikki
461 - Carrot Chips	462 - "Bikini" Ham & Cheese Sandwich	467 - "American Panko Fish Nuggets "	468 - Charred Broccolini with Lemon-Caper Sauce

469 - Cheese Rounds	470 - Raspberry & Vanilla Pancakes	471 - "Golden Cod Fish Fillets"	472 - "Tomato Sandwiches with Feta & Pesto"
473 - Bacon Candy	474 - Cinnamon French Toast Sticks	475 - Cod Finger Pesto Sandwich	476 - "Vegetable Tortilla Pizza"
477 - Fried Kale Chips	478 - Masala Omelet The Indian Way	479 - "Korean Kimchi-Spiced Salmon"	480 - "Baked Mediterranean Shakshuka"
481 - Garlic-cream Cheese Wontons	482 - Baked Kale Omelet	483 - "Easy Salmon with Greek Sauce"	484 - Traditional Swedish Meatballs
485 - Croutons	486 - Vienna Sausage & Cherry Tomato Frittata	487 - Wild Salmon with Creamy Parsley Sauce	488 - Serbian Pork Skewers with Yogurt Sauce
489 - Mini Greek Meatballs	490 - Buttered Eggs in Hole	491 - "Sweet Caribbean Salmon Fillets"	492 - Pork Chops with Mustard-Apricot Glaze
493 - Garlic Parmesan Kale Chips	494 - Loaded Egg Pepper Rings	495 - "Classic Mediterranean Salmon"	496 - Spicy-Sweet Pork Chops
497 - Herbed Cheese Brittle	498 - French Toast with Vanilla Filling	499 - "French Trout Meunière"	500 - Bavarian-Style Crispy Pork Schnitzel
501 - Easy Crispy Prawns	502 - Brioche Toast with Nutella	503 - "Rosemary Catfish"	504 - Beef Koftas in Tomato Sauce
505 - Grilled Cheese Sandwiches	506 - Soppressata Pizza	507 - "Jamaican Fish Fillets"	508 - Beef Meatballs with Cranberry Sauce
509 - Tortilla Chips	510 - Blueberry & Maple Toast	511 - "Peppery & Lemony Haddock"	512 - South American Arepas with Cilantro Sauce
513 - Roasted Red Salsa	514 - Spicy Egg & Bacon Tortilla Wraps	515 - "Roasted Tomatoes with Cheese Topping"	516 - Healthy Burgers
517 - Spicy Cheese-stuffed Mushrooms	518 - Paprika Rarebit	519 - "Indian Fried Okra"	520 - Homemade Hot Beef Satay
521 - Pita Chips	522 - Flaxseed Porridge	523 - "Mediterranean Eggplant Burgers"	524 - Garlic Steak with Mexican Salsa
525 - Sweet Chili Peanuts	526 - Avocado Tempura	527 - "Teriyaki Cauliflower"	528 - Gorgonzola Rib Eye Steak
529 - Green Olive And Mushroom Tapenade	530 - Quick Pickle Chips	531 - "Almond-Crusted Cauliflower Florets"	532 - Parsley Crumbed Beef Strips
533 - Ham And Cheese Sliders	534 - Green Bean Crisps	535 - Party Crispy Nachos	536 - Lamb Meatballs with Roasted Veggie Bake
537 - Turkey Bacon Dates	538 - Crispy Bacon with Butter Bean Dip	539 - "Air Fried Cheesy Ravioli"	540 - Herby Roast Beef
541 - Lemon Tofu Cubes	542 - Fried Sausage Ravioli	543 - "Egg & Cauliflower Rice Casserole"	544 - Beef Liver with Onions
545 - Bacon-wrapped Goat Cheese Poppers	546 - Roasted Coconut Carrots	547 - "Cheesy Vegetable Quesadilla"	548 - Lamb Chops with Lemony Couscous
549 - Hot Dogs	550 - Brie Cheese Croutons with Herbs	551 - "Mexican Chile Relleno"	552 - Easy Lamb Chop Bites
553 - Marinated Steak Kebabs	554 - French Beans with Toasted Almonds	555 - "Cinnamon Grilled Pineapples"	556 - Lamb Taquitos

557 - Grilled Prosciutto Wrapped Fig	558 - Spiced Almonds	559 - Italian Pork Scallopini	560 - One-Tray Parmesan Chicken Wings
561 - Corn Dogs	562 - Spiced Almond	563 - Spicy Sweet Beef with Veggie Topping	564 - Quinoa Chicken Nuggets
565 - Steak Bites And Spicy Dipping Sauce	566 - Sweet Mixed Nuts	567 - Wiener Beef Schnitzel	568 - San Antonio Taco Chicken Strips
569 - Blackened Steak Nuggets	570 - "Effortless Beef Short Ribs"	571 - Sweet & Sour Lamb Strips	572 - Cajun Chicken Tenders
573 - Turkey & Mushroom Sandwich	574 - "Fiery Prawns"	575 - Spiced Chicken Tacos	576 - Almond-Fried Crispy Chicken
577 - Bacon & Egg Sandwich	578 - "Crispy Prawns in Bacon Wraps"	579 - Rice Krispies Chicken Goujons	580 - Lemony Chicken Breast
581 - Mediterranean Avocado Toast	582 - "Cajun-Rubbed Jumbo Shrimp"	583 - Crispy Chicken Tenders with Hot Aioli	584 - Chicken Parmigiana with Fresh Rosemary
585 - Prosciutto & Mozzarella Bruschetta	586 - "Breaded Scallops"	587 - Greek Chicken Gyros	588 - Spinach Loaded Chicken Breasts
589 - Toasted Herb & Garlic Bagel	590 - "Buttered Crab Legs"	591 - French-Style Sweet Chicken Breasts	592 - Chicken Breasts "En Papillote"
593 - Grilled Apple & Brie Sandwich	594 - "Soy Sauce-Glazed Cod"	595 - French-Style Chicken Thighs	596 - Ham & Cheese Chicken Breasts
597 - Cheddar Black Bean Burritos	598 - "Smoked Salmon & Cheddar Taquitos"	599 - Air Fried Chicken Bowl with Black Beans	600 - Restaurant-Style Chicken with Yogurt Sauce

INTRODUCTION

Do you love the taste of crispy, golden fries... but hate the guilt that comes with deep-frying?

Do you wish you could prepare wholesome, flavorful meals in less than 30 minutes, even on your busiest days?

Welcome to **"Time Saving Air Fryer Cookbook For Beginners: 600 Quick, Easy & Healthy Recipes for Busy People"** — the ultimate guide to transforming the way you cook.

In today's fast-paced lifestyle, time is our most valuable resource. Yet, the desire for healthy eating has never been stronger. The air fryer is the perfect solution, using advanced rapid hot-air circulation technology to produce that irresistible crunch with up to 80% less oil than traditional frying. The result? Food that's lighter, healthier, and every bit as delicious.

This cookbook combines scientific cooking principles with practical, real-life recipes. Every one of the 600 recipes has been tested for:
- **Speed:** Ready in just 10–30 minutes from prep to plate.
- **Nutrition:** Designed with balanced macros and fresh, wholesome ingredients.
- **Simplicity:** Step-by-step instructions tailored for beginners, with no complicated techniques.

Inside, you'll discover:
- Flavor-packed breakfasts, hearty mains, and guilt-free snacks.
- Week-by-week meal plans to eliminate decision fatigue.
- Expert tips for maximizing your air fryer's performance.

Whether you're a complete beginner or a seasoned home cook, this book will help you save time, eat better, and enjoy the process of cooking like never before.

It's not just a cookbook — it's your roadmap to faster, healthier, and happier meals.

1. Moon Pie

Servings: 4 | **10 Minutes**

Ingredients:
- 8 large marshmallows
- 8 squares each of dark, milk and white chocolate

Directions:
Arrange the cracker halves on a cutting board. Put 2 marshmallows onto half of the graham cracker halves. Place 2 squares of chocolate onto the cracker with the marshmallows. Put the remaining crackers on top to create 4 sandwiches. Wrap each one in the baking paper so it resembles a parcel. Cook in the fryer for 5 minutes at 340°F.

Nutrition Facts (per serving):
Calories: 330 | Carbohydrates: 34g | Protein: 3g | Fat: 20g | Fiber: 2g | Sugar: 28g

---

2. Brownies For Two

Servings: 2 | **15 Minutes**

Ingredients:
- ½ cup blanched finely ground almond flour
- 3 tablespoons granular erythritol
- 3 tablespoons unsweetened cocoa powder
- ½ teaspoon baking powder
- 1 teaspoon vanilla extract
- 2 large eggs, whisked
- 2 tablespoons salted butter, melted

Directions:
In a medium bowl, combine flour, erythritol, cocoa powder, and baking powder.
Add in vanilla, eggs, and butter, and stir until a thick batter forms.
Pour batter into two 4" ramekins greased with cooking spray and place ramekins into air fryer basket. Adjust the temperature to 325°F and set the timer for 15 minutes. Centers will be firm when done. Let ramekins cool 5 minutes before serving.

Nutrition Facts (per serving):
Calories: 205 | Carbohydrates: 5g | Protein: 7g | Fat: 18g | Fiber: 2.5g | Sugar: 0.5g

---

3. Banana Chips With Chocolate Glaze

Servings: 2 | **20 Minutes**

Ingredients:
- 2 banana, cut into slices
- 1/4 teaspoon lemon zest
- 1 tablespoon agave syrup
- 1 tablespoon cocoa powder
- 1 tablespoon coconut oil, melted

Directions:
Toss the bananas with the lemon zest and agave syrup. Transfer your bananas to the parchment-lined cooking basket.
Bake in the preheated Air Fryer at 370°F for 12 minutes, turning them over halfway through the cooking time. In the meantime, melt the coconut oil in your microwave; add the cocoa powder and whisk to combine well.
Serve the baked banana chips.

Nutrition Facts (per serving):
Calories: 153 | Carbohydrates: 23.5g | Protein: 1g | Fat: 7g | Fiber: 2.5g | Sugar: 15.5g

---

4. Cinnamon Canned Biscuit Donuts

Servings: 4 | **25 Minutes**

Ingredients:
- 1 can jumbo biscuits
- 1 cup cinnamon sugar

Directions:
Preheat air fryer to 360°F. Divide biscuit dough into 8 biscuits and place on a flat work surface. Cut a small circle in the center of the biscuit with a small cookie cutter. Place a batch of 4 donuts in the air fryer. Spray with oil and Bake for 8 minutes, flipping once. Drizzle the cinnamon sugar over the donuts and serve.

Nutrition Facts (per serving):
Calories: 410 | Carbohydrates: 54g | Protein: 6g | Fat: 18g | Fiber: 1g | Sugar: 31g

5 Dark Chocolate Cake

Servings: 4 | 10 Minutes

Ingredients:
1½ tablespoons almond flour
3½ oz. unsalted butter
3½ oz. sugar free dark chocolate, chopped
2 eggs
3½ tablespoons swerve

Directions:
Preheat the Air fryer to 375°F and grease 4 regular sized ramekins.
Microwave all chocolate bits with butter in a bowl for about 3 minutes.
Remove from the microwave and whisk in the eggs and swerve.
Stir in the flour and mix well until smooth.
Transfer the mixture into the ramekins and arrange in the Air fryer basket.
Cook for about 10 minutes and dish out to serve.

Nutrition Facts (per serving):
Calories: 243 | Carbohydrates: 5.5g | Protein: 4.25g | Fat: 22.5g | Fiber: 2.75g | Sugar: 0.5g

6 Grilled Banana Boats

Servings: 3 | 15 Minutes

Ingredients:
3 large bananas
1 tablespoon ginger snaps
2 tablespoons mini chocolate chips
3 tablespoons mini marshmallows
3 tablespoons crushed vanilla wafers

Directions:
In the peel, slice your banana lengthwise; make sure not to slice all the way through the banana. Divide the remaining ingredients between the banana pockets. Place in the Air Fryer grill pan. Cook at 395°F for 7 minutes.
Let the banana boats cool for 5 to 6 minutes, and then eat with a spoon. Bon appétit!

Nutrition Facts (per serving):
Calories: 190 | Carbohydrates: 37g | Protein: 1.7g | Fat: 5g | Fiber: 3g | Sugar: 21g

7 Shortbread Fingers

Servings: 1 | 20 Minutes

Ingredients:
1 ½ cups butter
1 cup flour
¾ cup sugar
Cooking spray

Directions:
Pre-heat your Air Fryer to 350°F.
In a bowl. combine the flour and sugar.
Cut each stick of butter into small chunks. Add the chunks into the flour and the sugar.
Blend the butter into the mixture to combine everything well.
Use your hands to knead the mixture, forming a smooth consistency.
Shape the mixture into 10 equal-sized finger shapes, marking them with the tines of a fork for decoration if desired.
Lightly spritz the Air Fryer basket with the cooking spray. Place the cookies inside, spacing them out well. Bake the cookies for 12 minutes.
Let cool slightly before serving. Alternatively, you can store the cookies in an airtight container for up to 3 days.

Nutrition Facts (per serving):
Calories: 366 | Carbohydrates: 18g | Protein: 0.8g | Fat: 33.6g | Fiber: 0.1g | Sugar: 15g

8 Lemon Iced Donut Balls

Servings: 6 | 25 Minutes

Ingredients:
1 can jumbo biscuit dough
2 tsp lemon juice
½ cup icing sugar, sifted

Directions:
Preheat air fryer to 360°F. Divide the biscuit dough into 16 equal portions. Roll the dough into balls of 1½ inches thickness. Place the donut holes in the greased frying basket and Air Fry for 8 minutes, flipping once. Mix the icing sugar and lemon juice until smooth. Spread the icing over the top of the donuts. Leave to set a bit. Serve.

Nutrition Facts (per serving):
Calories: 217 | Carbohydrates: 33g | Protein: 3.3g | Fat: 8.3g | Fiber: 0.3g | Sugar: 8.3g

9 Mini Crustless Peanut Butter Cheesecake

Servings: 2 | 10 Minutes

Ingredients:
4 ounces cream cheese, softened
2 tablespoons confectioners' erythritol
1 tablespoon all-natural, no-sugar-added peanut butter
½ teaspoon vanilla extract
1 large egg, whisked

Directions:
In a medium bowl, mix cream cheese and erythritol until smooth. Add peanut butter and vanilla, mixing until smooth. Add egg and stir just until combined. Spoon mixture into an ungreased 4" springform nonstick pan and place into air fryer basket. Adjust the temperature to 300°F and set the timer for 10 minutes. Edges will be firm, but center will be mostly set with only a small amount of jiggle when done.
Let pan cool at room temperature 30 minutes, cover with plastic wrap, then place into refrigerator at least 2 hours. Serve chilled.

Nutrition Facts (per serving):
Calories: 185 | Carbohydrates: 2.5g | Protein: 5.5g | Fat: 17.5g | Fiber: 0.5g | Sugar: 1g

10 Chocolate Lava Cakes

Servings: 2 | 15 Minutes

Ingredients:
2 large eggs, whisked
¼ cup blanched finely ground almond flour
½ teaspoon vanilla extract
2 ounces low-carb chocolate chips, melted

Directions:
In a medium bowl, mix eggs with flour and vanilla. Fold in chocolate until fully combined.
Pour batter into two 4" ramekins greased with cooking spray. Place ramekins into air fryer basket. Adjust the temperature to 320°F and set the timer for 15 minutes. Cakes will be set at the edges and firm in the center when done. Let cool 5 minutes before serving.

Nutrition Facts (per serving):
Calories: 255 | Carbohydrates: 5g | Protein: 10g | Fat: 21g | Fiber: 2.5g | Sugar: 1g

11 Delicious Vanilla Custard

Servings: 2 | 20 Minutes

Ingredients:
5 eggs
2 tbsp swerve
1 tsp vanilla
½ cup unsweetened almond milk
½ cup cream cheese

Directions:
Add eggs in a bowl and beat using a hand mixer. Add cream cheese, sweetener, vanilla, and almond milk and beat for 2 minutes more.
Spray two ramekins with cooking spray.
Pour batter into the prepared ramekins.
Preheat the air fryer to 350°F.
Place ramekins into the air fryer and cook for 20 minutes.
Serve and enjoy.

Nutrition Facts (per serving):
Calories: 295 | Carbohydrates: 3g | Protein: 16.5g | Fat: 24g | Fiber: 0.5g | Sugar: 1.5g

12 Apple Pie Crumble

Servings: 4 | 25 Minutes

Ingredients:
1 can apple pie
¼ cup butter, softened
9 tablespoons self-rising flour
7 tablespoons caster sugar
Pinch of salt

Directions:
Preheat the Air fryer to 320°F and grease a baking dish.
Mix all the ingredients in a bowl until a crumbly mixture is formed.
Arrange the apple pie in the baking dish and top with the mixture.
Transfer the baking dish into the Air fryer basket and cook for about 25 minutes.
Dish out in a platter and serve.

Nutrition Facts (per serving):
Calories: 333 | Carbohydrates: 49.5g | Protein: 1.5g | Fat: 14g | Fiber: 0.75g | Sugar: 31.5g

13 Pumpkin Pie-spiced Pork Rinds

Servings: 4 | 5 Minutes

Ingredients:
- 3 ounces plain pork rinds
- 2 tablespoons salted butter, melted
- 1 teaspoon pumpkin pie spice
- ¼ cup confectioners' erythritol

Directions:
In a large bowl, toss pork rinds in butter. Sprinkle with pumpkin pie spice, then toss to evenly coat. Place pork rinds into ungreased air fryer basket. Adjust the temperature to 400°F and set the timer for 5 minutes. Pork rinds will be golden when done. Transfer rinds to a medium serving bowl and sprinkle with erythritol. Serve immediately.

Nutrition Facts (per serving):
Calories: 135 | Carbohydrates: 0.5g | Protein: 12g | Fat: 9.5g | Fiber: 0g | Sugar: 0g

---

14 Party S'mores

Servings: 6 | 15 Minutes

Ingredients:
- 2 dark chocolate bars, cut into 12 pieces
- 12 buttermilk biscuits
- 12 marshmallows

Directions:
Preheat air fryer to 350°F. Place 6 biscuits in the air fryer. Top each square with a piece of dark chocolate. Bake for 2 minutes. Add a marshmallow to each piece of chocolate. Cook for another minute. Remove and top with another piece of biscuit. Serve warm.

Nutrition Facts (per serving):
Calories: 473 | Carbohydrates: 63g | Protein: 6g | Fat: 23g | Fiber: 2g | Sugar: 24g

---

15 Monkey Bread

Servings: 6 | 20 Minutes

Ingredients:
- 1 can refrigerated biscuit dough
- ½ cup granulated sugar
- 1 tablespoon ground cinnamon
- ¼ cup salted butter, melted
- ¼ cup brown sugar
- Cooking spray

Directions:
Preheat the air fryer to 325°F. Spray a 6" round cake pan with cooking spray. Separate biscuits and cut each into four pieces.
In a large bowl, stir granulated sugar with cinnamon. Toss biscuit pieces in the cinnamon and sugar mixture until well coated. Place each biscuit piece in prepared pan.
In a medium bowl, stir together butter and brown sugar. Pour mixture evenly over the biscuit pieces. Place pan in the air fryer basket and cook 20 minutes until brown. Let cool 10 minutes before flipping bread out of the pan and serving.

Nutrition Facts (per serving):
Calories: 283 | Carbohydrates: 36.7g | Protein: 3.3g | Fat: 14g | Fiber: 0.7g | Sugar: 18.3g

---

16 Crunchy Roasted Potatoes

Servings: 5 | 25 Minutes

Ingredients:
- 2 pounds Small red, white, or purple potatoes
- 2 tablespoons Olive oil
- 2 teaspoons Table salt
- ¾ teaspoon Garlic powder
- ½ teaspoon Ground black pepper

Directions:
Preheat the air fryer to 400°F.
Toss the potatoes, oil, salt, garlic powder, and pepper in a large bowl until the spuds are evenly and thoroughly coated.
When the machine is at temperature, pour the potatoes into the basket, spreading them into an even layer. Air-fry for 25 minutes, tossing twice, until the potatoes are tender but crunchy.
Pour the contents of the basket into a serving bowl. Cool for 5 minutes before serving.

Nutrition Facts (per serving):
Calories: 178 | Carbohydrates: 22g | Protein: 3.6g | Fat: 8.4g | Fiber: 2.2g | Sugar: 0.8g

17 Peanut Cookies

Servings: 4 | 5 Minutes

Ingredients:
4 tablespoons peanut butter
4 teaspoons Erythritol
1 egg, beaten
¼ teaspoon vanilla extract

Directions:
In the mixing bowl mix up peanut butter, Erythritol, egg, and vanilla extract. Stir the mixture with the help of the fork. Then make 4 cookies. Preheat the air fryer to 355°F. Place the cookies in the air fryer and cook them for 5 minutes.

Nutrition Facts (per serving):
Calories: 118 | Carbohydrates: 2.25g | Protein: 4.75g | Fat: 10g | Fiber: 1g | Sugar: 0.5g

---

18 Nutella And Banana Pastries

Servings: 4 | 12 Minutes

Ingredients:
1 puff pastry sheet, cut into 4 equal squares
½ cup Nutella
2 bananas, sliced
2 tablespoons icing sugar

Directions:
Preheat the Air fryer to 375°F and grease an Air fryer basket.
Spread Nutella on each pastry square and top with banana slices and icing sugar.
Fold each square into a triangle and slightly press the edges with a fork.
Arrange the pastries in the Air fryer basket and cook for about 12 minutes.
Dish out and serve immediately.

Nutrition Facts (per serving):
Calories: 458 | Carbohydrates: 48g | Protein: 5g | Fat: 27g | Fiber: 2.5g | Sugar: 23g

---

19 Baked Apple

Servings: 6 | 20 Minutes

Ingredients:
3 small Honey Crisp or other baking apples
3 tablespoons maple syrup
3 tablespoons chopped pecans
1 tablespoon firm butter, cut into 6 pieces

Directions:
Put ½ cup water in the drawer of the air fryer.
Wash apples well and dry them.
Split apples in half. Remove core and a little of the flesh to make a cavity for the pecans.
Place apple halves in air fryer basket, cut side up.
Spoon 1½ teaspoons pecans into each cavity.
Spoon ½ tablespoon maple syrup over pecans in each apple.
Top each apple with ½ teaspoon butter.
Cook at 360°F for 20 minutes, until apples are tender.

Nutrition Facts (per serving):
Calories: 85 | Carbohydrates: 13g | Protein: 0.3g | Fat: 4g | Fiber: 1.5g | Sugar: 10g

---

20 Cinnamon Roasted Pumpkin

Servings: 2 | 25 Minutes

Ingredients:
1 lb pumpkin, halved crosswise and seeded
1 tsp coconut oil
1 tsp sugar
½ tsp ground nutmeg
1 tsp ground cinnamon

Directions:
Prepare the pumpkin by rubbing coconut oil on the cut sides. In a small bowl, combine sugar, nutmeg and cinnamon. Sprinkle over the pumpkin. Preheat air fryer to 325°F. Put the pumpkin in the greased frying basket, cut sides up. Bake until the squash is soft in the center, 15 minutes. Test with a knife to ensure softness. Serve.

Nutrition Facts (per serving):
Calories: 63 | Carbohydrates: 13g | Protein: 1.5g | Fat: 1.25g | Fiber: 2g | Sugar: 5g

Servings: 6 | 8 Minutes

21 Cinnamon Apple Chips

Ingredients:
3 Granny Smith apples, wash, core and thinly slice
1 tsp ground cinnamon
Pinch of salt

Directions:
Rub apple slices with cinnamon and salt and place into the air fryer basket.
Cook at 390°F for 8 minutes. Turn halfway through.
Serve and enjoy.

Nutrition Facts (per serving):
Calories: 53 | Carbohydrates: 14g | Protein: 0.2g | Fat: 0g | Fiber: 2g | Sugar: 10.5g

---

Servings: 4 | 12 Minutes

22 Lemon Tempeh

Ingredients:
1 teaspoon lemon juice
1 tablespoon sunflower oil
¼ teaspoon ground coriander
6 oz tempeh, chopped

Directions:
Sprinkle the tempeh with lemon juice, sunflower oil, and ground coriander. Massage the tempeh gently with the help of the fingertips. After this, preheat the air fryer to 325°F. Put the tempeh in the air fryer and cook it for 12 minutes. Flip the tempeh every 2 minutes during cooking.

Nutrition Facts (per serving):
Calories: 93 | Carbohydrates: 3g | Protein: 8g | Fat: 6g | Fiber: 1.5g | Sugar: 0g

---

Servings: 12 | 20 Minutes

23 Cream Cheese Shortbread Cookies

Ingredients:
¼ cup coconut oil, melted
2 ounces cream cheese, softened
½ cup granular erythritol
1 large egg, whisked
2 cups blanched finely ground almond flour
1 teaspoon almond extract

Directions:
Combine all ingredients in a large bowl to form a firm ball.
Place dough on a sheet of plastic wrap and roll into a 12"-long log shape. Roll log in plastic wrap and place in refrigerator 30 minutes to chill.
Remove log from plastic and slice into twelve equal cookies. Cut two sheets of parchment paper to fit air fryer basket. Place six cookies on each ungreased sheet. Place one sheet with cookies into air fryer basket. Adjust the temperature to 320°F and set the timer for 10 minutes, turning cookies halfway through cooking. They will be lightly golden when done.
Repeat with remaining cookies.
Let cool 15 minutes before serving to avoid crumbling.

Nutrition Facts (per serving):
Calories: 120 | Carbohydrates: 1.7g | Protein: 3.2g | Fat: 11.3g | Fiber: 1g | Sugar: 0.3g

---

Servings: 4 | 25 Minutes

24 Cool Mini Zucchini's

Ingredients:
4 large eggs, beaten
1 medium zucchini, sliced
4 ounces feta cheese, drained and crumbled
2 tbsp fresh dill, chopped
Cooking spray
Salt and pepper as needed

Directions:
Preheat the air fryer to 360°F, and un a bowl, add the beaten eggs and season with salt and pepper.
Stir in zucchini, dill and feta cheese. Grease 8 muffin tins with cooking spray. Roll pastry and arrange them to cover the sides of the muffin tins. Divide the egg mixture evenly between the holes. Place the prepared tins in your air fryer and cook for 15 minutes. Serve and enjoy!

Nutrition Facts (per serving):
Calories: 150 | Carbohydrates: 4g | Protein: 10g | Fat: 11g | Fiber: 1g | Sugar: 2g

Servings: 4 — 10 Minutes

25 Keto Butter Balls

Ingredients:
- 1 tablespoon butter, softened
- 1 tablespoon Erythritol
- ½ teaspoon ground cinnamon
- 1 tablespoon coconut flour
- 1 teaspoon coconut flakes
- Cooking spray

Directions:
Put the butter, Erythritol, ground cinnamon, coconut flour, and coconut flakes. Then stir the mixture with the help of the fork until homogenous. Make 4 balls. Preheat the air fryer to 375°F. Spray the air fryer basket with cooking spray and place the balls inside. Cook the dessert for 10 minutes.

Nutrition Facts (per serving):
Calories: 30 | Carbohydrates: 1g | Protein: 0.25g | Fat: 3g | Fiber: 0.5g | Sugar: 0g

---

Servings: 4 — 12 Minutes

26 Roasted Asparagus

Ingredients:
- 1 tablespoon olive oil
- 1 pound asparagus spears, ends trimmed
- ¼ teaspoon salt
- ¼ teaspoon ground black pepper
- 1 tablespoon salted butter, melted

Directions:
In a large bowl, drizzle olive oil over asparagus spears and sprinkle with salt and pepper.
Place spears into ungreased air fryer basket. Adjust the temperature to 375°F and set the timer for 12 minutes, shaking the basket halfway through cooking. Asparagus will be lightly browned and tender when done.
Transfer to a large dish and drizzle with butter. Serve warm.

Nutrition Facts (per serving):
Calories: 63 | Carbohydrates: 3g | Protein: 1.5g | Fat: 5.5g | Fiber: 1.25g | Sugar: 1.25g

---

Servings: 4 — 20 Minutes

27 Roasted Brussels Sprouts With Bacon

Ingredients:
- 4 slices thick-cut bacon, chopped (about ¼ pound)
- 1 pound Brussels sprouts, halved (or quartered if large)
- freshly ground black pepper

Directions:
Preheat the air fryer to 380°F.
Air-fry the bacon for 5 minutes, shaking the basket once or twice during the cooking time.
Add the Brussels sprouts to the basket and drizzle a little bacon fat from the bottom of the air fryer drawer into the basket. Toss the sprouts to coat with the bacon fat. Air-fry for an additional 15 minutes, or until the Brussels sprouts are tender to a knifepoint. Season with freshly ground black pepper.

Nutrition Facts (per serving):
Calories: 128 | Carbohydrates: 6.5g | Protein: 6g | Fat: 9g | Fiber: 2.5g | Sugar: 2g

---

Servings: 4 — 25 Minutes

28 Ginger Turmeric Chicken Thighs

Ingredients:
- 2 tablespoons coconut oil, melted
- ½ teaspoon ground turmeric
- ½ teaspoon salt
- ½ teaspoon garlic powder
- ½ teaspoon ground ginger
- ¼ teaspoon ground black pepper

Directions:
Place chicken thighs in a large bowl and drizzle with coconut oil. Sprinkle with remaining ingredients and toss to coat both sides of thighs.
Place thighs skin side up into ungreased air fryer basket. Adjust the temperature to 400°F and set the timer for 25 minutes. After 10 minutes, turn thighs. When 5 minutes remain, flip thighs once more. Chicken will be done when skin is golden brown and the internal temperature is at least 165°F. Serve warm.

Nutrition Facts (per serving):
Calories: 223 | Carbohydrates: 0.5g | Protein: 9g | Fat: 19g | Fiber: 0g

Servings: 6   🕐 10 Minutes

29 Delicious Spiced Apples

Ingredients:
4 small apples, sliced
1 tsp apple pie spice
1/2 cup erythritol
2 tbsp coconut oil, melted

Directions:
Add apple slices in a mixing bowl and sprinkle sweetener, apple pie spice, and coconut oil over apple and toss to coat.
Transfer apple slices in air fryer dish. Place dish in air fryer basket and cook at 350°F for 10 minutes.
Serve and enjoy.

Nutrition Facts (per serving):
Calories: 73 | Carbohydrates: 11g | Protein: 0.2g | Fat: 2.3g | Fiber: 1.7g | Sugar: 7.3g

---

 Servings: 6   🕐 12 Minutes

30 Cheesy Garlic Bread

Ingredients:
1 cup self-rising flour
1 cup plain full-fat Greek yogurt
¼ cup salted butter, softened
1 tablespoon minced garlic
1 cup shredded mozzarella cheese

Directions:
Preheat the air fryer to 320°F. Cut parchment paper to fit the air fryer basket.
In a large bowl, mix flour and yogurt until a sticky, soft dough forms. Let sit 5 minutes.
Turn dough onto a lightly floured surface. Knead dough 1 minute, then transfer to prepared parchment. Press out into an 8" round.
In a small bowl, mix butter and garlic. Brush over dough. Sprinkle with mozzarella.
Place in the air fryer and cook 12 minutes until edges are golden and cheese is brown. Serve warm.

Nutrition Facts (per serving):
Calories: 167 | Carbohydrates: 9g | Protein: 6.3g | Fat: 11.7g | Fiber: 0.3g | Sugar: 0.8g

---

 Servings: 4   🕐 20 Minutes

31 Almond Green Beans

Ingredients:
2 cups green beans, trimmed
¼ cup slivered almonds
2 tbsp butter, melted
Salt and pepper to taste
2 tsp lemon juice
Lemon zest and slices

Directions:
Preheat air fryer at 375°F. Add almonds to the frying basket and Air Fry for 2 minutes, tossing once. Set aside in a small bowl. Combine the remaining ingredients, except 1 tbsp of butter, in a bowl. Place green beans in the frying basket and Air Fry for 10 minutes, tossing once. Then, transfer them to a large serving dish. Scatter with the melted butter, lemon juice and roasted almonds and toss. Serve immediately garnished with lemon zest and lemon slices.

Nutrition Facts (per serving):
Calories: 65 | Carbohydrates: 3.5g | Protein: 1.5g | Fat: 5.5g | Fiber: 1.5g | Sugar: 1.5g

---

 Servings: 4   🕐 25 Minutes

32 Chipotle Drumsticks

Ingredients:
1 tablespoon tomato paste
½ teaspoon chipotle powder
¼ teaspoon apple cider vinegar
¼ teaspoon garlic powder
8 chicken drumsticks
½ teaspoon salt
⅛ teaspoon ground black pepper

Directions:
In a small bowl, combine tomato paste, chipotle powder, vinegar, and garlic powder.
Sprinkle drumsticks with salt and pepper, then place into a large bowl and pour in tomato paste mixture. Toss or stir to evenly coat all drumsticks in mixture.
Place drumsticks into ungreased air fryer basket. Adjust the temperature to 400°F and set the timer for 25 minutes, turning drumsticks halfway through cooking. Drumsticks will be dark red with an internal temperature of at least 165°F when done. Serve warm.

Nutrition Facts (per serving):
Calories: 219 | Carbohydrates: 1.2g | Protein: 9g | Fat: 19g | Fiber: 0g

33 Chocolate Doughnut Holes

Servings: 20 | 6 Minutes

Ingredients:
- 1 cup blanched finely ground almond flour
- ½ cup low-carb vanilla protein powder
- ½ cup granular erythritol
- ¼ cup unsweetened cocoa powder
- ½ teaspoon baking powder
- 2 large eggs, whisked
- ½ teaspoon vanilla extract

Directions:
Mix all ingredients in a large bowl until a soft dough forms. Separate and roll dough into twenty balls, about 2 tablespoons each.

Cut a piece of parchment to fit your air fryer basket. Working in batches if needed, place doughnut holes into air fryer basket on ungreased parchment. Adjust the temperature to 380°F and set the timer for 6 minutes, flipping doughnut holes halfway through cooking. Doughnut holes will be golden and firm when done. Let cool completely before serving, about 10 minutes.

Nutrition Facts (per serving):
Calories: 41 | Carbohydrates: 1.5g | Protein: 3.2g | Fat: 2.6g | Fiber: 0.5g | Sugar: 0.2g

---

34 Baked Jalapeño And Cheese Cauliflower Mash

Servings: 6 | 15 Minutes

Ingredients:
- 1 steamer bag cauliflower florets, cooked according to package instructions
- 2 tablespoons salted butter, softened
- 2 ounces cream cheese, softened
- ½ cup shredded sharp Cheddar cheese
- ¼ cup pickled jalapeños
- ½ teaspoon salt
- ¼ teaspoon ground black pepper

Directions:
Place cooked cauliflower into a food processor with remaining ingredients. Pulse twenty times until cauliflower is smooth and all ingredients are combined.

Spoon mash into an ungreased 6" round nonstick baking dish. Place dish into air fryer basket. Adjust the temperature to 380°F and set the timer for 15 minutes. The top will be golden brown when done. Serve warm.

Nutrition Facts (per serving):
Calories: 87 | Carbohydrates: 3g | Protein: 2.7g | Fat: 7.3g | Fiber: 1g | Sugar: 1.2g

---

35 Easy Green Bean Casserole

Servings: 4 | 20 Minutes

Ingredients:
- 1 can condensed cream of mushroom soup
- ¼ cup heavy cream
- 2 cans cut green beans, drained
- 1 teaspoon minced garlic
- ½ teaspoon salt
- ¼ teaspoon ground black pepper
- 1 cup packaged French fried onions

Directions:
Preheat the air fryer to 320°F.

In a 4-quart baking dish, pour soup and cream over green beans and mix to combine.

Stir in garlic, salt, and pepper until combined. Top with French fried onions.

Place in the air fryer basket and cook 20 minutes until top is lightly brown and dish is heated through. Serve warm.

Nutrition Facts (per serving):
Calories: 195 | Carbohydrates: 12.5g | Protein: 2.5g | Fat: 15g | Fiber: 2g | Sugar: 2g

---

36 Garlic Parmesan Drumsticks

Servings: 4 | 25 Minutes

Ingredients:
- 8 chicken drumsticks
- ½ teaspoon salt
- ⅛ teaspoon ground black pepper
- ½ teaspoon garlic powder
- 2 tablespoons salted butter, melted
- ½ cup grated Parmesan cheese
- 1 tablespoon dried parsley

Directions:
Sprinkle drumsticks with salt, pepper, and garlic powder. Place drumsticks into ungreased air fryer basket.

Adjust the temperature to 400°F and set the timer for 25 minutes, turning drumsticks halfway through cooking. Drumsticks will be golden and have an internal temperature of at least 165°F when done. Transfer drumsticks to a large serving dish. Pour butter over drumsticks, and sprinkle with Parmesan and parsley. Serve warm.

Nutrition Facts (per serving):
Calories: 223 | Carbohydrates: 1.5g | Protein: 9g | Fat: 18.6g | Fiber: 0g

37 Fried Oreos

Servings: 12 | 6 Minutes Per Batch

Ingredients:
oil for misting or nonstick spray
1 cup complete pancake and waffle mix
1 teaspoon vanilla extract
½ cup water, plus 2 tablespoons
12 Oreos or other chocolate sandwich cookies
1 tablespoon confectioners' sugar

Directions:
Spray baking pan with oil or nonstick spray and place in basket.
Preheat air fryer to 390°F.
In a medium bowl, mix together the pancake mix, vanilla, and water.
Dip 4 cookies in batter and place in baking pan.
Cook for 6 minutes, until browned.
Repeat steps 4 and 5 for the remaining cookies.
Sift sugar over warm cookies.

Nutrition Facts (per serving):
Calories: 123 | Carbohydrates: 19g | Protein: 1g | Fat: 4.7g | Fiber: 0.3g | Sugar: 9.2g

---

38 Spicy Roasted Potatoes

Servings: 2 | 15 Minutes

Ingredients:
4 potatoes, peeled and cut into wedges
2 tablespoons olive oil
Sea salt and ground black pepper, to taste
1 teaspoon cayenne pepper
1/2 teaspoon ancho chili powder

Directions:
Toss all ingredients in a mixing bowl until the potatoes are well covered.
Transfer them to the Air Fryer basket and cook at 400°F for 6 minutes; shake the basket and cook for a further 6 minutes.
Serve warm with your favorite sauce for dipping. Bon appétit!

Nutrition Facts (per serving):
Calories: 350 | Carbohydrates: 55g | Protein: 5g | Fat: 12g | Fiber: 5g | Sugar: 2g

---

39 Buttered Garlic Broccolini

Servings: 2 | 20 Minutes

Ingredients:
1 bunch broccolini
2 tbsp butter, cubed
¼ tsp salt
2 minced cloves garlic
2 tsp lemon juice

Directions:
Preheat air fryer at 350°F. Place salted water in a saucepan over high heat and bring it to a boil. Then, add in broccolini and boil for 3 minutes. Drain it and transfer it into a bowl. Mix in butter, garlic, and salt. Place the broccolini in the frying basket and Air Fry for 6 minutes. Serve immediately garnished with lemon juice.

Nutrition Facts (per serving):
Calories: 115 | Carbohydrates: 5g | Protein: 2g | Fat: 10g | Fiber: 2g | Sugar: 1g

---

40 Barbecue Chicken Drumsticks

Servings: 4 | 25 Minutes

Ingredients:
1 teaspoon salt
1 teaspoon chili powder
1 teaspoon garlic powder
½ teaspoon ground black pepper
½ teaspoon onion powder
8 chicken drumsticks
1 cup barbecue sauce, divided

Directions:
Preheat the air fryer to 375°F.
In a large bowl, combine salt, chili powder, garlic powder, pepper, and onion powder. Add drumsticks and toss to fully coat.
Brush drumsticks with ¾ cup barbecue sauce to coat.
Place in the air fryer basket and cook 25 minutes, turning three times during cooking, until drumsticks are brown and internal temperature reaches at least 165°F.
Before serving, brush remaining ¼ cup barbecue sauce over drumsticks. Serve warm.

Nutrition Facts (per serving):
Calories: 224 | Carbohydrates: 2.4g | Protein: 9g | Fat: 18.5g | Fiber: 0g

Servings: 12 | 8 Minutes

41 Cocoa Bombs

Ingredients:
2 cups macadamia nuts, chopped
4 tablespoons coconut oil, melted
1 teaspoon vanilla extract
¼ cup cocoa powder
1/3 cup swerve

Directions:
In a bowl, mix all the ingredients and whisk well. Shape medium balls out of this mix, place them in your air fryer and cook at 300°F for 8 minutes. Serve cold.

Nutrition Facts (per serving):
Calories: 177 | Carbohydrates: 3.5g | Protein: 1.8g | Fat: 18g | Fiber: 2g | Sugar: 0.75g

---

Servings: 4 | 15 Minutes

42 Crunchy Green Beans

Ingredients:
1 tbsp tahini
1 tbsp lemon juice
1 tsp allspice
1 lb green beans, trimmed

Directions:
Preheat air fryer to 400°F. Whisk tahini, lemon juice, 1 tbsp of water, and allspice in a bowl. Put in the green beans and toss to coat. Roast for 5 minutes until golden brown and cooked. Serve immediately.

Nutrition Facts (per serving):
Calories: 45 | Carbohydrates: 5.5g | Protein: 2.3g | Fat: 2g | Fiber: 2.25g | Sugar: 2.5g

---

Servings: 4 | 20 Minutes

43 Potato Wedges

Ingredients:
6 cups water
4 large russet potatoes, sliced into wedges
2 teaspoons seasoned salt
½ cup whole milk
½ cup all-purpose flour

Directions:
In a large saucepan over medium-high heat, bring water to a boil.
Carefully place potato wedges into boiling water and cook 5 minutes.
Preheat the air fryer to 400°F.
Drain potatoes into a colander, then rinse under cold running water 1 minute until they feel cool to the touch.
Place potatoes in a large bowl and sprinkle with seasoned salt. Pour milk into bowl, then toss wedges to coat.
Place flour on a large plate. Gently dredge each potato wedge in flour on both sides to lightly coat.
Place wedges in the air fryer basket and spritz both sides with cooking spray. Cook 15 minutes, turning after 10 minutes, until wedges are golden brown. Serve warm.

Nutrition Facts (per serving):
Calories: 258 | Carbohydrates: 56g | Protein: 5.8g | Fat: 1.3g | Fiber: 3.8g | Sugar: 2.5g

---

Servings: 6 | 25 Minutes

44 Chicken Wrapped In Bacon

Ingredients:
6 rashers unsmoked back bacon
1 small chicken breast
1 tbsp. garlic soft cheese

Directions:
Cut the chicken breast into six bite-sized pieces.
Spread the soft cheese across one side of each slice of bacon.
Put the chicken on top of the cheese and wrap the bacon around it, holding it in place with a toothpick.
Transfer the wrapped chicken pieces to the Air Fryer and cook for 15 minutes at 350°F.

Nutrition Facts (per serving):
Calories: 220 | Carbohydrates: 0.6g | Protein: 9g | Fat: 18.6g | Fiber: 0g

Servings: 1 — 10 Minutes

45 Easy Mug Brownie

Ingredients:
- 1 scoop chocolate protein powder
- 1 tbsp cocoa powder
- 1/2 tsp baking powder
- 1/4 cup unsweetened almond milk

Directions:
Add baking powder, protein powder, and cocoa powder in a mug and mix well.
Add milk in a mug and stir well.
Place the mug in the air fryer and cook at 390°F for 10 minutes.
Serve and enjoy.

Nutrition Facts (per serving):
Calories: 160 | Carbohydrates: 5g | Protein: 20g | Fat: 6g | Fiber: 3g | Sugar: 1g

---

Servings: 5 — 15 Minutes

46 Garlic Knots

Ingredients:
- 1 cup self-rising flour
- 1 cup plain full-fat Greek yogurt
- ⅓ cup salted butter, melted
- 1 teaspoon garlic powder
- ¼ cup grated Parmesan cheese

Directions:
Preheat the air fryer to 320°F.
In a large bowl, mix flour and yogurt and let sit 5 minutes.
Turn dough onto a lightly floured surface and gently knead about 3 minutes until it's no longer sticky. Form dough into a rectangle and roll out until it measures 10" × 6". Cut dough into ten 1"× 6" strips.
Tie each dough strip into a knot. Brush each knot with butter and sprinkle with garlic powder.
Place in the air fryer basket and cook 8 minutes, turning after 6 minutes. Let cool 2 minutes, sprinkle with Parmesan, and serve.

Nutrition Facts (per serving):
Calories: 208 | Carbohydrates: 10g | Protein: 4g | Fat: 16.8g | Fiber: 0.2g | Sugar: 1g

---

 Servings: 3 20 Minutes

47 Sweet Potato Fries

Ingredients:
- 2 10-ounce sweet potato(es)
- Vegetable oil spray
- To taste Coarse sea salt or kosher salt

Directions:
Preheat the air fryer to 400°F.
Peel the sweet potato(es), then cut lengthwise into ¼-inch-thick slices. Cut these slices lengthwise into ¼-inch-thick matchsticks. Place these matchsticks in a bowl and coat them with vegetable oil spray. Toss well, spray them again, and toss several times to make sure they're all evenly coated.
When the machine is at temperature, pour the sweet potato matchsticks into the basket, spreading them out in as close to an even layer as possible. Air-fry for 20 minutes, tossing and rearranging the matchsticks every 5 minutes, until lightly browned and crisp.
Pour the contents of the basket into a bowl, add some salt to taste, and toss well to coat.

Nutrition Facts (per serving):
Calories: 153 | Carbohydrates: 35.7g | Protein: 1.3g | Fat: 0.2g | Fiber: 4.7g | Sugar: 6.3g

---

 Servings: 6 25 Minutes

48 Chipotle Aioli Wings

Ingredients:
- 2 pounds bone-in chicken wings
- ½ teaspoon salt
- ¼ teaspoon ground black pepper
- 2 tablespoons mayonnaise
- 2 teaspoons chipotle powder
- 2 tablespoons lemon juice

Directions:
In a large bowl, toss wings in salt and pepper, then place into ungreased air fryer basket. Adjust the temperature to 400°F and set the timer for 25 minutes, shaking the basket twice while cooking. Wings will be done when golden and have an internal temperature of at least 165°F.
In a small bowl, whisk together mayonnaise, chipotle powder, and lemon juice. Place cooked wings into a large serving bowl and drizzle with aioli. Toss to coat. Serve warm.

Nutrition Facts (per serving):
Calories: 218 | Carbohydrates: 1.2g | Protein: 9.1g | Fat: 18.4g | Fiber: 0g

Servings: 8 | 10 Minutes

49 Strawberry Cups

Ingredients:
16 strawberries, halved
2 tablespoons coconut oil
2 cups chocolate chips, melted

Directions:
In a pan that fits your air fryer, mix the strawberries with the oil and the melted chocolate chips, toss gently, put the pan in the air fryer and cook at 340°F for 10 minutes. Divide into cups and serve cold.

Nutrition Facts (per serving):
Calories: 251 | Carbohydrates: 26g | Protein: 1.25g | Fat: 16g | Fiber: 2g | Sugar: 21g

---

Servings: 4 | 12 Minutes

50 "faux-tato" Hash

Ingredients:
1 pound radishes, ends removed, quartered
¼ medium yellow onion, peeled and diced
½ medium green bell pepper, seeded and chopped
2 tablespoons salted butter, melted
½ teaspoon garlic powder
¼ teaspoon ground black pepper

Directions:
In a large bowl, combine radishes, onion, and bell pepper. Toss with butter.
Sprinkle garlic powder and black pepper over mixture in bowl, then spoon into ungreased air fryer basket. Adjust the temperature to 320°F and set the timer for 12 minutes. Shake basket halfway through cooking. Radishes will be tender when done. Serve warm.

Nutrition Facts (per serving):
Calories: 55 | Carbohydrates: 3.5g | Protein: 0.75g | Fat: 4.5g | Fiber: 1.25g | Sugar: 1.5g

---

 Servings: 4 20 Minutes

51 Parmesan Garlic Fries

Ingredients:
2 medium Yukon gold potatoes, washed
1 tablespoon extra-virgin olive oil
1 garlic clove, minced
2 tablespoons finely grated parmesan cheese
¼ teaspoon black pepper
¼ teaspoon salt
1 tablespoon freshly chopped parsley

Directions:
Preheat the air fryer to 400°F.
Slice the potatoes into long strips about ¼-inch thick. In a large bowl, toss the potatoes with the olive oil, garlic, cheese, pepper, and salt.
Place the fries into the air fryer basket and cook for 4 minutes; shake the basket and cook another 4 minutes.
Remove and serve warm.

Nutrition Facts (per serving):
Calories: 105 | Carbohydrates: 12.5g | Protein: 1.75g | Fat: 5.5g | Fiber: 1.25g | Sugar: 0.5g

---

 Servings: 4 25 Minutes

52 Crispy Italian Chicken Thighs

Ingredients:
½ cup mayonnaise
4 bone-in, skin-on chicken thighs
1 teaspoon salt
½ teaspoon ground black pepper
2 teaspoons Italian seasoning
1 cup Italian bread crumbs

Directions:
Preheat the air fryer to 370°F.
Brush mayonnaise over chicken thighs on both sides. Sprinkle thighs with salt, pepper, and Italian seasoning. Place bread crumbs into a resealable plastic bag and add thighs. Shake to coat.
Remove thighs from bag and spritz with cooking spray. Place in the air fryer basket and cook 25 minutes, turning thighs after 15 minutes, until skin is golden and crispy and internal temperature reaches at least 165°F.
Serve warm.

Nutrition Facts (per serving):
Calories: 224 | Carbohydrates: 2.4g | Protein: 9.2g | Fat: 18.6g | Fiber: 0.2g

53 Coconut Macaroons

Servings: 12 | 8 Minutes

Ingredients:
- 1⅓ cups shredded, sweetened coconut
- 4½ teaspoons flour
- 2 tablespoons sugar
- 1 egg white
- ½ teaspoon almond extract

Directions:
Preheat air fryer to 330ºF.
Mix all ingredients together.
Shape coconut mixture into 12 balls.
Place all 12 macaroons in air fryer basket. They won't expand, so you can place them close together, but they shouldn't touch.
Cook at 330ºF for 8 minutes, until golden.

Nutrition Facts (per serving):
Calories: 53 | Carbohydrates: 3.2g | Protein: 0.5g | Fat: 4.2g | Fiber: 0.5g | Sugar: 2.5g

54 Balsamic Green Beans With Bacon

Servings: 4 | 15 Minutes

Ingredients:
- 2 cups green beans, trimmed
- 1 tbsp butter, melted
- Salt and pepper to taste
- 1 bacon slice, diced
- 1 clove garlic, minced
- 1 tbsp balsamic vinegar

Directions:
Preheat air fryer to 375ºF. Combine green beans, butter, salt, and pepper in a bowl. Put the bean mixture in the frying basket and Air Fry for 5 minutes. Stir in bacon and Air Fry for 4 more minutes. Mix in garlic and cook for 1 minute. Transfer it to a serving dish, drizzle with balsamic vinegar and combine. Serve right away.

Nutrition Facts (per serving):
Calories: 40 | Carbohydrates: 2.5g | Protein: 1g | Fat: 3g | Fiber: 1g | Sugar: 1.25g

55 Roasted Fennel Salad

Servings: 3 | 20 Minutes

Ingredients:
- 3 cups (about ¾ pound) Trimmed fennel, roughly chopped
- 1½ tablespoons Olive oil
- ¼ teaspoon Table salt
- ¼ teaspoon Ground black pepper
- 1½ tablespoons White balsamic vinegar

Directions:
Preheat the air fryer to 400ºF.
Toss the fennel, olive oil, salt, and pepper in a large bowl until the fennel is well coated in the oil.
When the machine is at temperature, pour the fennel into the basket, spreading it out into as close to one layer as possible. Air-fry for 20 minutes, tossing and rearranging the fennel pieces twice so that any covered or touching parts get exposed to the air currents, until golden at the edges and softened.
Pour the fennel into a serving bowl. Add the vinegar while hot. Toss well, then cool a couple of minutes before serving. Or serve at room temperature.

Nutrition Facts (per serving):
Calories: 60 | Carbohydrates: 6g | Protein: 0.7g | Fat: 4g | Fiber: 2g | Sugar: 2g

56 Gingered Chicken Drumsticks

Servings: 3 | 25 Minutes

Ingredients:
- ¼ cup full-fat coconut milk
- 3 chicken drumsticks
- 2 teaspoons fresh ginger, minced
- 2 teaspoons galangal, minced
- 2 teaspoons ground turmeric
- Salt, to taste

Directions:
Preheat the Air fryer to 375ºF and grease an Air fryer basket.
Mix the coconut milk, galangal, ginger, and spices in a bowl.
Add the chicken drumsticks and coat generously with the marinade.
Refrigerate to marinate for at least 8 hours and transfer into the Air fryer basket.
Cook for about 25 minutes and dish out the chicken drumsticks onto a serving platter.

Nutrition Facts (per serving):
Calories: 212 | Carbohydrates: 1.8g | Protein: 9.2g | Fat: 18g | Fiber: 0.4g

57 Marshmallow Pastries

Servings: 8 | 5 Minutes

Ingredients:
- 4-ounce butter, melted
- 8 phyllo pastry sheets, thawed
- ½ cup chunky peanut butter
- 8 teaspoons marshmallow fluff
- Pinch of salt

Directions:
Preheat the Air fryer to 360ºF and grease an Air fryer basket.
Brush butter over 1 filo pastry sheet and top with a second filo sheet.
Brush butter over second filo pastry sheet and repeat with all the remaining sheets.
Cut the phyllo layers in 8 strips and put 1 tablespoon of peanut butter and 1 teaspoon of marshmallow fluff on the underside of a filo strip.
Fold the tip of the sheet over the filling to form a triangle and fold repeatedly in a zigzag manner.
Arrange the pastries into the Air fryer basket and cook for about 5 minutes.
Season with a pinch of salt and serve warm.

Nutrition Facts (per serving):
Calories: 228 | Carbohydrates: 13g | Protein: 3.5g | Fat: 17.5g | Fiber: 1g | Sugar: 4.5g

58 Foil Packet Lemon Butter Asparagus

Servings: 4 | 15 Minutes

Ingredients:
- 1 pound asparagus, ends trimmed
- ¼ cup salted butter, cubed
- Zest and juice of ½ medium lemon
- ½ teaspoon salt
- ¼ teaspoon ground black pepper

Directions:
Preheat the air fryer to 375ºF. Cut a 6" × 6" square of foil.
Place asparagus on foil square.
Dot asparagus with butter. Sprinkle lemon zest, salt, and pepper on top of asparagus. Drizzle lemon juice over asparagus.
Fold foil over asparagus and seal the edges closed to form a packet.
Place in the air fryer basket and cook 15 minutes until tender. Serve warm.

Nutrition Facts (per serving):
Calories: 113 | Carbohydrates: 4.5g | Protein: 2.5g | Fat: 10g | Fiber: 2g | Sugar: 2g

59 Colorful Vegetable Medley

Servings: 4 | 20 Minutes

Ingredients:
- 1 lb green beans, chopped
- 2 carrots, cubed
- Salt and pepper to taste
- 1 zucchini, cut into chunks
- 1 red bell pepper, sliced
- Cooking spray

Directions:
Preheat air fryer to 390ºF. Combine green beans, carrots, salt and pepper in a large bowl. Spray with cooking oil and transfer to the frying basket. Roast for 6 minutes.
Combine zucchini and red pepper in a bowl. Season to taste and spray with cooking oil; set aside. When the cooking time is up, add the zucchini and red pepper to the basket. Cook for another 6 minutes. Serve and enjoy.

Nutrition Facts (per serving):
Calories: 65 | Carbohydrates: 11g | Protein: 2g | Fat: 2g | Fiber: 3g | Sugar: 5g

60 Smoked Halibut And Eggs In Brioche

Servings: 4 | 25 Minutes

Ingredients:
- 4 brioche rolls
- 1 pound smoked halibut, chopped
- 4 eggs
- 1 teaspoon dried thyme
- 1 teaspoon dried basil
- Salt and black pepper, to taste
- Cooking spray

Directions:
Cut off the top of each brioche; then, scoop out the insides to make the shells.
Lay the prepared brioche shells in the lightly greased cooking basket.
Spritz with cooking oil; add the halibut. Crack an egg into each brioche shell; sprinkle with thyme, basil, salt, and black pepper.
Bake in the preheated Air Fryer at 325ºF for 20 minutes. Bon appétit!

Nutrition Facts (per serving):
Calories: 342 | Carbohydrates: 21.6g | Protein: 26.9g | Fat: 16.8g | Fiber: 1.1g

61 Toasted Coconut Flakes

Servings: 1 | 5 Minutes

Ingredients:
1 cup unsweetened coconut flakes
2 tsp. coconut oil, melted
¼ cup granular erythritol
Salt

Directions:
In a large bowl, combine the coconut flakes, oil, granular erythritol, and a pinch of salt, ensuring that the flakes are coated completely.
Place the coconut flakes in your fryer and cook at 300°F for three minutes, giving the basket a good shake a few times throughout the cooking time. Fry until golden and serve.

Nutrition Facts (per serving):
Calories: 520 | Carbohydrates: 10g | Protein: 5g | Fat: 50g | Fiber: 7g | Sugar: 2g

62 Fingerling Potatoes

Servings: 4 | 15 Minutes

Ingredients:
1 pound fingerling potatoes
1 tablespoon light olive oil
½ teaspoon dried parsley
½ teaspoon lemon juice
coarsely ground sea salt

Directions:
Cut potatoes in half lengthwise.
In a large bowl, combine potatoes, oil, parsley, and lemon juice. Stir well to coat potatoes.
Place potatoes in air fryer basket and cook at 360°F for 15 minutes or until lightly browned and tender inside.
Sprinkle with sea salt before serving.

Nutrition Facts (per serving):
Calories: 108 | Carbohydrates: 22.5g | Protein: 2.25g | Fat: 2.5g | Fiber: 2g | Sugar: 1g

63 Cottage And Mayonnaise Stuffed Peppers

Servings: 2 | 20 Minutes

Ingredients:
1 red bell pepper, top and seeds removed
1 yellow bell pepper, top and seeds removed
Salt and pepper, to taste
1 cup Cottage cheese
4 tablespoons mayonnaise
2 pickles, chopped

Directions:
Arrange the peppers in the lightly greased cooking basket. Cook in the preheated Air Fryer at 400°F for 15 minutes, turning them over halfway through the cooking time.
Season with salt and pepper.
Then, in a mixing bowl, combine the cream cheese with the mayonnaise and chopped pickles. Stuff the pepper with the cream cheese mixture and serve. Enjoy!

Nutrition Facts (per serving):
Calories: 190 | Carbohydrates: 8g | Protein: 11g | Fat: 13g | Fiber: 1.5g | Sugar: 5g

64 Almond Flour Battered Wings

Servings: 4 | 25 Minutes

Ingredients:
¼ cup butter, melted
¾ cup almond flour
16 pieces chicken wings
2 tablespoons stevia powder
4 tablespoons minced garlic
Salt and pepper to taste

Directions:
Preheat the air fryer for 5 minutes.
In a mixing bowl, combine the chicken wings, almond flour, stevia powder, and garlic Season with salt and pepper to taste.
Place in the air fryer basket and cook for 25 minutes at 400°F.
Halfway through the cooking time, make sure that you give the fryer basket a shake.
Once cooked, place in a bowl and drizzle with melted butter. Toss to coat.

Nutrition Facts (per serving):
Calories: 318 | Carbohydrates: 4.2g | Protein: 24.6g | Fat: 22.4g | Fiber: 1.6g

65 Nutty Fudge Muffins

Servings: 10 | 10 Minutes

Ingredients:
- 1 package fudge brownie mix
- 1 egg
- 2 teaspoons water
- ¼ cup walnuts, chopped
- 1/3 cup vegetable oil

Directions:
Preheat the Air fryer to 300ºF and grease 10 muffin tins lightly.
Mix brownie mix, egg, oil and water in a bowl.
Fold in the walnuts and pour the mixture in the muffin cups.
Transfer the muffin tins in the Air fryer basket and cook for about 10 minutes.
Dish out and serve immediately.

Nutrition Facts (per serving):
Calories: 232 | Carbohydrates: 29.6g | Protein: 2.4g | Fat: 12g | Fiber: 1.2g | Sugar: 20g

66 Roasted Heirloom Carrots With Orange And Thyme

Servings: 2 | 12 Minutes

Ingredients:
- 10 to 12 heirloom or rainbow carrots, scrubbed but not peeled
- 1 teaspoon olive oil
- salt and freshly ground black pepper
- 1 tablespoon butter
- 1 teaspoon fresh orange zest
- 1 teaspoon chopped fresh thyme

Directions:
Preheat the air fryer to 400ºF.
Scrub the carrots and halve them lengthwise. Toss them in the olive oil, season with salt and freshly ground black pepper and transfer to the air fryer.
Air-fry at 400ºF for 12 minutes, shaking the basket every once in a while to rotate the carrots as they cook.
As soon as the carrots have finished cooking, add the butter, orange zest and thyme and toss all the ingredients together in the air fryer basket to melt the butter and coat evenly. Serve warm.

Nutrition Facts (per serving):
Calories: 135 | Carbohydrates: 24g | Protein: 2g | Fat: 5g | Fiber: 5g | Sugar: 12g

67 Black Bean And Rice Burrito Filling

Servings: 4 | 20 Minutes

Ingredients:
- 1 cup uncooked instant long-grain white rice
- 1 cup salsa
- ½ cup vegetable broth
- 1 cup black beans
- ½ cup corn

Directions:
Preheat the air fryer to 400ºF.
Mix all ingredients in a 3-quart baking dish until well combined.
Cover with foil, being sure to tuck foil under the bottom of the pan to ensure the air fryer fan does not blow it off.
Cook 20 minutes, stirring twice during cooking. Serve warm.

Nutrition Facts (per serving):
Calories: 190 | Carbohydrates: 33g | Protein: 6g | Fat: 4g | Fiber: 4g | Sugar: 3g

68 Green Bean Sautée

Servings: 4 | 25 Minutes

Ingredients:
- 1 ½ lb green beans, trimmed
- 1 tbsp olive oil
- ½ tsp garlic powder
- Salt and pepper to taste
- 4 garlic cloves, thinly sliced
- 1 tbsp fresh basil, chopped

Directions:
Preheat the air fryer to 375ºF. Toss the beans with the olive oil, garlic powder, salt, and pepper in a bowl, then add to the frying basket. Air Fry for 6 minutes, shaking the basket halfway through the cooking time. Add garlic to the air fryer and cook for 3-6 minutes or until the green beans are tender and the garlic slices start to brown. Sprinkle with basil and serve warm.

Nutrition Facts (per serving):
Calories: 87 | Carbohydrates: 9.6g | Protein: 2.4g | Fat: 4.6g | Fiber: 3.7g

69 Grits Again

Servings: 2 | 10 Minutes

Ingredients:
- cooked grits
- plain breadcrumbs
- oil for misting or cooking spray
- honey or maple syrup for serving (optional)

Directions:
While grits are still warm, spread them into a square or rectangular baking pan, about ½-inch thick. If your grits are thicker than that, scoop some out into another pan.

Chill several hours or overnight, until grits are cold and firm.

When ready to cook, pour off any water that has collected in pan and cut grits into 2- to 3-inch squares. Dip grits squares in breadcrumbs and place in air fryer basket in single layer, close but not touching.

Cook at 390°F for 10 minutes, until heated through and crispy brown on the outside.

Serve while hot either plain or with a drizzle of honey or maple syrup.

Nutrition Facts (per serving):
Calories: 130 | Carbohydrates: 23g | Protein: 2.5g | Fat: 2g | Fiber: 1g | Sugar: 0.5g

70 Garlic Parmesan-roasted Cauliflower

Servings: 6 | 15 Minutes

Ingredients:
- 1 medium head cauliflower, leaves and core removed, cut into florets
- 2 tablespoons salted butter, melted
- ½ tablespoon salt
- 2 cloves garlic, peeled and finely minced
- ½ cup grated Parmesan cheese, divided

Directions:
Toss cauliflower in a large bowl with butter. Sprinkle with salt, garlic, and ¼ cup Parmesan.

Place florets into ungreased air fryer basket. Adjust the temperature to 350°F and set the timer for 15 minutes, shaking basket halfway through cooking. Cauliflower will be browned at the edges and tender when done. Transfer florets to a large serving dish and sprinkle with remaining Parmesan. Serve warm.

Nutrition Facts (per serving):
Calories: 62 | Carbohydrates: 3g | Protein: 2.8g | Fat: 4.7g | Fiber: 1.3g | Sugar: 1.2g

71 Roasted Cauliflower

 Servings: 2 | 20 Minutes

Ingredients:
- medium head cauliflower
- 2 tbsp. salted butter, melted
- 1 medium lemon
- 1 tsp. dried parsley
- ½ tsp. garlic powder

Directions:
Having removed the leaves from the cauliflower head, brush it with the melted butter. Grate the rind of the lemon over it and then drizzle some juice. Finally add the parsley and garlic powder on top.

Transfer the cauliflower to the basket of the fryer.

Cook for fifteen minutes at 350°F, checking regularly to ensure it doesn't overcook. The cauliflower is ready when it is hot and fork tender.

Take care when removing it from the fryer, cut up and serve.

Nutrition Facts (per serving):
Calories: 120 | Carbohydrates: 7g | Protein: 2g | Fat: 10g | Fiber: 3g | Sugar: 2g

72 Skewered Corn In Air Fryer

 Servings: 2 | 25 Minutes

Ingredients:
- 1-pound apricot, halved
- 2 ears of corn
- 2 medium green peppers, cut into large chunks
- 2 teaspoons prepared mustard
- Salt and pepper to taste

Directions:
Preheat the air fryer to 330°F.

Place the grill pan accessory in the air fryer.

On the double layer rack with the skewer accessories, skewer the corn, green peppers, and apricot. Season with salt and pepper to taste.

Place skewered corn on the double layer rack and cook for 25 minutes.

Once cooked, brush with prepared mustard.

Nutrition Facts (per serving):
Calories: 162 | Carbohydrates: 30.4g | Protein: 4.3g | Fat: 3.2g | Fiber: 4.1g

73 Cauliflower

Servings: 4 | 6 Minutes

Ingredients:
½ cup water
1 10-ounce package frozen cauliflower (florets)
1 teaspoon lemon pepper seasoning

Directions:
Pour the water into air fryer drawer.
Pour the frozen cauliflower into the air fryer basket and sprinkle with lemon pepper seasoning.
Cook at 390°F for approximately 6 minutes.

Nutrition Facts (per serving):
Calories: 18 | Carbohydrates: 3g | Protein: 1.25g | Fat: 0.1g | Fiber: 1.5g | Sugar: 1.25g

---

74 Polenta

Servings: 4 | 15 Minutes

Ingredients:
1 pound polenta
¼ cup flour
oil for misting or cooking spray

Directions:
Cut polenta into ½-inch slices.
Dip slices in flour to coat well. Spray both sides with oil or cooking spray.
Cook at 390°F for 5 minutes. Turn polenta and spray both sides again with oil.
Cook 10 more minutes or until brown and crispy.

Nutrition Facts (per serving):
Calories: 133 | Carbohydrates: 27.5g | Protein: 2.5g | Fat: 0.75g | Fiber: 1.5g | Sugar: 0.25g

---

75 Zucchini Topped With Coconut Cream 'n Bacon

Servings: 3 | 20 Minutes

Ingredients:
1 tablespoon lemon juice
3 slices bacon, fried and crumbled
3 tablespoons olive oil
3 zucchini squashes
4 tablespoons coconut cream
Salt and pepper to taste

Directions:
Preheat the air fryer for 5 minutes.
Line up chopsticks on both sides of the zucchini and slice thinly until you hit the stick. Brush the zucchinis with olive oil. Set aside.
Place the zucchini in the air fryer. Bake for 20 minutes at 350°F.
Meanwhile, combine the coconut cream and lemon juice in a mixing bowl. Season with salt and pepper to taste.
Once the zucchini is cooked, scoop the coconut cream mixture and drizzle on top.
Sprinkle with bacon bits.

Nutrition Facts (per serving):
Calories: 230 | Carbohydrates: 6g | Protein: 5g | Fat: 21g | Fiber: 2g | Sugar: 3g

---

76 White Wheat Walnut Bread

Servings: 8 | 25 Minutes

Ingredients:
1 cup lukewarm water
1 packet RapidRise yeast
1 tablespoon light brown sugar
2 cups whole-grain white wheat flour
1 egg, room temperature, beaten with a fork
2 teaspoons olive oil
½ teaspoon salt
½ cup chopped walnuts
cooking spray

Directions:
In a small bowl, mix the water, yeast, and brown sugar.
Pour yeast mixture over flour and mix until smooth. Add the egg, olive oil, and salt and beat with a wooden spoon for 2 minutes.
Stir in chopped walnuts. You will have very thick batter rather than stiff bread dough.
Spray air fryer baking pan with cooking spray and pour in batter, smoothing the top.
Let batter rise for 15 minutes.
Preheat air fryer to 360°F.
Cook bread for 25 minutes, until toothpick pushed into center comes out with crumbs clinging. Let bread rest for 10 minutes before removing from pan.

Nutrition Facts (per serving):
Calories: 180 | Carbohydrates: 21g | Protein: 6g | Fat: 9g | Fiber: 3g

Servings: 3 — 10 Minutes

77 Taco Okra

Ingredients:
9 oz okra, chopped
1 teaspoon taco seasoning
1 teaspoon sunflower oil

Directions:
In the mixing bowl mix up chopped okra, taco seasoning, and sunflower oil. Then preheat the air fryer to 385ºF. Put the okra mixture in the air fryer and cook it for 5 minutes. Then shake the vegetables well and cook them for 5 minutes more.

Nutrition Facts (per serving):
Calories: 37 | Carbohydrates: 5g | Protein: 1.3g | Fat: 1.7g | Fiber: 2g | Sugar: 1g

---

Servings: 4 — 12 Minutes

78 Rosemary Roasted Potatoes With Lemon

Ingredients:
1 pound small red-skinned potatoes, halved or cut into bite-sized chunks
1 tablespoon olive oil
1 teaspoon finely chopped fresh rosemary
¼ teaspoon salt
freshly ground black pepper
1 tablespoon lemon zest

Directions:
Preheat the air fryer to 400ºF.
Toss the potatoes with the olive oil, rosemary, salt and freshly ground black pepper.
Air-fry for 12 minutes, tossing the potatoes a few times throughout the cooking process.
As soon as the potatoes are tender to a knifepoint, toss them with the lemon zest and more salt if desired.

Nutrition Facts (per serving):
Calories: 105 | Carbohydrates: 18g | Protein: 2.5g | Fat: 3.5g | Fiber: 1.75g | Sugar: 1g

---

Servings: 4 — 20 Minutes

79 Cinnamon Sugar Tortilla Chips

Ingredients:
4 flour tortillas
1/4 cup vegan margarine, melted
1 ½ tablespoons ground cinnamon
1/4 cup caster sugar

Directions:
Slice each tortilla into eight slices. Brush the tortilla pieces with the melted margarine.
In a mixing bowl, thoroughly combine the cinnamon and sugar. Toss the cinnamon mixture with the tortillas.
Transfer to the cooking basket and cook at 360ºF for 8 minutes or until lightly golden. Work in batches.
They will crisp up as they cool. Serve and enjoy!

Nutrition Facts (per serving):
Calories: 200 | Carbohydrates: 26g | Protein: 3g | Fat: 10g | Fiber: 1g | Sugar: 8g

---

Servings: 6 — 25 Minutes

80 Whole-grain Cornbread

Ingredients:
1 cup stoneground cornmeal
½ cup brown rice flour
1 teaspoon sugar
2 teaspoons baking powder
¼ teaspoon salt
1 cup milk
2 tablespoons oil
2 eggs
cooking spray

Directions:
Preheat the air fryer to 360ºF.
In a medium mixing bowl, mix cornmeal, brown rice flour, sugar, baking powder, and salt together.
Add the remaining ingredients and beat with a spoon until batter is smooth.
Spray air fryer baking pan with nonstick cooking spray and add the cornbread batter.
Bake at 360ºF for 25 minutes, until center is done.

Nutrition Facts (per serving):
Calories: 165 | Carbohydrates: 22g | Protein: 5g | Fat: 6g | Fiber: 2g

Servings: 4 | 10 Minutes

81 Bacon-wrapped Asparagus

Ingredients:
1 tablespoon extra-virgin olive oil
½ teaspoon sea salt
¼ cup grated Parmesan cheese
1 pound asparagus, ends trimmed
8 slices bacon

Directions:
Preheat the air fryer to 380ºF.
In large bowl, mix together the olive oil, sea salt, and Parmesan cheese. Toss the asparagus in the olive oil mixture.
Evenly divide the asparagus into 8 bundles. Wrap 1 piece of bacon around each bundle, not overlapping the bacon but spreading it across the bundle.
Place the asparagus bundles into the air fryer basket, not touching. Work in batches as needed.
Cook for 8 minutes; check for doneness, and cook another 2 minutes.

Nutrition Facts (per serving):
Calories: 235 | Carbohydrates: 4g | Protein: 12g | Fat: 19g | Fiber: 2g | Sugar: 1.5g

---

Servings: 5 | 15 Minutes

82 Swiss Chard Mix

Ingredients:
7 oz Swiss chard, chopped
4 oz Swiss cheese, grated
4 teaspoons almond flour
½ cup heavy cream
½ teaspoon ground black pepper

Directions:
Mix up Swiss chard and Swiss cheese. Add almond flour, heavy cream, and ground black pepper. Stir the mixture until homogenous. After this, transfer it in 5 small ramekins. Preheat the air fryer to 365ºF. Place the ramekins with gratin in the air fryer basket and cook them for 15 minutes.

Nutrition Facts (per serving):
Calories: 114 | Carbohydrates: 1.6g | Protein: 4g | Fat: 10.4g | Fiber: 0.6g | Sugar: 0.6g

---

 Servings: 6 20 Minutes

83 Spice-rubbed Pork Loin

Ingredients:
1 teaspoon paprika
½ teaspoon ground cumin
½ teaspoon chili powder
½ teaspoon garlic powder
2 tablespoons coconut oil
1 boneless pork loin
½ teaspoon salt
¼ teaspoon ground black pepper

Directions:
In a small bowl, mix paprika, cumin, chili powder, and garlic powder.
Drizzle coconut oil over pork. Sprinkle pork loin with salt and pepper, then rub spice mixture evenly on all sides.
Place pork loin into ungreased air fryer basket. Adjust the temperature to 400ºF and set the timer for 20 minutes, turning pork halfway through cooking. Pork loin will be browned and have an internal temperature of at least 145ºF when done. Serve warm.

Nutrition Facts (per serving):
Calories: 223 | Carbohydrates: 1.2g | Protein: 14g | Fat: 18g | Fiber: 1g

---

 Servings: 4 25 Minutes

84 Italian Bruschetta With Mushrooms & Cheese

Ingredients:
½ cup button mushrooms, chopped
½ baguette, sliced
1 garlic clove, minced
3 oz sliced Parmesan cheese
1 tbsp extra virgin olive oil
Salt and pepper to taste

Directions:
Preheat air fryer to 350ºF. Add the mushrooms, olive oil, salt, pepper, and garlic to a mixing bowl and stir thoroughly to combine. Divide the mushroom mixture between the bread slices, drizzling all over the surface with olive oil, then cover with Parmesan slices. Place the covered bread slices in the greased frying basket and Bake for 15 minutes. Serve and enjoy!

Nutrition Facts (per serving):
Calories: 190 | Carbohydrates: 17g | Protein: 7g | Fat: 11g | Fiber: 1g

Servings: 4 — 8 Minutes

85 Crispy Green Beans

Ingredients:
- 2 teaspoons olive oil
- ½ pound fresh green beans, ends trimmed
- ¼ teaspoon salt
- ¼ teaspoon ground black pepper

Directions:
In a large bowl, drizzle olive oil over green beans and sprinkle with salt and pepper.
Place green beans into ungreased air fryer basket. Adjust the temperature to 350°F and set the timer for 8 minutes, shaking the basket two times during cooking. Green beans will be dark golden and crispy at the edges when done. Serve warm.

Nutrition Facts (per serving):
Calories: 25 | Carbohydrates: 2.5g | Protein: 0.6g | Fat: 1.75g | Fiber: 1g | Sugar: 1g

---

Servings: 8 — 15 Minutes

86 Sweet Butternut Squash

Ingredients:
- 1 medium butternut squash, peeled and cubed
- 2 tablespoons salted butter, melted
- ½ teaspoon salt
- 1 ½ tablespoons brown sugar
- ½ teaspoon ground cinnamon

Directions:
Preheat the air fryer to 400°F.
In a large bowl, place squash and add butter. Toss to coat. Sprinkle salt, brown sugar, and cinnamon over squash and toss to fully coat.
Place squash in the air fryer basket and cook 15 minutes, shaking the basket three times during cooking, until the edges are golden and the center is fork-tender. Serve warm.

Nutrition Facts (per serving):
Calories: 58 | Carbohydrates: 13g | Protein: 0.75g | Fat: 1.5g | Fiber: 2g | Sugar: 3g

---

Servings: 3 — 20 Minutes

87 Crispy Pierogi With Kielbasa And Onions

Ingredients:
- 6 Frozen potato and cheese pierogi, thawed
- ½ pound Smoked kielbasa, sliced into ½-inch-thick rounds
- ¾ cup Very roughly chopped sweet onion, preferably Vidalia
- Vegetable oil spray

Directions:
Preheat the air fryer to 375°F.
Put the pierogi, kielbasa rounds, and onion in a large bowl. Coat them with vegetable oil spray, toss well, spray again, and toss until everything is glistening. When the machine is at temperature, dump the contents of the bowl it into the basket. Air-fry, tossing and rearranging everything twice so that all covered surfaces get exposed, for 20 minutes, or until the sausages have begun to brown and the pierogi are crisp.
Pour the contents of the basket onto a serving platter. Wait a minute or two just to take make sure nothing's searing hot before serving.

Nutrition Facts (per serving):
Calories: 248 | Carbohydrates: 14g | Protein: 9g | Fat: 18g | Fiber: 1g

---

Servings: 4 — 25 Minutes

88 Honey Tater Tots With Bacon

Ingredients:
- 24 frozen tater tots
- 6 bacon slices
- 1 tbsp honey
- 1 cup grated cheddar

Directions:
Preheat air fryer to 400°F. Air Fry the tater tots for 10 minutes, shaking the basket once halfway through cooking. Cut the bacon into pieces. When the tater tots are done, remove them from the fryer to a baking pan. Top them with bacon and drizzle with honey. Air Fry for 5 minutes to crisp up the bacon. Top the tater tots with cheese and cook for 2 minutes to melt the cheese. Serve.

Nutrition Facts (per serving):
Calories: 320 | Carbohydrates: 16g | Protein: 10g | Fat: 24g | Fiber: 1g

Servings: 3 — 10 Minutes

89 Perfect Asparagus

Ingredients:
- 1 pound Very thin asparagus spears
- 2 tablespoons Olive oil
- 1 teaspoon Coarse sea salt or kosher salt
- ¾ teaspoon Finely grated lemon zest

Directions:
Preheat the air fryer to 400°F.
Trim just enough off the bottom of the asparagus spears so they'll fit in the basket. Put the spears on a large plate and drizzle them with some of the olive oil. Turn them over and drizzle more olive oil, working to get all the spears coated.
When the machine is at temperature, place the spears in one direction in the basket. They may be touching. Air-fry for 10 minutes, tossing and rearranging the spears twice, until tender.
Dump the contents of the basket on a serving platter. Spread out the spears. Sprinkle them with the salt and lemon zest while still warm. Serve at once.

Nutrition Facts (per serving):
Calories: 100 | Carbohydrates: 6.7g | Protein: 2.7g | Fat: 8g | Fiber: 3.3g | Sugar: 3g

---

Servings: 4 — 12 Minutes

90 Savory Roasted Carrots

Ingredients:
- 1 pound baby carrots
- 2 tablespoons dry ranch seasoning
- 3 tablespoons salted butter, melted

Directions:
Preheat the air fryer to 360°F.
Place carrots into a 6" round baking dish. Sprinkle carrots with ranch seasoning and drizzle with butter. Gently toss to coat.
Place in the air fryer basket and cook 12 minutes, stirring twice during cooking, until carrots are tender. Serve warm.

Nutrition Facts (per serving):
Calories: 100 | Carbohydrates: 8.8g | Protein: 0.75g | Fat: 7g | Fiber: 1.75g | Sugar: 4.5g

---

Servings: 6 — 20 Minutes

91 Crispy 'n Salted Chicken Meatballs

Ingredients:
- ½ cup almond flour
- ¾ pound skinless boneless chicken breasts, ground
- 1 ½ teaspoon herbs de Provence
- 1 tablespoon coconut milk
- 2 eggs, beaten
- Salt and pepper to taste

Directions:
Mix all ingredient in a bowl.
Form small balls using the palms of your hands.
Place in the fridge to set for at least 2 hours.
Preheat the air fryer for 5 minutes.
Place the chicken balls in the fryer basket.
Cook for 20 minutes at 325°F.
Halfway through the cooking time, give the fryer basket a shake to cook evenly on all sides.

Nutrition Facts (per serving):
Calories: 219 | Carbohydrates: 2.1g | Protein: 8g | Fat: 19g | Fiber: 1g

---

Servings: 3 — 25 Minutes

92 Smokehouse-style Beef Ribs

Ingredients:
- ¼ teaspoon Mild smoked paprika
- ¼ teaspoon Garlic powder
- ¼ teaspoon Onion powder
- ¼ teaspoon Table salt
- ¼ teaspoon Ground black pepper
- 3 10- to 12-ounce beef back ribs (not beef short ribs)

Directions:
Preheat the air fryer to 350°F.
Mix the smoked paprika, garlic powder, onion powder, salt, and pepper in a small bowl until uniform. Massage and pat this mixture onto the ribs.
When the machine is at temperature, set the ribs in the basket in one layer, turning them on their sides if necessary, sort of like they're spooning but with at least ¼ inch air space between them. Air-fry for 25 minutes, turning once, until deep brown and sizzling. Use kitchen tongs to transfer the ribs to a wire rack. Cool for 5 minutes before serving.

Nutrition Facts (per serving):
Calories: 400 | Carbohydrates: 0g | Protein: 28g | Fat: 32g | Fiber: 0g

Servings: 4 | 10 Minutes

93 Buttery Mushrooms

Ingredients:
8 ounces cremini mushrooms, halved
2 tablespoons salted butter, melted
¼ teaspoon salt
¼ teaspoon ground black pepper

Directions:
In a medium bowl, toss mushrooms with butter, then sprinkle with salt and pepper. Place into ungreased air fryer basket. Adjust the temperature to 400°F and set the timer for 10 minutes, shaking the basket halfway through cooking. Mushrooms will be tender when done. Serve warm.

Nutrition Facts (per serving):
Calories: 65 | Carbohydrates: 2g | Protein: 1.25g | Fat: 6g | Fiber: 0.5g | Sugar: 0.75g

---

Servings: 4 | 12 Minutes

94 Bacon-balsamic Brussels Sprouts

Ingredients:
2 cups trimmed and halved fresh Brussels sprouts
2 tablespoons olive oil
¼ teaspoon salt
¼ teaspoon ground black pepper
2 tablespoons balsamic vinegar
2 slices cooked sugar-free bacon, crumbled

Directions:
In a large bowl, toss Brussels sprouts in olive oil, then sprinkle with salt and pepper. Place into ungreased air fryer basket. Adjust the temperature to 375°F and set the timer for 12 minutes, shaking the basket halfway through cooking. Brussels sprouts will be tender and browned when done.
Place sprouts in a large serving dish and drizzle with balsamic vinegar. Sprinkle bacon over top. Serve warm.

Nutrition Facts (per serving):
Calories: 63 | Carbohydrates: 4.5g | Protein: 1.5g | Fat: 4.5g | Fiber: 1.5g | Sugar: 1g

---

 Servings: 4 20 Minutes

95 Chicken Sausage In Dijon Sauce

Ingredients:
4 chicken sausages
1/4 cup mayonnaise
2 tablespoons Dijon mustard
1 tablespoon balsamic vinegar
1/2 teaspoon dried rosemary

Directions:
Arrange the sausages on the grill pan and transfer it to the preheated Air Fryer.
Grill the sausages at 350°F for approximately 13 minutes. Turn them halfway through cooking. Meanwhile, prepare the sauce by mixing the remaining ingredients with a wire whisk. Serve the warm sausages with chilled Dijon sauce. Enjoy!

Nutrition Facts (per serving):
Calories: 222 | Carbohydrates: 2.2g | Protein: 9g | Fat: 19g | Fiber: 0g

---

 Servings: 4 25 minutes

96 Bacon-Wrapped Chicken Breasts

Ingredients:
2 chicken breasts
8 oz cream cheese
1 tbsp butter
6 turkey bacon slices
Salt to taste
1 tbsp fresh parsley, chopped

Directions:
Preheat the air fryer to 390 F. Stretch out the bacon and lay the slices in 2 sets; 3 bacon strips together on each side. Place the chicken on each bacon set. Use a knife to smear the cream cheese on both.
Spread the butter on top and sprinkle with salt. Wrap the turkey bacon around the chicken and secure the ends into the wrap. Place the wrapped chicken in the greased frying basket and AirFry for 16-18 minutes, turning halfway through. Top with fresh parsley and serve with steamed greens (optional).

Nutrition Facts (per serving):
Calories: 330 | Carbohydrates: 2g | Protein: 31g | Fat: 21g | Fiber: 0g

97 Brussels Sprouts

Servings: 3 | 5 Minutes

Ingredients:
1 10-ounce package frozen brussels sprouts, thawed and halved
2 teaspoons olive oil
salt and pepper

Directions:
Toss the brussels sprouts and olive oil together. Place them in the air fryer basket and season to taste with salt and pepper.
Cook at 360°F for approximately 5 minutes, until the edges begin to brown.

Nutrition Facts (per serving):
Calories: 43 | Carbohydrates: 4g | Protein: 1.7g | Fat: 3g | Fiber: 1.7g | Sugar: 0.7g

98 Southwest-style Corn Cobs

Servings: 6 | 15 Minutes

Ingredients:
½ cup sour cream
1 ½ teaspoons chili powder
Juice and zest of 1 medium lime
¼ teaspoon salt
6 mini corn cobs
½ cup crumbled cotija cheese

Directions:
Preheat the air fryer to 350°F.
In a medium bowl, mix sour cream, chili powder, lime zest and juice, and salt.
Brush mixture all over corn cobs and place them in the air fryer basket. Cook 15 minutes until corn is tender. Sprinkle with cotija and serve.

Nutrition Facts (per serving):
Calories: 85 | Carbohydrates: 6.5g | Protein: 2g | Fat: 6g | Fiber: 0.8g | Sugar: 1g

99 Buffalo Chicken Sandwiches

Servings: 4 | 20 Minutes

Ingredients:
4 boneless, skinless chicken thighs
1 packet dry ranch seasoning
¼ cup buffalo sauce
4 slices pepper jack cheese
4 sandwich buns

Directions:
Preheat the air fryer to 375°F.
Sprinkle each chicken thigh with ranch seasoning and spritz with cooking spray.
Place chicken in the air fryer basket and cook 20 minutes, turning chicken halfway through, until chicken is brown at the edges and internal temperature reaches at least 165°F.
Drizzle buffalo sauce over chicken, top with a slice of cheese, and place on buns to serve.

Nutrition Facts (per serving):
Calories: 224 | Carbohydrates: 2.4g | Protein: 9g | Fat: 19g | Fiber: 0g

100 Effortless Chicken Drumsticks

Servings: 4 | 25 minutes

Ingredients:
1 lb chicken drumsticks
1 tsp garlic powder
1 tsp cayenne pepper
½ cup flour
¼ cup milk
Salt and black pepper to taste

Directions:
Preheat the air fryer to 390 F. Spray the frying basket with cooking spray. In a small bowl, mix garlic powder, cayenne pepper, salt, and black pepper. Rub the chicken drumsticks with the mixture.
In a separate bowl, pour the flour. Dunk the chicken in the milk, then roll in the flour to coat. Place the drumsticks in the frying basket and spray with cooking spray. AirFry for 14-16 minutes, flipping once.

Nutrition Facts (per serving):
Calories: 210 | Carbohydrates: 9g | Protein: 22g | Fat: 10g | Fiber: 0g

Servings: 2 — 8 Minutes

101 Spicy Fried Green Beans

Ingredients:
12 ounces green beans, trimmed
2 small dried hot red chili peppers (like árbol)
¼ cup panko breadcrumbs
1 tablespoon olive oil
½ teaspoon salt
⅛ teaspoon crushed red pepper flakes
2 scallions, thinly sliced

Directions:
Preheat the air fryer to 400°F.
Toss the green beans, chili peppers and panko breadcrumbs with the olive oil, salt and crushed red pepper flakes.
Air-fry for 8 minutes, shaking the basket once during the cooking process. The crumbs will fall into the bottom drawer – don't worry.
Transfer the green beans to a serving dish, sprinkle the scallions and the toasted crumbs from the air fryer drawer on top and serve. The dried peppers are not to be eaten, but they do look nice with the green beans. You can leave them in, or take them out as you please.

Nutrition Facts (per serving):
Calories: 100 | Carbohydrates: 9g | Protein: 2g | Fat: 7g | Fiber: 2.5g | Sugar: 2.5g

Servings: 4 — 12 Minutes

102 Perfect Broccoli

Ingredients:
5 cups 1- to 1½-inch fresh broccoli florets (not frozen)
Olive oil spray
¾ teaspoon Table salt

Directions:
Preheat the air fryer to 375°F.
Put the broccoli florets in a big bowl, coat them generously with olive oil spray, then toss to coat all surfaces, even down into the crannies, spraying them in a couple of times more. Sprinkle the salt on top and toss again.
When the machine is at temperature, pour the florets into the basket. Air-fry for 10 minutes, tossing and rearranging the pieces twice so that all the covered or touching bits are eventually exposed to the air currents, until lightly browned but still crunchy.
Pour the florets into a serving bowl. Cool for a minute or two, then serve hot.

Nutrition Facts (per serving):
Calories: 35 | Carbohydrates: 6g | Protein: 2.75g | Fat: 0.75g | Fiber: 2.5g | Sugar: 1.25g

Servings: 4 — 20 Minutes

103 Creamy Onion Chicken

Ingredients:
1 ½ cup onion soup mix
1 cup mushroom soup
½ cup cream

Directions:
Preheat Fryer to 400°F. Add mushrooms, onion mix and cream in a frying pan. Heat on low heat for 1 minute. Pour the warm mixture over chicken slices and allow to sit for 25 minutes. Place the marinated chicken in the air fryer cooking basket and cook for 15 minutes. Serve with the remaining cream.

Nutrition Facts (per serving):
Calories: 223 | Carbohydrates: 2.8g | Protein: 9g | Fat: 18.5g | Fiber: 0g

Servings: 4 — 25 minutes

104 Gambas al Ajillo (Garlic Shrimp)

Ingredients:
1 lb shrimp, peeled and deveined
½ tsp Cajun seasoning
10 lettuce leaves
1 tbsp olive oil
¼ tsp garlic powder
2 tbsp lemon juice, chopped

Directions:
Mix the garlic powder, half of the lemon juice, olive oil, and Cajun seasoning in a bowl to make a marinade. Toss the shrimp to coat thoroughly. Cover with a plastic wrap and refrigerate for 30 minutes.
Preheat the air fryer to 400 F. Place the shrimp in the greased frying basket and AirFry for 5 minutes. Shake the basket and cook for 7-8 more minutes, until cooked through. Arrange the lettuce leaves on a plate and top with the shrimp. Drizzle with the remaining lemon juice and serve.

Nutrition Facts (per serving):
Calories: 150 | Carbohydrates: 2g | Protein: 25g | Fat: 5g | Fiber: 1g

Servings: 2   7 Minutes

105 Roasted Belgian Endive With Pistachios And Lemon

Ingredients:
2 Medium 3-ounce Belgian endive head(s)
2 tablespoons Olive oil
½ teaspoon Table salt
¼ cup Finely chopped unsalted shelled pistachios
Up to 2 teaspoons Lemon juice

Directions:
Preheat the air fryer to 325°F.
Trim the Belgian endive head(s), removing the little bit of dried-out stem end but keeping the leaves intact. Quarter the head(s) through the stem. Brush the endive quarters with oil, getting it down between the leaves. Sprinkle the quarters with salt.
When the machine is at temperature, set the endive quarters cut sides up in the basket with as much air space between them as possible. They should not touch. Air-fry undisturbed for 7 minutes, or until lightly browned along the edges.
Use kitchen tongs to transfer the endive quarters to serving plates or a platter. Sprinkle with the pistachios and lemon juice. Serve warm or at room temperature.

Nutrition Facts (per serving):
Calories: 195 | Carbohydrates: 5.5g | Protein: 2.5g | Fat: 18.5g | Fiber: 2.5g | Sugar: 1.5g

---

 Servings: 2   15 Minutes

106 Zucchini Gratin

Ingredients:
5 oz. parmesan cheese, shredded
1 tbsp. coconut flour
1 tbsp. dried parsley
2 zucchinis
1 tsp. butter, melted

Directions:
Mix the parmesan and coconut flour together in a bowl, seasoning with parsley to taste.
Cut the zucchini in half lengthwise and chop the halves into four slices.
Pre-heat the fryer at 400°F.
Pour the melted butter over the zucchini and then dip the zucchini into the parmesan-flour mixture, coating it all over. Cook the zucchini in the fryer for thirteen minutes.

Nutrition Facts (per serving):
Calories: 160 | Carbohydrates: 3g | Protein: 10g | Fat: 13g | Fiber: 1g | Sugar: 1.5g

---

 Servings: 8   20 Minutes

107 Buttermilk Brined Turkey Breast

Ingredients:
¾ cup brine from a can of olives
3½ pounds boneless, skinless turkey breast
2 fresh thyme sprigs
1 fresh rosemary sprig
½ cup buttermilk

Directions:
Preheat the Air fryer to 350°F and grease an Air fryer basket.
Mix olive brine and buttermilk in a bowl until well combined.
Place the turkey breast, buttermilk mixture and herb sprigs in a resealable plastic bag.
Seal the bag and refrigerate for about 12 hours.
Remove the turkey breast from bag and arrange the turkey breast into the Air fryer basket.
Cook for about 20 minutes, flipping once in between.
Dish out the turkey breast onto a cutting board and cut into desired size slices to serve.

Nutrition Facts (per serving):
Calories: 218 | Carbohydrates: 1.5g | Protein: 10g | Fat: 18g | Fiber: 0g

---

Servings: 4   25 minutes

108 Omelet Bread Cups

Ingredients:
4 crusty rolls
5 eggs, beaten
½ tsp thyme, dried
3 strips cooked bacon, chopped
2 tbsp heavy cream
4 Gouda cheese thin slices

Directions:
Preheat the air fryer to 330 F. Cut the tops off the rolls and remove the inside with your fingers. Line the rolls with a slice of cheese and press down, so the cheese conforms to the inside of the roll.
In a bowl, mix the eggs, heavy cream, bacon, and thyme. Stuff the rolls with the egg mixture. Lay them in the greased frying basket and Bake for 6-8 minutes or until the eggs become puffy, and the roll shows a golden brown texture. Remove and let them cool for a few minutes before serving.

Nutrition Facts (per serving):
Calories: 400 | Carbohydrates: 28g | Protein: 18g | Fat: 23g | Fiber: 1g

Servings: 4 | 10 Minutes

109 Glazed Carrots

Ingredients:
- 2 teaspoons honey
- 1 teaspoon orange juice
- ½ teaspoon grated orange rind
- ⅛ teaspoon ginger
- 1 pound baby carrots
- 2 teaspoons olive oil
- ¼ teaspoon salt

Directions:
Combine honey, orange juice, grated rind, and ginger in a small bowl and set aside.
Toss the carrots, oil, and salt together to coat well and pour them into the air fryer basket.
Cook at 390°F for 5 minutes. Shake basket to stir a little and cook for 4 minutes more, until carrots are barely tender.
Pour carrots into air fryer baking pan.
Stir the honey mixture to combine well, pour glaze over carrots, and stir to coat.
Cook at 360°F for 1 minute or just until heated through.

Nutrition Facts (per serving):
Calories: 56 | Carbohydrates: 7.3g | Protein: 0.75g | Fat: 2.5g | Fiber: 1.75g | Sugar: 4.25g

---

Servings: 6 | 12 Minutes

110 Alfredo Eggplant Stacks

Ingredients:
- 1 large eggplant, ends trimmed, cut into ¼" slices
- 1 medium beefsteak tomato, cored and cut into ¼" slices
- 1 cup Alfredo sauce
- 8 ounces fresh mozzarella cheese, cut into 18 slices
- 2 tablespoons fresh parsley leaves

Directions:
Place 6 slices eggplant in bottom of an ungreased 6" round nonstick baking dish. Place 1 slice tomato on top of each eggplant round, followed by 1 tablespoon Alfredo and 1 slice mozzarella. Repeat with remaining ingredients, about three repetitions.
Cover dish with aluminum foil and place dish into air fryer basket. Adjust the temperature to 350°F and set the timer for 12 minutes. Eggplant will be tender when done.
Sprinkle parsley evenly over each stack. Serve warm.

Nutrition Facts (per serving):
Calories: 160 | Carbohydrates: 4g | Protein: 8g | Fat: 12g | Fiber: 1g | Sugar: 2g

---

Servings: 6 | 20 Minutes

111 Bacon-wrapped Chicken

Ingredients:
- 1 chicken breast, cut into 6 pieces
- 6 rashers back bacon
- 1 tbsp. soft cheese

Directions:
Put the bacon rashers on a flat surface and cover one side with the soft cheese.
Lay the chicken pieces on each bacon rasher. Wrap the bacon around the chicken and use a toothpick stick to hold each one in place. Put them in Air Fryer basket.
Air fry at 350°F for 15 minutes.

Nutrition Facts (per serving):
Calories: 222 | Carbohydrates: 0.8g | Protein: 9g | Fat: 18.7g | Fiber: 0g

---

Servings: 4 | 25 minutes

112 Zucchini Muffins

Ingredients:
- 1 ½ cups flour
- 1 tsp cinnamon
- 3 eggs
- 2 tsp baking powder
- ½ tsp sugar
- 1 cup milk
- 2 tbsp butter, melted
- 1 tbsp yogurt
- 1 zucchini, shredded
- A pinch of salt
- 2 tbsp cream cheese

Directions:
Preheat the air fryer to 350 F. In a bowl, whisk the eggs with sugar, salt, cinnamon, cream cheese, flour, and baking powder. In another bowl, combine the remaining ingredients, except for the zucchini. Gently combine the dry and liquid mixtures. Stir in the zucchini. Grease 4 muffin tins with oil and pour the batter inside them. Place them in the air fryer and Bake for 18-20 minutes until golden. Serve.

Nutrition Facts (per serving):
Calories: 348 | Carbohydrates: 41.5g | Protein: 12g | Fat: 14.6g | Fiber: 2g

Servings: 2 — 5 Minutes

113 Parmesan Asparagus

Ingredients:
1 bunch asparagus, stems trimmed
1 teaspoon olive oil
salt and freshly ground black pepper
¼ cup coarsely grated Parmesan cheese
½ lemon

Directions:
Preheat the air fryer to 400°F.
Toss the asparagus with the oil and season with salt and freshly ground black pepper.
Transfer the asparagus to the air fryer basket and air-fry at 400°F for 5 minutes, shaking the basket to turn the asparagus once or twice during the cooking process.
When the asparagus is cooked to your liking, sprinkle the asparagus generously with the Parmesan cheese and close the air fryer drawer again. Let the asparagus sit for 1 minute in the turned-off air fryer. Then, remove the asparagus, transfer it to a serving dish and finish with a grind of black pepper and a squeeze of lemon juice.

Nutrition Facts (per serving):
Calories: 95 | Carbohydrates: 6g | Protein: 6.5g | Fat: 5g | Fiber: 3g | Sugar: 2g

---

Servings: 4 — 12 Minutes

114 White Cheddar And Mushroom Soufflés

Ingredients:
3 large eggs, whites and yolks separated
½ cup sharp white Cheddar cheese
3 ounces cream cheese, softened
¼ teaspoon cream of tartar
¼ teaspoon salt
¼ teaspoon ground black pepper
½ cup cremini mushrooms, sliced

Directions:
In a large bowl, whip egg whites until stiff peaks form, about 2 minutes. In a separate large bowl, beat Cheddar, egg yolks, cream cheese, cream of tartar, salt, and pepper together until combined.
Fold egg whites into cheese mixture, being careful not to stir. Fold in mushrooms, then pour mixture evenly into four ungreased 4" ramekins.
Place ramekins into air fryer basket. Adjust the temperature to 350°F and set the timer for 12 minutes. Eggs will be browned on the top and firm in the center when done. Serve warm.

Nutrition Facts (per serving):
Calories: 160 | Carbohydrates: 2g | Protein: 9g | Fat: 13g | Fiber: 0.3g | Sugar: 1g

---

Servings: 2 — 20 Minutes

115 Teriyaki Chicken Legs

Ingredients:
4 tablespoons teriyaki sauce
1 tablespoon orange juice
1 teaspoon smoked paprika
4 chicken legs
cooking spray

Directions:
Mix together the teriyaki sauce, orange juice, and smoked paprika. Brush on all sides of chicken legs. Spray air fryer basket with nonstick cooking spray and place chicken in basket.
Cook at 360°F for 6 minutes. Turn and baste with sauce. Cook for 6 more minutes, turn and baste. Cook for 8 minutes more, until juices run clear when chicken is pierced with a fork.

Nutrition Facts (per serving):
Calories: 224 | Carbohydrates: 2.6g | Protein: 9g | Fat: 18.5g | Fiber: 0g

---

Servings: 4 — 25 minutes

116 Kiwi Muffins with Pecans

Ingredients:
1 cup flour
1 kiwi, mashed
¼ cup powdered sugar
1 tbsp milk
1 tbsp pecans, chopped
½ tsp baking powder
¼ cup oats
¼ cup butter, room temperature

Directions:
Preheat the air fryer to 350 F. Place the sugar, pecans, kiwi, and butter in a bowl and mix well. In another bowl, mix the flour, baking powder, and oats and stir well. Combine the two mixtures and stir in the milk. Pour the batter into a greased muffin tin that fits in the fryer and Bake for 15 minutes. Remove to a wire rack and leave to cool for a few minutes before removing the muffin from the tin. Enjoy!

Nutrition Facts (per serving):
Calories: 290 | Carbohydrates: 37.5g | Protein: 4.4g | Fat: 13.5g | Fiber: 1.9g

Servings: 4 — 7 Minutes

117 Roasted Broccoli Salad

Ingredients:
2 cups fresh broccoli florets, chopped
1 tablespoon olive oil
¼ teaspoon salt
⅛ teaspoon ground black pepper
¼ cup lemon juice, divided
¼ cup shredded Parmesan cheese
¼ cup sliced roasted almonds

Directions:
In a large bowl, toss broccoli and olive oil together. Sprinkle with salt and pepper, then drizzle with 2 tablespoons lemon juice.
Place broccoli into ungreased air fryer basket. Adjust the temperature to 350°F and set the timer for 7 minutes, shaking the basket halfway through cooking. Broccoli will be golden on the edges when done.
Place broccoli into a large serving bowl and drizzle with remaining lemon juice. Sprinkle with Parmesan and almonds. Serve warm.

Nutrition Facts (per serving):
Calories: 83 | Carbohydrates: 3.5g | Protein: 3g | Fat: 6.5g | Fiber: 1.5g | Sugar: 1g

---

Servings: 4 — 15 Minutes

118 Lemon Caper Cauliflower Steaks

Ingredients:
1 small head cauliflower, leaves and core removed, cut into 4 (½"-thick) "steaks"
4 tablespoons olive oil, divided
1 medium lemon, zested and juiced, divided
¼ teaspoon salt
⅛ teaspoon ground black pepper
1 tablespoon salted butter, melted
1 tablespoon capers, rinsed

Directions:
Brush each cauliflower "steak" with ½ tablespoon olive oil on both sides and sprinkle with lemon zest, salt, and pepper on both sides.
Place cauliflower into ungreased air fryer basket. Adjust the temperature to 400°F and set the timer for 15 minutes, turning cauliflower halfway through cooking. Steaks will be golden at the edges and browned when done.
Transfer steaks to four medium plates. In a small bowl, whisk remaining olive oil, butter, lemon juice, and capers, and pour evenly over steaks. Serve warm.

Nutrition Facts (per serving):
Calories: 130 | Carbohydrates: 7g | Protein: 2g | Fat: 11g | Fiber: 2.5g | Sugar: 2g

---

 Servings: 4 20 Minutes

119 Chicken Gruyere

Ingredients:
¼ cup Gruyere cheese, grated
1 pound chicken breasts, boneless, skinless
½ cup flour
2 eggs, beaten
Sea salt and black pepper to taste
4 lemon slices
Cooking spray

Directions:
Preheat your Air Fryer to 370°F. Spray the air fryer basket with cooking spray.
Mix the breadcrumbs with Gruyere cheese in a bowl, pour the eggs in another bowl, and the flour in a third bowl. Toss the chicken in the flour, then in the eggs, and then in the breadcrumb mixture. Place in the fryer basket, close and cook for 12 minutes. At the 6-minute mark, turn the chicken over. Once golden brown, remove onto a serving plate and serve topped with lemon slices.

Nutrition Facts (per serving):
Calories: 221 | Carbohydrates: 2.3g | Protein: 9.2g | Fat: 18.4g | Fiber: 0.1g

---

 Servings: 4 25 minutes

120 Crispy Alfredo Chicken Wings

Ingredients:
1 ½ lb chicken wings, pat-dried
Salt to taste
½ cup Alfredo sauce

Directions:
Preheat the air fryer to 370 F. Season the wings with salt. Arrange them in the greased frying basket, without overlapping, and AirFry for 12 minutes until no longer pink in the center. Flip them, increase the heat to 390 F, and cook for 5 more minutes. Work in batches if needed. Plate the wings and drizzle with Alfredo sauce to serve.

Nutrition Facts (per serving):
Calories: 455 | Carbohydrates: 1.3g | Protein: 35g | Fat: 34.3g

Servings: 4 | 8 Minutes

121 Roasted Broccoli

Ingredients:
12 ounces broccoli florets
2 tablespoons olive oil
½ teaspoon salt
¼ teaspoon ground black pepper

Directions:
Preheat the air fryer to 360°F.
In a medium bowl, place broccoli and drizzle with oil. Sprinkle with salt and pepper.
Place in the air fryer basket and cook 8 minutes, shaking the basket twice during cooking, until the edges are brown and the center is tender. Serve warm.

Nutrition Facts (per serving):
Calories: 75 | Carbohydrates: 4.5g | Protein: 2.25g | Fat: 6g | Fiber: 2g | Sugar: 1g

---

Servings: 4 | 14 Minutes

122 Crouton-breaded Pork Chops

Ingredients:
4 boneless pork chops
1 teaspoon salt
½ teaspoon ground black pepper
2 cups croutons
½ teaspoon dried thyme
¼ teaspoon dried sage
1 large egg, whisked
Cooking spray

Directions:
Preheat the air fryer to 400°F.
Sprinkle pork chops with salt and pepper on both sides.
In a food processor, add croutons, thyme, and sage. Pulse five times until croutons are mostly broken down with a few medium-sized pieces remaining. Transfer to a medium bowl.
In a separate medium bowl, place egg. Dip each pork chop into egg, then press into crouton mixture to coat both sides. Spritz with cooking spray.
Place pork in the air fryer basket and cook 14 minutes, turning halfway through cooking time, until chops are golden brown and internal temperature reaches at least 145°F. Serve warm.

Nutrition Facts (per serving):
Calories: 290 | Carbohydrates: 10g | Protein: 25g | Fat: 17g | Fiber: 1g | Sugar: 1g

---

Servings: 4 | 20 Minutes

123 Chicken Parmesan Casserole

Ingredients:
2 cups cubed cooked chicken breast
½ teaspoon salt
¼ teaspoon ground black pepper
¾ cup marinara sauce
2 teaspoons Italian seasoning, divided
1 cup shredded mozzarella cheese
½ cup grated Parmesan cheese

Directions:
Preheat the air fryer to 320°F.
In a large bowl, toss chicken with salt, pepper, marinara, and 1 teaspoon Italian seasoning.
Scrape mixture into a 6" round baking dish. Top with mozzarella, Parmesan, and remaining 1 teaspoon Italian seasoning.
Place in the air fryer basket and cook 20 minutes until the sauce is bubbling and cheese is brown and melted. Serve warm.

Nutrition Facts (per serving):
Calories: 216 | Carbohydrates: 2.7g | Protein: 9.5g | Fat: 17.5g

---

Servings: 4 | 25 minutes

124 Crunchy Ranch Chicken Wings

Ingredients:
2 lb chicken wings
2 tbsp olive oil
1 tbsp ranch seasoning mix
Salt to taste

Directions:
Preheat the air fryer to 390 F. Put the ranch seasoning, olive oil, and salt in a large, resealable bag and mix well. Add the wings, seal the bag, and toss until the wings are thoroughly coated.
Put the wings in the greased frying basket in one layer, spritz them with a nonstick cooking spray, and AirFry for 7 minutes. Turn them over and fry for 5-8 more minutes until the wings are light brown and crispy. Test for doneness with a meat thermometer. Serve with your favorite dipping sauce and enjoy!

Nutrition Facts (per serving):
Calories: 500 | Carbohydrates: 0.5g | Protein: 45g | Fat: 35.5g

Servings: 12   🕐 10 Minutes

125 Corn Muffins

Ingredients:
½ cup all-purpose flour
½ cup cornmeal
¼ cup granulated sugar
½ teaspoon baking powder
¼ cup salted butter, melted
½ cup buttermilk
1 large egg

Directions:
Preheat the air fryer to 350°F.
In a large bowl, whisk together flour, cornmeal, sugar, and baking powder.
Add butter, buttermilk, and egg to dry mixture. Stir until well combined.
Divide batter evenly among twelve silicone or aluminum muffin cups, filling cups about halfway. Working in batches as needed, place in the air fryer and cook 10 minutes until golden brown. Let cool 5 minutes before serving.

Nutrition Facts (per serving):
Calories: 67 | Carbohydrates: 7.1g | Protein: 1.2g | Fat: 3.7g | Fiber: 0.3g | Sugar: 1.8g

 Servings: 8   🕐 12 Minutes

126 Spinach And Provolone Steak Rolls

Ingredients:
1 flank steak, butterflied
8 deli slices provolone cheese
1 cup fresh spinach leaves
½ teaspoon salt
¼ teaspoon ground black pepper

Directions:
Place steak on a large plate. Place provolone slices to cover steak, leaving 1" at the edges. Lay spinach leaves over cheese. Gently roll steak and tie with kitchen twine or secure with toothpicks. Carefully slice into eight pieces. Sprinkle each with salt and pepper. Place rolls into ungreased air fryer basket, cut side up. Adjust the temperature to 400°F and set the timer for 12 minutes. Steak rolls will be browned and cheese will be melted when done and have an internal temperature of at least 150°F for medium steak and 180°F for well-done steak. Serve warm.

Nutrition Facts (per serving):
Calories: 240 | Carbohydrates: 1g | Protein: 28g | Fat: 14g | Fiber: 0g | Sugar: 0g

 Servings: 4   🕐 20 Minutes

127 Fish Sticks

Ingredients:
1 lb. tilapia fillets, cut into strips
1 large egg, beaten
2 tsp. Old Bay seasoning
1 tbsp. olive oil
1 cup friendly bread crumbs

Directions:
Pre-heat the Air Fryer at 400°F.
In a shallow dish, combine together the bread crumbs, Old Bay, and oil. Put the egg in a small bowl. Dredge the fish sticks in the egg. Cover them with bread crumbs and put them in the fryer's basket. Cook the fish for 10 minutes or until they turn golden brown.
Serve hot.

Nutrition Facts (per serving):
Calories: 192 | Carbohydrates: 2.3g | Protein: 14.5g | Fat: 12.8g | Fiber: 0.3g

 Servings: 4   🕐 25 minutes

128 Crispy Chicken Nuggets

Ingredients:
1 lb chicken breasts, cut into large cubes
Salt and black pepper to taste
2 tbsp olive oil
5 tbsp plain breadcrumbs
2 tbsp panko breadcrumbs
2 tbsp grated Parmesan cheese

Directions:
Preheat the air fryer to 380 F. Season the chicken with black pepper and salt. In a bowl, mix the breadcrumbs and Parmesan cheese. Coat the chicken pieces with the olive oil. Then dip into the breadcrumb mixture, shake off the excess, and place in the greased frying basket. Lightly spray the nuggets with cooking spray and AirFry for 13-15 minutes, flipping once. Serve warm

Nutrition Facts (per serving):
Calories: 298 | Carbohydrates: 7.3g | Protein: 27g | Fat: 12.5g | Fiber: 0.4g

129 Asparagus

Servings: 4 | 9 Minutes

Ingredients:
- 1 bunch asparagus, washed and trimmed
- ⅛ teaspoon dried tarragon, crushed
- salt and pepper
- 1 to 2 teaspoons extra-light olive oil

Directions:
Spread asparagus spears on cookie sheet or cutting board.
Sprinkle with tarragon, salt, and pepper.
Drizzle with 1 teaspoon of oil and roll the spears or mix by hand. If needed, add up to 1 more teaspoon of oil and mix again until all spears are lightly coated.
Place spears in air fryer basket. If necessary, bend the longer spears to make them fit. It doesn't matter if they don't lie flat.
Cook at 390°F for 5 minutes. Shake basket or stir spears with a spoon.
Cook for an additional 4 minutes or just until crisp-tender.

Nutrition Facts (per serving):
Calories: 25 | Carbohydrates: 2g | Protein: 1.25g | Fat: 1.75g | Fiber: 1g | Sugar: 0.75g

130 Cheddar Bacon Ranch Pinwheels

Servings: 5 | 12 Minutes Per Batch

Ingredients:
- 4 ounces full-fat cream cheese, softened
- 1 tablespoon dry ranch seasoning
- ½ cup shredded Cheddar cheese
- 1 sheet frozen puff pastry dough, thawed
- 6 slices bacon, cooked and crumbled

Directions:
Preheat the air fryer to 320°F. Cut parchment paper to fit the air fryer basket.
In a medium bowl, mix cream cheese, ranch seasoning, and Cheddar. Unfold puff pastry and gently spread cheese mixture over pastry.
Sprinkle crumbled bacon on top. Starting from a long side, roll dough into a log, pressing in the edges to seal.
Cut log into ten pieces, then place on parchment in the air fryer basket, working in batches as necessary.
Cook 12 minutes, turning each piece after 7 minutes.
Let cool 5 minutes before serving.

Nutrition Facts (per serving):
Calories: 290 | Carbohydrates: 13g | Protein: 8g | Fat: 23g | Fiber: 1g | Sugar: 2g

 Servings: 4 | 20 Minutes

131 Almond Topped Trout

Ingredients:
- 4 trout fillets
- 2 tbsp olive oil
- Salt and pepper to taste
- 2 garlic cloves, sliced
- 1 lemon, sliced
- 1 tbsp flaked almonds

Directions:
Preheat air fryer to 380°F. Lightly brush each fillet with olive oil on both sides and season with salt and pepper. Put the fillets in a single layer in the frying basket. Put the sliced garlic over the tops of the trout fillets, then top with lemon slices and cook for 12-15 minutes. Serve topped with flaked almonds and enjoy!

Nutrition Facts (per serving):
Calories: 212 | Carbohydrates: 1.5g | Protein: 25g | Fat: 12g | Fiber: 0.7

 Servings: 4 | 25 minutes

132 Corn-Crusted Chicken Tenders

Ingredients:
- 2 chicken breasts, cut into strips
- Salt and black pepper to taste
- 2 eggs
- 1 cup ground cornmeal

Directions:
Preheat the air fryer to 390 F. In a bowl, mix cornmeal, salt, and black pepper. In another bowl, beat the eggs; season with salt and pepper. Dip the chicken in the eggs and then coat in the cornmeal. Spray the strips with cooking spray and place them in the frying basket in a single layer. AirFry for 6 minutes, slide the basket out, and flip the sticks. Cook for 6-8 more minutes until golden brown. Serve hot.

Nutrition Facts (per serving):
Calories: 285 | Carbohydrates: 15g | Protein: 26g | Fat: 12g | Fiber: 1.1g

Servings: 6 | 10 Minutes

133 Roasted Brussels Sprouts

Ingredients:
1 pound fresh Brussels sprouts, trimmed and halved
2 tablespoons coconut oil
½ teaspoon salt
¼ teaspoon ground black pepper
½ teaspoon garlic powder
1 tablespoon salted butter, melted

Directions:
Place Brussels sprouts into a large bowl. Drizzle with coconut oil and sprinkle with salt, pepper, and garlic powder.
Place Brussels sprouts into ungreased air fryer basket. Adjust the temperature to 350°F and set the timer for 10 minutes, shaking the basket three times during cooking. Brussels sprouts will be dark golden and tender when done.
Place cooked sprouts in a large serving dish and drizzle with butter. Serve warm.

Nutrition Facts (per serving):
Calories: 60 | Carbohydrates: 4g | Protein: 1g | Fat: 5g | Fiber: 1.5g | Sugar: 0.8g

---

Servings: 4 | 14 Minutes

134 Breaded Air Fryer Pork Chops

Ingredients:
4 boneless pork chops
1 teaspoon salt
½ teaspoon ground black pepper
2 cups croutons
½ teaspoon dried thyme
¼ teaspoon dried sage
1 large egg, whisked
Cooking spray

Directions:
Preheat the air fryer to 400°F.
Sprinkle pork chops with salt and pepper on both sides.
In a food processor, add croutons, thyme, and sage. Pulse five times until croutons are mostly broken down with a few medium-sized pieces remaining. Transfer to a medium bowl.
In a separate medium bowl, place egg. Dip each pork chop into egg, then press into crouton mixture to coat both sides. Spritz with cooking spray.
Place pork in the air fryer basket and cook 14 minutes, turning halfway through cooking time, until chops are golden brown and internal temperature reaches at least 145°F. Serve warm.

Nutrition Facts (per serving):
Calories: 228 | Carbohydrates: 2.3g | Protein: 9.5g | Fat: 20g | Fiber: 2g

---

Servings: 2 | 20 Minutes

135 Lime Flaming Halibut

Ingredients:
2 tbsp butter, melted
½ tsp chili powder
½ cup bread crumbs
2 halibut fillets

Directions:
Preheat air fryer to 350°F. In a bowl, mix the butter, chili powder and bread crumbs. Press mixture onto tops of halibut fillets. Place halibut in the greased frying basket and Air Fry for 10 minutes or until the fish is opaque and flake easily with a fork. Serve right away.

Nutrition Facts (per serving):
Calories: 276 | Carbohydrates: 9.6g | Protein: 28.1g | Fat: 14.8g | Fiber: 0.6g

---

Servings: 4 | 25 minutes

136 Air Fried Asparagus with Romesco Sauce

Ingredients:
1 cup panko breadcrumbs
Salt and black pepper to taste
½ cup almond flour
1 lb asparagus spears, trimmed and washed
2 eggs
2 tomatoes, chopped
Romesco Sauce
2 roasted peppers, chopped
½ cup almond flour
½ tsp garlic powder
1 tbsp vinegar
2 slices toasted bread, torn into pieces
½ tsp paprika
1 tsp crushed red chili flakes
1 tbsp tomato purée
½ cup extra-virgin olive oil

Directions:
Preheat the air fryer to 390 F. On a plate, combine panko breadcrumbs, salt, and black pepper. On another shallow plate, whisk the eggs with salt and black pepper. On a third plate, pour the almond flour. Dip asparagus in the almond flour, followed by a dip in the eggs, and finally, coat with breadcrumbs. Place in the greased frying basket and AirFry for 10 minutes, turning once halfway. Pulse all romesco sauce ingredients in a food processor until smooth. Serve asparagus with romesco sauce.

Nutrition Facts (per serving):
Calories: 330 | Carbohydrates: 16g | Protein: 8.5g | Fat: 26g | Fiber: 4.2g

Servings: 4 — 8 Minutes

137 Pesto Vegetable Kebabs

Ingredients:
- 12 ounces button mushrooms
- 12 ounces cherry tomatoes
- 2 medium zucchini, cut into ¼" slices
- 1 medium red onion, peeled and cut into 1" cubes
- 1 cup pesto, divided
- ½ teaspoon salt
- ¼ teaspoon ground black pepper

Directions:
Soak eight 6" skewers in water 10 minutes to avoid burning. Preheat the air fryer to 350°F.
Place a mushroom on a skewer, followed by a tomato, zucchini slice, and red onion piece. Repeat to fill up the skewer, then follow the same pattern for remaining skewers.
Brush each skewer evenly using ½ cup pesto. Sprinkle kebabs with salt and pepper. Place in the air fryer basket and cook 10 minutes, turning halfway through cooking time, until vegetables are tender. Brush kebabs with remaining ½ cup pesto before serving.

Nutrition Facts (per serving):
Calories: 188 | Carbohydrates: 10.5g | Protein: 3.5g | Fat: 15g | Fiber: 3g | Sugar: 4.5g

---

Servings: 4 — 15 Minutes

138 Rib Eye Steak

Ingredients:
- 4 rib eye steaks
- 1 teaspoon salt
- ½ teaspoon ground black pepper
- 2 tablespoons salted butter

Directions:
Preheat the air fryer to 400°F.
Sprinkle steaks with salt and pepper and place in the air fryer basket.
Cook 15 minutes, turning halfway through cooking time, until edges are firm, and the internal temperature reaches at least 160°F for well-done.
Top each steak with ½ tablespoon butter immediately after removing from the air fryer. Let rest 5 minutes before cutting. Serve warm.

Nutrition Facts (per serving):
Calories: 229 | Carbohydrates: 0g | Protein: 11g | Fat: 20g | Fiber: 0g

---

Servings: 4 20 Minutes

139 Broccoli With Cauliflower

Ingredients:
- 1½ cups broccoli, cut into 1-inch pieces
- 1½ cups cauliflower, cut into 1-inch pieces
- 1 tablespoon olive oil
- Salt, as required

Directions:
Preheat the Air fryer to 375°F and grease an Air fryer basket.
Mix the vegetables, olive oil, and salt in a bowl and toss to coat well.
Arrange the veggie mixture in the Air fryer basket and cook for about 20 minutes, tossing once in between.
Dish out in a bowl and serve hot.

Nutrition Facts (per serving):
Calories: 78 | Carbohydrates: 6.9g | Protein: 2.6g | Fat: 5.1g | Fiber: 2.8g

---

 Servings: 4 25 minutes

140 Parmesan Artichoke Hearts

Ingredients:
- 1 can (14-oz) artichoke hearts, drained
- 2 eggs
- ¼ cup flour
- ¼ Parmesan cheese, grated
- ⅓ cup panko breadcrumbs
- 1 tsp garlic powder
- Salt and black pepper to taste

Directions:
Preheat the air fryer to 390 F. Pat dry the artichokes with a paper towel and cut them into wedges. In a bowl, whisk the eggs with a pinch of salt. In another bowl, combine Parmesan cheese, breadcrumbs, and garlic powder. In a third bowl, pour the flour mixed with salt and black pepper.
Dip the artichokes in the flour, followed by a dip in the eggs, and finally coat with breadcrumbs. Place them in the frying basket and AirFry for 10 minutes, flipping once. Serve with mayo sauce if desired.

Nutrition Facts (per serving):
Calories: 145 | Carbohydrates: 10g | Protein: 8g | Fat: 8g | Fiber: 3g

Servings: 4 — 6 Minutes

141 Sesame Seeds Bok Choy

Ingredients:
- 4 bunches baby bok choy, bottoms removed and leaves separated
- Olive oil cooking spray
- 1 teaspoon garlic powder
- 1 teaspoon sesame seeds

Directions:
Set the temperature of air fryer to 325ºF.
Arrange bok choy leaves into the air fryer basket in a single layer.
Spray with the cooking spray and sprinkle with garlic powder.
Air fry for about 5-6 minutes, shaking after every 2 minutes.
Remove from air fryer and transfer the bok choy onto serving plates.
Garnish with sesame seeds and serve hot.

Nutrition Facts (per serving):
Calories: 25 | Carbohydrates: 2g | Protein: 1g | Fat: 1.5g | Fiber: 1g | Sugar: 0.75g

---

Servings: 2 — 12 Minutes

142 Perfect Grill Chicken Breast

Ingredients:
- 2 chicken breast, skinless and boneless
- 2 tsp olive oil
- Pepper
- Salt

Directions:
Remove air fryer basket and replace it with air fryer grill pan.
Place chicken breast to the grill pan. Season chicken with pepper and salt. Drizzle with oil.
Cook chicken for 375ºF for 12 minutes.
Serve and enjoy.

Nutrition Facts (per serving):
Calories: 218 | Carbohydrates: 0g | Protein: 10g | Fat: 19g | Fiber: 0g

---

Servings: 4 — 20 Minutes

143 Crustless Spinach And Cheese Frittata

Ingredients:
- 6 large eggs
- ½ cup heavy whipping cream
- 1 cup frozen chopped spinach, drained
- 1 cup shredded sharp Cheddar cheese
- ¼ cup peeled and diced yellow onion
- ½ teaspoon salt
- ¼ teaspoon ground black pepper

Directions:
In a large bowl, whisk eggs and cream together. Whisk in spinach, Cheddar, onion, salt, and pepper.
Pour mixture into an ungreased 6" round nonstick baking dish. Place dish into air fryer basket. Adjust the temperature to 320ºF and set the timer for 20 minutes. Eggs will be firm and slightly browned when done. Serve immediately.

Nutrition Facts (per serving):
Calories: 267 | Carbohydrates: 2.9g | Protein: 13.6g | Fat: 22.1g | Fiber: 0.5g

---

Servings: 4 — 25 minutes

144 Crunchy Cauliflower Bites

Ingredients:
- 1 tbsp Italian seasoning
- 1 cup flour
- 1 cup milk
- 1 egg, beaten
- 1 head cauliflower, cut into florets

Directions:
Preheat the air fryer to 390 F. Grease the frying basket with cooking spray. In a bowl, mix flour, milk, egg, and Italian seasoning. Coat the cauliflower in the mixture and drain the excess liquid.
Place the florets in the frying basket, spray with cooking spray, and AirFry for 7 minutes. Shake and continue cooking for another 5 minutes. Allow to cool before serving.

Nutrition Facts (per serving):
Calories: 165 | Carbohydrates: 21g | Protein: 6g | Fat: 6g | Fiber: 2.5g

Servings: 4   8 Minutes Per Batch

145 Spinach Pesto Flatbread

Ingredients:
1 cup basil pesto
4 round flatbreads
½ cup chopped frozen spinach, thawed and drained
8 ounces fresh mozzarella cheese, sliced
1 teaspoon crushed red pepper flakes

Directions:
Preheat the air fryer to 350°F.
For each flatbread, spread ¼ cup pesto across flatbread, then scatter 2 tablespoons spinach over pesto. Top with 2 ounces mozzarella slices and ¼ teaspoon red pepper flakes. Repeat with remaining flatbread and toppings.
Place in the air fryer basket, working in batches as necessary, and cook 8 minutes until cheese is brown and bubbling. Serve warm.

Nutrition Facts (per serving):
Calories: 230 | Carbohydrates: 12g | Protein: 8g | Fat: 16g | Fiber: 1g | Sugar: 1g

 Servings: 4   15 Minutes

146 Jumbo Buffalo Chicken Meatballs

Ingredients:
1 pound ground chicken thighs
1 large egg, whisked
½ cup hot sauce, divided
½ cup crumbled blue cheese
2 tablespoons dry ranch seasoning
¼ teaspoon salt
¼ teaspoon ground black pepper

Directions:
In a large bowl, combine ground chicken, egg, ¼ cup hot sauce, blue cheese, ranch seasoning, salt, and pepper.
Divide mixture into eight equal sections of about ¼ cup each and form each section into a ball. Place meatballs into ungreased air fryer basket. Adjust the temperature to 370°F and set the timer for 15 minutes. Meatballs will be done when golden and have an internal temperature of at least 165°F.
Transfer meatballs to a large serving dish and toss with remaining hot sauce. Serve warm.

Nutrition Facts (per serving):
Calories: 224 | Carbohydrates: 2.3g | Protein: 9g | Fat: 19g | Fiber: 0g

 Servings: 4   20 Minutes

147 Chives Omelet

Ingredients:
6 eggs, whisked
1 cup chives, chopped
Cooking spray
1 cup mozzarella, shredded
Salt and black pepper to the taste

Directions:
In a bowl, mix all the ingredients except the cooking spray and whisk well. Grease a pan that fits your air fryer with the cooking spray, pour the eggs mix, spread, put the pan into the machine and cook at 350°F for 20 minutes. Divide the omelet between plates and serve for breakfast.

Nutrition Facts (per serving):
Calories: 195 | Carbohydrates: 2g | Protein: 13g | Fat: 15g | Fiber: 0g

 Servings: 4   25 minutes

148 Crispy Yellow Squash Chips

Ingredients:
2 yellow squash, sliced into rounds
½ cup flour
Salt and black pepper to taste
2 eggs
1 tbsp soy sauce
¾ cup panko breadcrumbs
¼ tsp dried dill
¼ cup Parmesan cheese, grated
Greek yogurt dressing, for serving

Directions:
Preheat the air fryer to 380 F. Spray the frying basket with cooking spray.
In a bowl, mix the flour, dill, salt, and black pepper. In another bowl, beat the eggs with soy sauce. In a third, pour the breadcrumbs and Parmesan cheese, mix well.
Dip the squash rounds in the flour, then in the eggs, and then coat with breadcrumbs. Place in the frying basket and AirFry for 10 minutes, flipping once halfway through. Serve with Greek yogurt dressing.

Nutrition Facts (per serving):
Calories: 210 | Carbohydrates: 18g | Protein: 9g | Fat: 12g | Fiber: 2g

149 Italian Seasoned Easy Pasta Chips

Servings: 2 | **10 Minutes**

Ingredients:
- ½ teaspoon salt
- 1 ½ teaspoon Italian seasoning blend
- 1 tablespoon nutritional yeast
- 1 tablespoon olive oil
- 2 cups whole wheat bowtie pasta

Directions:
Place the baking dish accessory in the air fryer.
Give a good stir.
Close the air fryer and cook for 10 minutes at 390°F.

Nutrition Facts (per serving):
Calories: 230 | Carbohydrates: 34g | Protein: 7g | Fat: 7g | Fiber: 5g | Sugar: 1.5g

150 Pecan-crusted Chicken Tenders

Servings: 4 | **12 Minutes**

Ingredients:
- 2 tablespoons mayonnaise
- 1 teaspoon Dijon mustard
- 1 pound boneless, skinless chicken tenders
- ½ teaspoon salt
- ¼ teaspoon ground black pepper
- ½ cup chopped roasted pecans, finely ground

Directions:
In a small bowl, whisk mayonnaise and mustard until combined. Brush mixture onto chicken tenders on both sides, then sprinkle tenders with salt and pepper. Place pecans in a medium bowl and press each tender into pecans to coat each side.
Place tenders into ungreased air fryer basket in a single layer, working in batches if needed. Adjust the temperature to 375°F and set the timer for 12 minutes, turning tenders halfway through cooking. Tenders will be golden brown and have an internal temperature of at least 165°F when done. Serve warm.

Nutrition Facts (per serving):
Calories: 224 | Carbohydrates: 2.1g | Protein: 9g | Fat: 19g | Fiber: 0.6g

151 Goat Cheese, Beet, And Kale Frittata

Servings: 6 | **20 Minutes**

Ingredients:
- 6 large eggs
- ½ teaspoon garlic powder
- ¼ teaspoon black pepper
- ¼ teaspoon salt
- 1 cup chopped kale
- 1 cup cooked and chopped red beets
- ⅓ cup crumbled goat cheese

Directions:
Preheat the air fryer to 320°F.
In a medium bowl, whisk the eggs with the garlic powder, pepper, and salt. Mix in the kale, beets, and goat cheese.
Spray an oven-safe 7-inch springform pan with cooking spray. Pour the egg mixture into the pan and place it in the air fryer basket.
Cook for 20 minutes, or until the internal temperature reaches 145°F.
When the frittata is cooked, let it set for 5 minutes before removing from the pan.
Slice and serve immediately.

Nutrition Facts (per serving):
Calories: 115 | Carbohydrates: 3g | Protein: 8g | Fat: 8g | Fiber: 1g

152 Kielbasa & Mushroom Pierogi

Servings: 4 | **25 minutes**

Ingredients:
- ½ package puff pastry dough, at room temperature
- ½ lb Kielbasa smoked sausage, chopped
- ½ onion, chopped
- ½ lb mushrooms, chopped
- ½ tsp ground cumin
- ¼ tsp paprika
- Salt and black pepper to taste
- 1 egg, beaten

Directions:
Preheat the air fryer to 360 F. In a bowl, mix Kielbasa sausage, onion, mushrooms, cumin, paprika, salt, and pepper. Place the pastry on a lightly floured surface. Using a glass, cut out 8 circles of the pastry.
Place 1 tbsp of the sausage mixture on each pastry circle, brush the edges with the beaten egg, and fold over. Seal the edges with a fork. Brush the empanadas with the remaining egg and spray with cooking spray. Place in the greased frying basket and Bake for 12-14 minutes until golden brown.

Nutrition Facts (per serving):
Calories: 390 | Carbohydrates: 22g | Protein: 10g | Fat: 29g | Fiber: 1.2g

Servings: 8 — 8 Minutes

153 Pesto Vegetable Skewers

Ingredients:
1 medium zucchini, trimmed and cut into ½" slices
½ medium yellow onion, peeled and cut into 1" squares
1 medium red bell pepper, seeded and cut into 1" squares
16 whole cremini mushrooms
⅓ cup basil pesto
½ teaspoon salt
¼ teaspoon ground black pepper

Directions:
Divide zucchini slices, onion, and bell pepper into eight even portions. Place on 6" skewers for a total of eight kebabs. Add 2 mushrooms to each skewer and brush kebabs generously with pesto.
Sprinkle each kebab with salt and black pepper on all sides, then place into ungreased air fryer basket. Adjust the temperature to 375°F and set the timer for 8 minutes, turning kebabs halfway through cooking. Vegetables will be browned at the edges and tender-crisp when done. Serve warm.

Nutrition Facts (per serving):
Calories: 55 | Carbohydrates: 2.8g | Protein: 1g | Fat: 4.5g | Fiber: 0.8g | Sugar: 1g

Servings: 4 — 14 Minutes

154 Rosemary Partridge

Ingredients:
10 oz partridges
1 teaspoon dried rosemary
1 tablespoon butter, melted
1 teaspoon salt

Directions:
Cut the partridges into the halves and sprinkle with dried rosemary and salt. Then brush them with melted butter. Preheat the air fryer to 385°F. Put the partridge halves in the air fryer and cook them for 8 minutes. Then flip the poultry on another side and cook for 6 minutes more.

Nutrition Facts (per serving):
Calories: 217 | Carbohydrates: 0g | Protein: 9g | Fat: 19g | Fiber: 0g

Servings: 4 — 20 Minutes

155 Tomatoes Frittata

Ingredients:
4 eggs, whisked
1 pound cherry tomatoes, halved
1 tablespoon parsley, chopped
Cooking spray
1 tablespoon cheddar, grated
Salt and black pepper to the taste

Directions:
Put the tomatoes in the air fryer's basket, cook at 360°F for 5 minutes and transfer them to the baking pan that fits the machine greased with cooking spray. In a bowl, mix the eggs with the remaining ingredients, whisk, pour over the tomatoes an cook at 360°F for 15 minutes. Serve right away for breakfast.

Nutrition Facts (per serving):
Calories: 103 | Carbohydrates: 3g | Protein: 7g | Fat: 7g | Fiber: 1g

Servings: 2 — 25 minutes

156 Crispy Pepperoni Pizza

Ingredients:
8 oz fresh pizza dough
⅓ cup tomato sauce
⅓ cup mozzarella cheese, shredded
8 pepperonis, sliced
1 tsp oregano, dried
Flour to dust

Directions:
On a floured surface, place pizza dough and dust with flour. Stretch with hands into greased frying basket. Spray the dish with cooking spray and place the pizza dough inside.
Spread the tomato sauce, leaving some space at the border. Scatter with mozzarella cheese and oregano and top with pepperoni slices. Bake for 14-16 minutes or until crispy at 340 F. Serve sliced.

Nutrition Facts (per serving):
Calories: 410 | Carbohydrates: 38g | Protein: 16g | Fat: 21g | Fiber: 2g

157 Vegetable Nuggets

Servings: 6 | 10 Minutes Per Batch

Ingredients:
- 1 cup shredded carrots
- 2 cups broccoli florets
- 2 large eggs
- 1 cup shredded Cheddar cheese
- 1 cup Italian bread crumbs
- 1 teaspoon salt
- ½ teaspoon ground black pepper

Directions:
Preheat the air fryer to 400°F.
In a food processor, combine carrots and broccoli and pulse five times. Add eggs, Cheddar, bread crumbs, salt, and pepper, and pulse ten times.
Carefully scoop twenty-four balls, about 1 heaping tablespoon each, out of the mixture. Spritz balls with cooking spray.
Place balls in the air fryer basket, working in batches as necessary, and cook 10 minutes, shaking the basket twice during cooking to ensure even browning. Serve warm.

Nutrition Facts (per serving):
Calories: 130 | Carbohydrates: 7.5g | Protein: 6.3g | Fat: 8g | Fiber: 1g | Sugar: 1g

158 Yummy Shredded Chicken

Servings: 2 | 15 Minutes

Ingredients:
- 2 large chicken breasts
- ¼ tsp Pepper
- 1 tsp garlic puree
- 1 tsp mustard
- Salt

Directions:
Add all ingredients to the bowl and toss well.
Transfer chicken into the air fryer basket and cook at 360°F for 15 minutes.
Remove chicken from air fryer and shred using a fork. Serve and enjoy.

Nutrition Facts (per serving):
Calories: 216 | Carbohydrates: 0.4g | Protein: 10g | Fat: 18.5g | Fiber: 0g

159 Crispy Spiced Chickpeas

Servings: 2 | 20 Minutes

Ingredients:
- 1 can chickpeas, drained
- ½ teaspoon salt
- ½ teaspoon chili powder
- ¼ teaspoon ground cinnamon
- ⅛ teaspoon smoked paprika
- pinch ground cayenne pepper
- 1 tablespoon olive oil

Directions:
Preheat the air fryer to 400°F.
Dry the chickpeas as well as you can with a clean kitchen towel, rubbing off any loose skins as necessary. Combine the spices in a small bowl. Toss the chickpeas with the olive oil and then add the spices and toss again.
Air-fry for 15 minutes, shaking the basket a couple of times while they cook.
Check the chickpeas to see if they are crispy enough and if necessary, air-fry for another 5 minutes to crisp them further. Serve warm, or cool to room temperature and store in an airtight container for up to two weeks.

Nutrition Facts (per serving):
Calories: 200 | Carbohydrates: 20g | Protein: 7g | Fat: 10g | Fiber: 6g

160 Bacon-Wrapped Dates

Servings: 4 | 25 minutes

Ingredients:
- 2 tbsp maple syrup
- 16 dates, pits removed
- ⅓ cup blue cheese, softened
- 8 bacon slices, cut in half crosswise

Directions:
Preheat the air fryer to 370 F. Grease the frying basket with cooking oil. Using a sharp knife, make a deep cut into each date to create a pocket. Stuff the dates with blue cheese and pinch to lock up.
Lay the bacon slices on the chopping board. Put a date on one side of each slice and roll up. Secure with toothpicks. Brush the wrapped dates with maple syrup and AirFry for 10-12 minutes, turning halfway through cooking until the bacon is crispy. Let cool for 5 minutes and serve.

Nutrition Facts (per serving):
Calories: 260 | Carbohydrates: 22g | Protein: 6g | Fat: 17g | Fiber: 2g

Servings: 2 | 8 Minutes

161 Savory Herb Cloud Eggs

Ingredients:
- 2 large eggs, whites and yolks separated
- ¼ teaspoon salt
- ¼ teaspoon dried oregano
- 2 tablespoons chopped fresh chives
- 2 teaspoons salted butter, melted

Directions:
In a large bowl, whip egg whites until stiff peaks form, about 3 minutes. Place egg whites evenly into two ungreased 4" ramekins. Sprinkle evenly with salt, oregano, and chives. Place 1 whole egg yolk in center of each ramekin and drizzle with butter.
Place ramekins into air fryer basket. Adjust the temperature to 350°F and set the timer for 8 minutes. Egg whites will be fluffy and browned when done. Serve warm.

Nutrition Facts (per serving):
Calories: 80 | Carbohydrates: 0.5g | Protein: 5.5g | Fat: 6g | Fiber: 0g | Sugar: 0.5g

---

Servings: 4 | 12 Minutes

162 Parmesan Chicken Tenders

Ingredients:
- 1 pound boneless, skinless chicken breast tenderloins
- ½ cup mayonnaise
- 1 cup grated Parmesan cheese
- 1 cup panko bread crumbs
- ½ teaspoon garlic powder
- 1 teaspoon salt
- ½ teaspoon ground black pepper
- Cooking spray

Directions:
Preheat the air fryer to 400°F.
In a large bowl, add chicken and mayonnaise and toss to coat.
In a medium bowl, mix Parmesan, bread crumbs, garlic powder, salt, and pepper. Press chicken into bread crumb mixture to fully coat. Spritz with cooking spray and place in the air fryer basket.
Cook 12 minutes, turning halfway through cooking time, until tenders are golden and crisp on the edges and internal temperature reaches at least 165°F. Serve warm.

Nutrition Facts (per serving):
Calories: 224 | Carbohydrates: 2.6g | Protein: 9g | Fat: 19g | Fiber: 0.3g

---

Servings: 5 | 20 Minutes

163 Cheddar Cheese Lumpia Rolls

Ingredients:
- 5 ounces mature cheddar cheese, cut into 15 sticks
- 15 pieces spring roll lumpia wrappers
- 2 tablespoons sesame oil

Directions:
Wrap the cheese sticks in the lumpia wrappers.
Transfer to the Air Fryer basket. Brush with sesame oil.
Bake in the preheated Air Fryer at 395°F for 10 minutes or until the lumpia wrappers turn golden brown. Work in batches.
Shake the Air Fryer basket occasionally to ensure even cooking. Bon appétit!

Nutrition Facts (per serving):
Calories: 250 | Carbohydrates: 16g | Protein: 9g | Fat: 16g | Fiber: 1g

---

Servings: 4 | 25 minutes

164 South Asian Pork Momos

Ingredients:
- 1 lb ground pork
- 2 tbsp olive oil
- 1 carrot, shredded
- 1 onion, chopped
- 1 tsp soy sauce
- 16 wonton wrappers
- Salt and black pepper to taste

Directions:
Preheat the air fryer to 320 F. Warm olive oil in a pan over medium heat and stir-fry ground pork, onion, carrot, soy sauce, salt, and black pepper for 8-10 minutes or until the meat is browned.
Divide the filling between the wrappers. Tuck them around the mixture to form momo shapes and seal the edges. Spritz the momos with cooking spray and AirFry them for 9-11 minutes, flipping once.

Nutrition Facts (per serving):
Calories: 350 | Carbohydrates: 18g | Protein: 20g | Fat: 22g | Fiber: 1.5g

165 Almond Asparagus

Servings: 3 **Time:** 6 Minutes

Ingredients:
- 1 pound asparagus
- 1/3 cup almonds, sliced
- 2 tablespoons olive oil
- 2 tablespoons balsamic vinegar
- Salt and black pepper, to taste

Directions:
Preheat the Air fryer to 400ºF and grease an Air fryer basket.
Mix asparagus, oil, vinegar, salt, and black pepper in a bowl and toss to coat well.
Arrange asparagus into the Air fryer basket and sprinkle with the almond slices.
Cook for about 6 minutes and dish out to serve hot.

Nutrition Facts (per serving):
Calories: 110 | Carbohydrates: 4.7g | Protein: 2g | Fat: 9.3g | Fiber: 2g | Sugar: 1.3g

166 Basic Chicken Breasts

Servings: 4 **Time:** 15 Minutes

Ingredients:
- 2 tsp olive oil
- 2 chicken breasts
- Salt and pepper to taste
- ½ tsp garlic powder
- ½ tsp rosemary

Directions:
Preheat air fryer to 350ºF. Rub the chicken breasts with olive oil over tops and bottom and sprinkle with garlic powder, rosemary, salt, and pepper. Place the chicken in the frying basket and Air Fry for 9 minutes, flipping once. Let rest onto a serving plate for 5 minutes before cutting into cubes. Serve and enjoy!

Nutrition Facts (per serving):
Calories: 219 | Carbohydrates: 0.3g | Protein: 10g | Fat: 18.8g | Fiber: 0g

167 Lamb Chops

Servings: 2 **Time:** 20 Minutes

Ingredients:
- 2 teaspoons oil
- ½ teaspoon ground rosemary
- ½ teaspoon lemon juice
- 1 pound lamb chops, approximately 1-inch thick
- salt and pepper
- cooking spray

Directions:
Mix the oil, rosemary, and lemon juice together and rub into all sides of the lamb chops. Season to taste with salt and pepper.
For best flavor, cover lamb chops and allow them to rest in the fridge for 20 minutes.
Spray air fryer basket with nonstick spray and place lamb chops in it.
Cook at 360ºF for approximately 20minutes. This will cook chops to medium. The meat will be juicy but have no remaining pink. Cook for a minute or two longer for well done chops. For rare chops, stop cooking after about 12minutes and check for doneness.

Nutrition Facts (per serving):
Calories: 430 | Carbohydrates: 0g | Protein: 30g | Fat: 34g | Fiber: 0g

168 Crispy Hasselback Potatoes

Servings: 4 **Time:** 25 minutes

Ingredients:
- 2 tbsp lard, melted
- 1 lb russet potatoes
- 1 tbsp olive oil
- Salt and black pepper to taste
- 1 garlic clove, crushed
- 1 tbsp fresh dill, chopped

Directions:
Preheat the air fryer to 400 F. On the potatoes, make thin vertical slits, around 1/5 inch apart. Make sure to cut the potatoes 3/4-the way down, so that they can hold together. Mix together the lard, olive oil, and garlic in a bowl. Brush the potatoes with some of the mixture.
Season with salt and pepper and place them in the greased frying basket. AirFry for 25-30 minutes, brushing once halfway through so they don't dry during cooking, until golden and crispy around the edges. Sprinkle with dill. Serve and enjoy!

Nutrition Facts (per serving):
Calories: 230 | Carbohydrates: 26g | Protein: 3g | Fat: 13g | Fiber: 2.2g

Servings: 2   10 Minutes

169 Curried Eggplant

Ingredients:
1 large eggplant, cut into ½-inch thick slices
1 garlic clove, minced
½ fresh red chili, chopped
1 tablespoon vegetable oil
¼ teaspoon curry powder
Salt, to taste

Directions:
Preheat the Air fryer to 300°F and grease an Air fryer basket.
Mix all the ingredients in a bowl and toss to coat well. Arrange the eggplant slices in the Air fryer basket and cook for about 10 minutes, tossing once in between. Dish out onto serving plates and serve hot.

Nutrition Facts (per serving):
Calories: 100 | Carbohydrates: 6g | Protein: 1g | Fat: 8g | Fiber: 3g | Sugar: 3g

---

 Servings: 6   12 Minutes

170 Chicken Adobo

Ingredients:
6 boneless chicken thighs
¼ cup soy sauce or tamari
½ cup rice wine vinegar
4 cloves garlic, minced
⅛ teaspoon crushed red pepper flakes
½ teaspoon black pepper

Directions:
Place the chicken thighs into a resealable plastic bag with the soy sauce or tamari, the rice wine vinegar, the garlic, and the crushed red pepper flakes. Seal the bag and let the chicken marinate at least 1 hour in the refrigerator.
Preheat the air fryer to 400°F.
Drain the chicken and pat dry with a paper towel. Season the chicken with black pepper and liberally spray with cooking spray.
Place the chicken in the air fryer basket and cook for 9 minutes, turn over at 9 minutes and check for an internal temperature of 165°F, and cook another 3 minutes.

Nutrition Facts (per serving):
Calories: 221 | Carbohydrates: 1.4g | Protein: 9g | Fat: 18.6g | Fiber: 0g

---

 Servings: 4 20 Minutes

171 Crispy Pork Belly

Ingredients:
1 pound pork belly, cut into 1" cubes
¼ cup soy sauce
1 tablespoon Worcestershire sauce
2 teaspoons sriracha hot chili sauce
½ teaspoon salt
¼ teaspoon ground black pepper

Directions:
Place pork belly into a medium sealable bowl or bag and pour in soy sauce, Worcestershire sauce, and sriracha. Seal and let marinate 30 minutes in the refrigerator.
Remove pork from marinade, pat dry with a paper towel, and sprinkle with salt and pepper.
Place pork in ungreased air fryer basket. Adjust the temperature to 360°F and set the timer for 20 minutes, shaking the basket halfway through cooking. Pork belly will be done when it has an internal temperature of at least 145°F and is golden brown. Let pork belly rest on a large plate 10 minutes. Serve warm.

Nutrition Facts (per serving):
Calories: 520 | Carbohydrates: 2g | Protein: 17g | Fat: 47g | Fiber: 0g

---

 Servings: 4 25 minutes

172 Sweet Potato Boats

Ingredients:
4 sweet potatoes, boiled and halved lengthwise
2 tbsp olive oil
1 shallot, chopped
1 cup canned mixed beans
¼ cup mozzarella cheese, grated
Salt and black pepper to taste

Directions:
Preheat the air fryer to 400 F. Grease the frying basket with olive oil.
Scoop out the flesh from the potatoes, so shells are formed. Chop the potato flesh and put it in a bowl. Add in shallot, mixed beans, salt, and pepper; mix to combine. Fill the potato shells with the mixture and top with the cheese. Arrange on the basket and place inside the fryer. Bake for 10-12 minutes.

Nutrition Facts (per serving):
Calories: 270 | Carbohydrates: 38g | Protein: 6.5g | Fat: 10g | Fiber: 6g

Servings: 2 | 10 Minutes

173 Basil Tomatoes

Ingredients:
- 2 tomatoes, halved
- 1 tablespoon fresh basil, chopped
- Olive oil cooking spray
- Salt and black pepper, as required

Directions:
Preheat the Air fryer to 320°F and grease an Air fryer basket.
Spray the tomato halves evenly with olive oil cooking spray and season with salt, black pepper and basil.
Arrange the tomato halves into the Air fryer basket, cut sides up.
Cook for about 10 minutes and dish out onto serving plates.

Nutrition Facts (per serving):
Calories: 45 | Carbohydrates: 4g | Protein: 1g | Fat: 3g | Fiber: 1g | Sugar: 3g

---

Servings: 4 | 12 Minutes

174 Garlic Ginger Chicken

Ingredients:
- 1 pound boneless, skinless chicken thighs, cut into 1" pieces
- ¼ cup soy sauce
- 2 cloves garlic, peeled and finely minced
- 1 tablespoon minced ginger
- ¼ teaspoon salt

Directions:
Place all ingredients in a large sealable bowl or bag. Place sealed bowl or bag into refrigerator and let marinate at least 30 minutes up to overnight. Remove chicken from marinade and place into ungreased air fryer basket. Adjust the temperature to 375°F and set the timer for 12 minutes, shaking the basket twice during cooking. Chicken will be golden and have an internal temperature of at least 165°F when done. Serve warm.

Nutrition Facts (per serving):
Calories: 220 | Carbohydrates: 1.3g | Protein: 9g | Fat: 18.7g | Fiber: 0g

---

 Servings: 6 20 Minutes

175 Mustard Herb Pork Tenderloin

Ingredients:
- ¼ cup mayonnaise
- 2 tablespoons Dijon mustard
- ½ teaspoon dried thyme
- ¼ teaspoon dried rosemary
- 1 pork tenderloin
- ½ teaspoon salt
- ¼ teaspoon ground black pepper

Directions:
In a small bowl, mix mayonnaise, mustard, thyme, and rosemary. Brush tenderloin with mixture on all sides, then sprinkle with salt and pepper on all sides. Place tenderloin into ungreased air fryer basket. Adjust the temperature to 400°F and set the timer for 20 minutes, turning tenderloin halfway through cooking. Tenderloin will be golden and have an internal temperature of at least 145°F when done. Serve warm.

Nutrition Facts (per serving):
Calories: 210 | Carbohydrates: 1g | Protein: 24g | Fat: 12g | Fiber: 0g

---

 Servings: 4 25 minutes

176 Roasted Hot Chickpeas

Ingredients:
- 1 (19-oz) can chickpeas, drained and rinsed
- 2 tbsp olive oil
- ½ tsp ground cumin
- ¼ tsp mustard powder
- ¼ tsp onion powder
- ½ tsp chili powder
- ¼ tsp cayenne pepper
- ¼ tsp salt

Directions:
Preheat the air fryer to 385 F. In a mixing bowl, thoroughly combine the olive oil, cumin, mustard powder, onion powder, chili powder, cayenne pepper, and salt. Add in the chickpeas.
Toss them until evenly coated. Transfer the chickpeas to the frying basket and Air Fry, shaking the basket every 2-3 minutes. Cook until they're as crunchy as you like them, about 15-20 minutes. Serve.

Nutrition Facts (per serving):
Calories: 180 | Carbohydrates: 20g | Protein: 6g | Fat: 8g | Fiber: 6g

Servings: 2 — 5 Minutes

177 Sweet Pepper Nachos

Ingredients:
6 mini sweet peppers, seeded and sliced in half
¾ cup shredded Colby jack cheese
¼ cup sliced pickled jalapeños
½ medium avocado, peeled, pitted, and diced
2 tablespoons sour cream

Directions:
Place peppers into an ungreased 6" round nonstick baking dish. Sprinkle with Colby and top with jalapeños.
Place dish into air fryer basket. Adjust the temperature to 350°F and set the timer for 5 minutes. Cheese will be melted and bubbly when done.
Remove dish from air fryer and top with avocado. Drizzle with sour cream. Serve warm.

Nutrition Facts (per serving):
Calories: 220 | Carbohydrates: 8g | Protein: 8g | Fat: 18g | Fiber: 2g | Sugar: 4g

Servings: 4 — 12 Minutes

178 Cajun-breaded Chicken Bites

Ingredients:
1 pound boneless, skinless chicken breasts, cut into 1" cubes
½ cup heavy whipping cream
½ teaspoon salt
¼ teaspoon ground black pepper
1 ounce plain pork rinds, finely crushed
¼ cup unflavored whey protein powder
½ teaspoon Cajun seasoning

Directions:
Place chicken in a medium bowl and pour in cream. Stir to coat. Sprinkle with salt and pepper.
In a separate large bowl, combine pork rinds, protein powder, and Cajun seasoning. Remove chicken from cream, shaking off any excess, and toss in dry mix until fully coated.
Place bites into ungreased air fryer basket. Adjust the temperature to 400°F and set the timer for 12 minutes, shaking the basket twice during cooking. Bites will be done when golden brown and have an internal temperature of at least 165°F. Serve warm.

Nutrition Facts (per serving):
Calories: 219 | Carbohydrates: 1.4g | Protein: 9.2g | Fat: 18g | Fiber: 0.1g

 Servings: 4 20 Minutes

179 Friday Night Cheeseburgers

Ingredients:
1 lb ground beef
1 tsp Worcestershire sauce
1 tbsp allspice
Salt and pepper to taste
4 cheddar cheese slices
4 buns

Directions:
Preheat air fryer to 360°F. Combine beef, Worcestershire sauce, allspice, salt and pepper in a large bowl. Divide into 4 equal portions and shape into patties. Place the burgers in the greased frying basket and Air Fry for 8 minutes. Flip and cook for another 3-4 minutes. Top each burger with cheddar cheese and cook for another minute so the cheese melts. Transfer to a bun and serve.

Nutrition Facts (per serving):
Calories: 520 | Carbohydrates: 26g | Protein: 30g | Fat: 33g | Fiber: 1g

 Servings: 4 25 minutes

180 Roasted Pumpkin Seeds with Cardamom

Ingredients:
1 cup pumpkin seeds, pulp removed, rinsed
1 tbsp butter, melted
1 tbsp brown sugar
1 tsp orange zest
½ tsp cardamom
½ tsp salt

Directions:
Preheat air fryer to 320 F. Place the pumpkin seeds in a greased baking dish and place the dish in the fryer. AirFry for 4-5 minutes to avoid moisture. In a bowl, whisk butter, sugar, zest, cardamom, and salt. Add the seeds to the bowl and toss to coat well. Transfer the seeds to the baking dish inside the fryer and Bake for 13-15 minutes, shaking the basket every 5 minutes, until lightly browned. Serve warm.

Nutrition Facts (per serving):
Calories: 170 | Carbohydrates: 6g | Protein: 7g | Fat: 14g | Fiber: 2g

Servings: 4 | 10 Minutes

181 Crispy Cabbage Steaks

Ingredients:
1 small head green cabbage, cored and cut into ½"-thick slices
¼ teaspoon salt
¼ teaspoon ground black pepper
2 tablespoons olive oil
1 clove garlic, peeled and finely minced
½ teaspoon dried thyme
½ teaspoon dried parsley

Directions:
Sprinkle each side of cabbage with salt and pepper, then place into ungreased air fryer basket, working in batches if needed.
Drizzle each side of cabbage with olive oil, then sprinkle with remaining ingredients on both sides.
Adjust the temperature to 350°F and set the timer for 10 minutes, turning "steaks" halfway through cooking. Cabbage will be browned at the edges and tender when done. Serve warm.

Nutrition Facts (per serving):
Calories: 120 | Carbohydrates: 8g | Protein: 2g | Fat: 9g | Fiber: 3g | Sugar: 4g

---

Servings: 8 | 15 Minutes

182 Air Fried Chicken Tenderloin

Ingredients:
½ cup almond flour
1 egg, beaten
2 tablespoons coconut oil
8 chicken tenderloins
Salt and pepper to taste

Directions:
Preheat the air fryer for 5 minutes.
Season the chicken tenderloin with salt and pepper to taste.
Soak in beaten eggs then dredge in almond flour.
Place in the air fryer and brush with coconut oil.
Cook for 15 minutes at 375°F.
Halfway through the cooking time, give the fryer basket a shake to cook evenly.

Nutrition Facts (per serving):
Calories: 221 | Carbohydrates: 2.2g | Protein: 9g | Fat: 18.5g | Fiber: 0.8g

---

Servings: 2 | 20 minutes

183 Balsamic Brussels Sprouts

Ingredients:
½ lb Brussels sprouts, trimmed and halved
1 tbsp butter, melted
Salt and black pepper to taste
1 tbsp balsamic vinegar

Directions:
Preheat the air fryer to 380 F. In a bowl, mix Brussels sprouts with butter, salt, and black pepper. Place the sprouts in the greased frying basket and AirFry for 5-7 minutes. Shake and cook until the sprouts are caramelized but tender on the inside, 5-7 more minutes. Drizzle with balsamic vinegar to serve.

Nutrition Facts (per serving):
Calories: 90 | Carbohydrates: 9g | Protein: 3g | Fat: 6g | Fiber: 3.5g

---

Servings: 4 | 25 minutes

184 Roasted Pumpkin Seeds with Cardamom

Ingredients:
1 cup pumpkin seeds, pulp removed, rinsed
1 tbsp butter, melted
1 tbsp brown sugar
1 tsp orange zest
½ tsp cardamom
½ tsp salt

Directions:
Preheat air fryer to 320 F. Place the pumpkin seeds in a greased baking dish and place the dish in the fryer. AirFry for 4-5 minutes to avoid moisture. In a bowl, whisk butter, sugar, zest, cardamom, and salt. Add the seeds to the bowl and toss to coat well. Transfer the seeds to the baking dish inside the fryer and Bake for 13-15 minutes, shaking the basket every 5 minutes, until lightly browned. Serve warm.

Nutrition Facts (per serving):
Calories: 195 | Carbohydrates: 5g | Protein: 9g | Fat: 16g | Fiber: 1g

Servings: 2 — 8 Minutes

185 Mediterranean Pan Pizza

Ingredients:
- 1 cup shredded mozzarella cheese
- ¼ medium red bell pepper, seeded and chopped
- ½ cup chopped fresh spinach leaves
- 2 tablespoons chopped black olives
- 2 tablespoons crumbled feta cheese

Directions:
Sprinkle mozzarella into an ungreased 6" round nonstick baking dish in an even layer. Add remaining ingredients on top.
Place dish into air fryer basket. Adjust the temperature to 350°F and set the timer for 8 minutes, checking halfway through to avoid burning. Top of pizza will be golden brown and the cheese melted when done. Remove dish from fryer and let cool 5 minutes before slicing and serving.

Nutrition Facts (per serving):
Calories: 180 | Carbohydrates: 4g | Protein: 11g | Fat: 14g | Fiber: 1.5g | Sugar: 2g

---

Servings: 4 — 15 Minutes

186 15-minute Chicken

Ingredients:
- 4 boneless, skinless chicken breasts
- 2 tablespoons olive oil
- 1 teaspoon salt
- 1 teaspoon garlic powder
- 1 teaspoon paprika
- ½ teaspoon ground black pepper

Directions:
Preheat the air fryer to 375°F. Carefully butterfly chicken breasts lengthwise, leaving the two halves connected. Drizzle chicken with oil, then sprinkle with salt, garlic powder, paprika, and pepper. Place in the air fryer basket and cook 15 minutes, turning halfway through cooking time, until chicken is golden brown and the internal temperature reaches at least 165°F. Serve warm.

Nutrition Facts (per serving):
Calories: 220 | Carbohydrates: 0.5g | Protein: 9g | Fat: 18.6g | Fiber: 0g

---

 Servings: 4 20 minutes

187 Zucchini-Parmesan Chips

Ingredients:
- 2 medium zucchinis, sliced
- 1 cup breadcrumbs
- 2 eggs, beaten
- 1 cup Parmesan cheese, grated
- Salt and black pepper to taste
- 1 tsp smoked paprika

Directions:
Preheat the air fryer to 390 F. In a bowl, mix breadcrumbs, salt, pepper, Parmesan, and paprika. Dip zucchini slices in the eggs and then in the cheese mix; press to coat well. Spray the coated slices with cooking spray and place them in the frying basket. AirFry for 12-14 minutes, flipping once. Serve hot.

Nutrition Facts (per serving):
Calories: 240 | Carbohydrates: 16g | Protein: 13g | Fat: 14g | Fiber: 2g

---

 Servings: 4 25 minutes

188 Traditional Swedish Meatballs

Ingredients:
- 1 lb ground pork
- 1 tbsp fresh dill, chopped
- ½ tsp nutmeg
- ⅓ cup seasoned breadcrumbs
- 1 egg, beaten
- Salt and white pepper to taste
- 2 tbsp butter
- ⅓ cup sour cream
- 2 tbsp flour

Directions:
Preheat the air fryer to 360 F. In a bowl, combine the ground pork, dill, nutmeg, breadcrumbs, egg, salt, and pepper and mix well. Shape the mixture into small balls. AirFry them in the greased frying basket for 12-14 minutes, flipping once.
Meanwhile, melt butter in a saucepan over medium heat and stir in the flour until lightly browned, about 2 minutes. Gradually pour 1 cup of water and whisk until the sauce thickens. Stir in sour cream and cook for 1 minute. Pour the sauce over the meatballs to serve.

Nutrition Facts (per serving):
Calories: 325 | Carbohydrates: 4g | Protein: 19g | Fat: 26g | Fiber: 0g

Servings: 4 | 8 Minutes

189 Pesto Spinach Flatbread

Ingredients:
- 1 cup blanched finely ground almond flour
- 2 ounces cream cheese
- 2 cups shredded mozzarella cheese
- 1 cup chopped fresh spinach leaves
- 2 tablespoons basil pesto

Directions:
Place flour, cream cheese, and mozzarella in a large microwave-safe bowl and microwave on high 45 seconds, then stir.
Fold in spinach and microwave an additional 15 seconds. Stir until a soft dough ball forms.
Cut two pieces of parchment paper to fit air fryer basket. Separate dough into two sections and press each out on ungreased parchment to create 6" rounds.
Spread 1 tablespoon pesto over each flatbread and place rounds on parchment into ungreased air fryer basket. Adjust the temperature to 350°F and set the timer for 8 minutes, turning crusts halfway through cooking. Flatbread will be golden when done.
Let cool 5 minutes before slicing and serving.

Nutrition Facts (per serving):
Calories: 300 | Carbohydrates: 6g | Protein: 15g | Fat: 25g | Fiber: 2g | Sugar: 2g

---

Servings: 4 | 12 Minutes

190 Blackened Chicken Tenders

Ingredients:
- 1 pound boneless, skinless chicken tenders
- 2 teaspoons paprika
- 1 teaspoon garlic powder
- 1 teaspoon salt
- ½ teaspoon cayenne pepper
- ½ teaspoon dried thyme
- ½ teaspoon ground black pepper
- Cooking spray

Directions:
Preheat the air fryer to 400°F.
Place chicken tenders into a large bowl.
In a small bowl, mix paprika, garlic powder, salt, cayenne, thyme, and black pepper. Add spice mixture to chicken and toss to coat. Spritz chicken with cooking spray.
Place chicken in the air fryer basket and cook 12 minutes, turning halfway through cooking time, until chicken is brown at the edges and internal temperature reaches at least 165°F. Serve warm.

Nutrition Facts (per serving):
Calories: 219 | Carbohydrates: 0.8g | Protein: 9g | Fat: 18.5g | Fiber: 0g

---

 Servings: 2 20 minutes

191 Onion Rings

Ingredients:
- 1 onion, sliced into 1-inch rings
- 1 egg, beaten
- ¼ cup milk
- Salt and garlic powder to taste
- ½ cup all-purpose flour
- ¼ cup panko breadcrumbs

Directions:
Preheat the air fryer to 350 F. Dust the onion rings with some flour and set aside. In a bowl, mix the remaining flour, garlic powder, and salt. Stir in the egg and milk. Dip onion rings into the flour mixture, then coat them in the crumbs. Lay the rings into the frying basket and spray with cooking spray. AirFry for 8-11 minutes until golden and crispy, shaking once. Serve with honey-mustard dipping sauce.

Nutrition Facts (per serving):
Calories: 190 | Carbohydrates: 26g | Protein: 5g | Fat: 7g | Fiber: 2g

---

Servings: 4 25 minutes

192 Serbian Pork Skewers with Yogurt Sauce

Ingredients:
- 1 lb pork sausage meat
- Salt and black pepper to taste
- 1 onion, chopped
- ½ tsp garlic puree
- 1 tsp ground cumin
- 1 cup Greek yogurt
- 2 tbsp walnuts, finely chopped
- 1 tbsp fresh dill, chopped

Directions:
Preheat the air fryer to 340 F. In a bowl, mix the sausage meat, onion, garlic puree, ground cumin, salt, and pepper. Knead until everything is well incorporated. Form patties out the mixture, about ½ inch thick, and thread them onto flat skewers. Lay them on the greased frying basket.
AirFry for 14-16 minutes, turning them over once or twice until golden. Whisk the yogurt, walnuts, garlic, dill, and salt in a small bowl to obtain a sauce. Serve the skewers with the yogurt sauce.

Nutrition Facts (per serving):
Calories: 330 | Carbohydrates: 4g | Protein: 16g | Fat: 27g | Fiber: 0.5g

Servings: 4 — 8 Minutes

193 Stuffed Portobellos

Ingredients:
3 ounces cream cheese, softened
½ medium zucchini, trimmed and chopped
¼ cup seeded and chopped red bell pepper
1½ cups chopped fresh spinach leaves
4 large portobello mushrooms, stems removed
2 tablespoons coconut oil, melted
½ teaspoon salt

Directions:
In a medium bowl, mix cream cheese, zucchini, pepper, and spinach.
Drizzle mushrooms with coconut oil and sprinkle with salt. Scoop ¼ zucchini mixture into each mushroom. Place mushrooms into ungreased air fryer basket. Adjust the temperature to 400°F and set the timer for 8 minutes. Portobellos will be tender and tops will be browned when done. Serve warm.

Nutrition Facts (per serving):
Calories: 140 | Carbohydrates: 5g | Protein: 4g | Fat: 11g | Fiber: 2g | Sugar: 3g

---

Servings: 4 — 15 Minutes

194 Pulled Turkey Quesadillas

Ingredients:
¾ cup pulled cooked turkey breast
6 tortilla wraps
1/3 cup grated Swiss cheese
1 small red onion, sliced
2 tbsp Mexican chili sauce

Directions:
Preheat air fryer to 400°F. Lay 3 tortilla wraps on a clean workspace, then spoon equal amounts of Swiss cheese, turkey, Mexican chili sauce, and red onion on the tortillas. Spritz the exterior of the tortillas with cooking spray. Air Fry the quesadillas, one at a time, for 5-8 minutes. The cheese should be melted and the outsides crispy. Serve.

Nutrition Facts (per serving):
Calories: 223 | Carbohydrates: 2.5g | Protein: 9.2g | Fat: 18.2g | Fiber: 0.4g

---

 Servings: 4 20 minutes

195 Herb & Cheese Stuffed Mushrooms

Ingredients:
1 lb brown mushrooms, stems removed
1 cup Grana Padano cheese, grated
½ tsp dried thyme
½ tsp dried rosemary
Salt and black pepper to taste
1 tbsp olive oil

Directions:
Preheat the air fryer to 360 F. In a bowl, mix Grana Padano cheese, herbs, salt, and black pepper. Spoon the mixture into the mushrooms and press down so that it sticks. Drizzle with olive oil and place in the air fryer. Bake for 8-10 minutes or until the cheese has melted. Serve warm.

Nutrition Facts (per serving):
Calories: 170 | Carbohydrates: 5g | Protein: 12g | Fat: 12g | Fiber: 1g

---

 Servings: 4 25 minutes

196 Veggies & Pork Pinchos

Ingredients:
1 lb pork tenderloin, cubed
2 tbsp olive oil
1 lime, juiced and zested
2 cloves garlic, minced
1 tsp chili powder
1 tsp ground fennel seeds
½ tsp ground cumin
Salt and white pepper to taste
1 red pepper, cut into chunks
½ cup mushrooms, quartered

Directions:
In a bowl, mix half of the olive oil, lime zest and juice, garlic, chili, ground fennel, cumin, salt, and white pepper. Add in the pork and stir to coat. Cover with cling film and place in the fridge for 1 hour.
Preheat the air fryer to 380 F. Season the mushrooms and red pepper with salt and black pepper and drizzle with the remaining olive oil. Thread alternating the pork, mushroom and red pepper pieces onto short skewers. Place in the greased frying basket and AirFry for 15 minutes, turning once. Serve hot.

Nutrition Facts (per serving):
Calories: 215 | Carbohydrates: 2g | Protein: 24g | Fat: 12g | Fiber: 0.5g

Servings: 12 — 10 Minutes

197 Falafels

Ingredients:
1 pouch falafel mix
2-3 tablespoons plain breadcrumbs
oil for misting or cooking spray

Directions:
Prepare falafel mix according to package directions. Preheat air fryer to 390°F.
Place breadcrumbs in shallow dish or on wax paper. Shape falafel mixture into 12 balls and flatten slightly. Roll in breadcrumbs to coat all sides and mist with oil or cooking spray.
Place falafels in air fryer basket in single layer and cook for 5 minutes. Shake basket, and continue cooking for 5 minutes, until they brown and are crispy.

Nutrition Facts (per serving):
Calories: 90 | Carbohydrates: 12g | Protein: 3g | Fat: 3g | Fiber: 2g | Sugar: 1g

---

Servings: 4 — 15 Minutes

198 Chicken Cordon Bleu

Ingredients:
4 boneless, skinless chicken breasts
¾ teaspoon salt
½ teaspoon ground black pepper
8 slices deli Black Forest ham
8 slices Gruyère cheese
1 large egg, beaten
2 cups panko bread crumbs

Directions:
Preheat the air fryer to 375°F.
Cut each chicken breast in half lengthwise. Use a mallet to pound to ¼" thickness. Sprinkle salt and pepper on each side of chicken.
Place a slice of ham and a slice of cheese on each piece of chicken. Roll up chicken and secure with toothpicks.
In a medium bowl, add egg. In a separate medium bowl, add bread crumbs. Dip each chicken roll into egg, then into bread crumbs, pressing gently to adhere.
Spritz rolls with cooking spray and place in the air fryer basket. Cook 15 minutes, turning halfway through cooking time, until rolls are golden brown and internal temperature reaches at least 165°F. Serve warm.

Nutrition Facts (per serving):
Calories: 224 | Carbohydrates: 2.4g | Protein: 9g | Fat: 18.9g | Fiber: 0.2g

---

Servings: 2 — 20 minutes

199 Classic Zucchini Fries

Ingredients:
1 zucchini, cut lengthways into strips
½ cup panko breadcrumbs
½ cup all-purpose flour
1 egg
Salt and garlic powder to taste
½ cup garlic mayonnaise

Directions:
Preheat the air fryer to 400 F. Sift the flour into a bowl with a pinch of salt. Whisk the egg in another bowl with some salt. Pour the breadcrumbs in a third one and mix with garlic powder. Coat the zucchini strips in the flour, then in the beaten egg, and finally in the crumbs. Lightly spray the strips with cooking spray and AirFry until crispy, 10-12 minutes, flipping once halfway through. Serve with garlic mayo.

Nutrition Facts (per serving):
Calories: 310 | Carbohydrates: 23g | Protein: 5g | Fat: 22g | Fiber: 2g

---

Servings: 4 — 25 minutes

200 Spicy Tricolor Pork Kebabs

Ingredients:
1 lb pork steak, cut into cubes
¼ cup soy sauce
2 tsp smoked paprika
1 tsp chili powder
1 tsp garlic salt
1 tsp red chili flakes
1 tbsp white wine vinegar
3 tbsp steak sauce
Skewing:
1 green pepper, cut into cubes
1 red pepper, cut into cubes
1 yellow squash, seeded and cut into cubes
1 green squash, seeded and cut into cubes
Salt and black pepper to taste
A bunch of skewers

Directions:
In a mixing bowl, add the pork cubes, soy sauce, smoked paprika, chili powder, garlic salt, red chili flakes, wine vinegar, and steak sauce. Mix with a spoon and marinate for 1 hour in the fridge.
Preheat the air fryer to 370 F. On each skewer, stick the pork cubes and vegetables alternating them. Arrange the skewers on the greased frying basket and Bake them for 12-14 minutes, flipping once.

Nutrition Facts (per serving):
Calories: 208 | Carbohydrates: 4g | Protein: 21g | Fat: 11g | Fiber: 1.5g

Servings: 4   🕒 10 Minutes

201 Stuffed Mushrooms

Ingredients:
- 12 baby bella mushrooms, stems removed
- 4 ounces full-fat cream cheese, softened
- ¼ cup grated vegetarian Parmesan cheese
- ¼ cup Italian bread crumbs
- 1 teaspoon crushed red pepper flakes

Directions:
Preheat the air fryer to 400ºF.
Use a spoon to hollow out mushroom caps.
In a medium bowl, combine cream cheese, Parmesan, bread crumbs, and red pepper flakes. Scoop approximately 1 tablespoon mixture into each mushroom cap.
Place stuffed mushrooms in the air fryer basket and cook 10 minutes until stuffing is brown. Let cool 5 minutes before serving.

Nutrition Facts (per serving):
Calories: 160 | Carbohydrates: 7g | Protein: 6g | Fat: 13g | Fiber: 1g | Sugar: 2g

 Servings: 4   🕒 12 Minutes

202 Pretzel-crusted Chicken

Ingredients:
- 2 cups mini twist pretzels
- ½ cup mayonnaise
- 2 tablespoons honey
- 2 tablespoons yellow mustard
- 4 boneless, skinless chicken breasts, sliced in half lengthwise
- 1 teaspoon salt
- ½ teaspoon ground black pepper
- Cooking spray

Directions:
Preheat the air fryer to 375ºF.
In a food processor, place pretzels and pulse ten times.
In a medium bowl, mix mayonnaise, honey, and mustard.
Sprinkle chicken with salt and pepper, then brush with sauce mixture until well coated.
Pour pretzel crumbs onto a shallow plate and press each piece of chicken into them until well coated.
Spritz chicken with cooking spray and place in the air fryer basket. Cook 12 minutes, turning halfway through cooking time, until edges are golden brown and the internal temperature reaches at least 165ºF. Serve warm.

Nutrition Facts (per serving):
Calories: 223 | Carbohydrates: 2.5g | Protein: 9g | Fat: 18.6g | Fiber: 0.3g

 Servings: 6   20 minutes

203 Perfect Air Fryer Eggs

Ingredients:
- 6 large eggs
- Salt and black pepper to taste

Directions:
Preheat the air fryer to 270 F. Lay the eggs in the basket (or in a muffin tray) and cook for 10 minutes for runny or 15 minutes for hard. Using tongs, place the eggs in a bowl with cold water to cool for 5 minutes. When cooled, remove the shells, cut them in half, and sprinkle with salt and pepper. Serve.

Nutrition Facts (per serving):
Calories: 70 | Carbohydrates: 0g | Protein: 6g | Fat: 5g | Fiber: 0g

 Servings: 4   25 minutes

204 Pork Chops with Mustard-Apricot Glaze

Ingredients:
- 4 pork chops, ½-inch thick
- Salt and black pepper to taste
- 1 tbsp apricot jam
- 1 ½ tbsp minced, finely chopped
- 2 tbsp wholegrain mustard

Directions:
In a bowl, add apricot jam, garlic, mustard, salt, and black pepper; mix well. Add the pork chops and toss to coat. Place the chops in the greased frying basket and Bake for 10 minutes at 350 F. Turn the chops with a spatula and cook further for 6-8 minutes until golden and crispy. Once ready, remove the chops to a serving platter and serve with a side of steamed green veggies if desired.

Nutrition Facts (per serving):
Calories: 248 | Carbohydrates: 2.5g | Protein: 22g | Fat: 15g | Fiber: 0.2g

Servings: 4 | 8 Minutes

205 Toasted Ravioli

Ingredients:
1 cup Italian bread crumbs
2 tablespoons grated vegetarian Parmesan cheese
1 large egg
¼ cup whole milk
1 package fresh cheese ravioli
Cooking spray

Directions:
Preheat the air fryer to 400°F.
In a large bowl, whisk together bread crumbs and Parmesan.
In a medium bowl, whisk together egg and milk. Dip each ravioli into egg mixture, shaking off the excess, then press into bread crumb mixture until well coated. Spritz each side with cooking spray.
Place in the air fryer basket and cook 8 minutes, turning halfway through cooking time, until ravioli is brown at the edges and crispy. Serve warm.

Nutrition Facts (per serving):
Calories: 230 | Carbohydrates: 24g | Protein: 9g | Fat: 10g | Fiber: 2g | Sugar: 2g

---

Servings: 6 | 14 Minutes

206 Italian Roasted Chicken Thighs

Ingredients:
6 boneless chicken thighs
½ teaspoon dried oregano
½ teaspoon garlic powder
½ teaspoon sea salt
½ teaspoon black pepper
¼ teaspoon crushed red pepper flakes

Directions:
Pat the chicken thighs with paper towel.
In a small bowl, mix the oregano, garlic powder, salt, pepper, and crushed red pepper flakes. Rub the spice mixture onto the chicken thighs.
Preheat the air fryer to 400°F.
Place the chicken thighs in the air fryer basket and spray with cooking spray. Cook for 10 minutes, turn over, and cook another 4 minutes. When cooking completes, the internal temperature should read 165°F.

Nutrition Facts (per serving):
Calories: 218 | Carbohydrates: 0.6g | Protein: 9g | Fat: 18.3g | Fiber: 0g

---

Servings: 4 | 20 minutes

207 Sweet Garlicky Chicken Wings

Ingredients:
16 chicken wings
¼ cup butter
1 tsp honey
½ tbsp salt
4 garlic cloves, minced
¾ cup potato starch

Directions:
Preheat the air fryer to 370 F. Coat the chicken with potato starch and place in the greased frying basket. Bake for 5 minutes. Whisk the rest of the ingredients in a bowl. Remove the wings from the fryer, pour the sauce over them, and Bake for another 10 minutes, until crispy. Serve immediately.

Nutrition Facts (per serving):
Calories: 340 | Carbohydrates: 10g | Protein: 22g | Fat: 24g | Fiber: 0g

---

Servings: 4 | 25 minutes

208 Southeast-Asian Pork Chops

Ingredients:
4 pork chops
2 garlic cloves, minced
½ tbsp sugar
4 stalks lemongrass, trimmed and chopped
2 shallots, chopped
2 tbsp olive oil
1 ¼ tsp soy sauce
1 ¼ tsp fish sauce
Salt and black pepper to taste

Directions:
In a bowl, add garlic, sugar, lemongrass, shallots, olive oil, soy sauce, fish sauce, salt, and pepper; mix well. Add in the pork chops, coat them with the mixture and marinate for 2 hours in the fridge.
Preheat the air fryer to 400 F. Remove the chops from the marinade and place them in the frying basket. Bake for 14-16 minutes, flipping once, until golden. Serve with sautéed asparagus if desired.

Nutrition Facts (per serving):
Calories: 250 | Carbohydrates: 1.5g | Protein: 22g | Fat: 17g | Fiber: 0g

Servings: 2 | 10 Minutes

209 Bacon With Shallot And Greens

Ingredients:
7 ounces mixed greens
8 thick slices pork bacon
2 shallots, peeled and diced
Nonstick cooking spray

Directions:
Begin by preheating the air fryer to 345°F.
Now, add the shallot and bacon to the Air Fryer cooking basket; set the timer for 2 minutes. Spritz with a nonstick cooking spray.
After that, pause the Air Fryer; throw in the mixed greens; give it a good stir and cook an additional 5 minutes. Serve warm.

Nutrition Facts (per serving):
Calories: 240 | Carbohydrates: 4g | Protein: 9g | Fat: 20g | Fiber: 1.5g | Sugar: 2g

---

Servings: 4 | 15 Minutes Per Batch

210 Barbecue Chicken Enchiladas

Ingredients:
1 ½ cups barbecue sauce, divided
3 cups shredded cooked chicken
8 flour tortillas
1 ½ cups shredded Mexican-blend cheese, divided
⅓ cup diced red onion

Directions:
Preheat the air fryer to 350°F.
In a large bowl, mix 1 cup barbecue sauce and shredded chicken.
Place ¼ cup chicken onto each tortilla and top with 2 tablespoons cheese.
Roll each tortilla and place seam side down into two 6" round baking dishes. Brush tortillas with remaining sauce, top with remaining cheese, and sprinkle with onion.
Working in batches, place in the air fryer basket and cook 15 minutes until the sauce is bubbling and cheese is melted. Serve warm.

Nutrition Facts (per serving):
Calories: 223 | Carbohydrates: 2.5g | Protein: 9g | Fat: 18.2g | Fiber: 0.3g

---

 Servings: 4 20 minutes

211 Turkey Scotch Eggs

Ingredients:
4 hard-boiled eggs, peeled
1 cup panko breadcrumbs
1 egg, beaten in a bowl
1 lb ground turkey
½ tsp dried rosemary
Salt and black pepper to taste

Directions:
Preheat the air fryer to 400 F. In a bowl, mix panko breadcrumbs with rosemary. In another bowl, pour the ground turkey and mix it with salt and pepper. Shape into 4 balls.
Wrap the balls around the boiled eggs to form a large ball with the egg in the center. Dip in the beaten egg and coat with breadcrumbs. Place in the greased frying basket and Bake for 12-14 minutes, shaking once. Serve and enjoy!

Nutrition Facts (per serving):
Calories: 340 | Carbohydrates: 12g | Protein: 28g | Fat: 20g | Fiber: 1g

---

 Servings: 4 25 minutes

212 Spicy-Sweet Pork Chops

Ingredients:
4 thin boneless pork chops
3 tbsp brown sugar
½ tsp cayenne pepper
½ tsp ancho chili powder
½ tsp garlic powder
1 tbsp olive oil
½ cup Cholula hot sauce
Salt and black pepper to taste

Directions:
Preheat your Air Fryer to 375 F.
To make the marinade, mix brown sugar, olive oil, cayenne pepper, garlic powder, salt, and pepper in a small bowl. Dip each pork chop into the marinade, shaking off, and placing them in the frying basket in a single layer. AirFry for 7 minutes. Slide the basket out, turn the chops, and brush them with marinade. Cook for another 5 to 8 minutes until golden brown. Plate and top with hot sauce to serve.

Nutrition Facts (per serving):
Calories: 240 | Carbohydrates: 9g | Protein: 18g | Fat: 14g | Fiber: 0g

Servings: 6 — 8 Minutes

213 Beef Al Carbon (street Taco Meat)

Ingredients:
1½ pounds sirloin steak, cut into ½-inch cubes
¾ cup lime juice
½ cup extra-virgin olive oil
1 teaspoon ground cumin
2 teaspoons garlic powder
1 teaspoon salt

Directions:
In a large bowl, toss together the steak, lime juice, olive oil, cumin, garlic powder, and salt. Allow the meat to marinate for 30 minutes. Drain off all the marinade and pat the meat dry with paper towels.
Preheat the air fryer to 400°F.
Place the meat in the air fryer basket and spray with cooking spray. Cook the meat for 5 minutes, toss the meat, and continue cooking another 3 minutes, until slightly crispy.

Nutrition Facts (per serving):
Calories: 218 | Carbohydrates: 1.1g | Protein: 12g | Fat: 19g | Fiber: 0g

---

Servings: 6 — 15 Minutes

214 Air Fried Cheese Chicken

Ingredients:
6 tbsp seasoned breadcrumbs
2 tbsp Parmesan cheese, grated
1 tbsp melted butter
½ cup mozzarella cheese, shredded
1 tbsp marinara sauce
Cooking spray as needed

Directions:
Preheat your air fryer to 390°F. Grease the cooking basket with cooking spray. In a small bowl, mix breadcrumbs and Parmesan cheese. Brush the chicken pieces with butter and dredge into the breadcrumbs. Add chicken to the cooking basket and cook for 6 minutes. Turn over and top with marinara sauce and shredded mozzarella; cook for 3 more minutes.

Nutrition Facts (per serving):
Calories: 218 | Carbohydrates: 2.4g | Protein: 9g | Fat: 18g | Fiber: 0.3g

---

Servings: 4 — 20 minutes

215 Air Fried Pork Popcorn Bites

Ingredients:
4 boneless pork chops, cut into 1-inch cubes
Salt and black pepper to taste
1 cup flour
¼ tsp garlic powder
¼ tsp onion powder
1 tsp paprika
2 eggs
1 cup ranch sauce

Directions:
Preheat the Air fryer to 390 F. Spray the basket with cooking spray. In a bowl, combine the flour, garlic and onion powders, paprika, salt, and black pepper and mix well. In another bowl, whisk the eggs with a bit of salt. Dip the pork in the flour first, then in the eggs, and back again in the flour; coat well.
Spray with cooking spray and place in the frying basket. AirFry for 15 minutes, shaking once halfway through. Remove to a serving plate and serve with ranch sauce.

Nutrition Facts (per serving):
Calories: 430 | Carbohydrates: 17g | Protein: 30g | Fat: 27g | Fiber: 1g

---

Servings: 4 — 25 minutes

216 Juicy Double Cut Pork Chops

Ingredients:
4 pork chops
½ cup green mole sauce
2 tbsp tamarind paste
1 garlic clove, minced
2 tbsp corn syrup
1 tbsp olive oil
2 tbsp molasses
4 tbsp southwest seasoning
2 tbsp ketchup
2 tbsp water

Directions:
In a bowl, mix all ingredients, except for the pork chops and mole sauce. Add in the pork chops and toss to coat. Let them marinate for 30 minutes. Preheat the air fryer to 350 F. Place the chops in the greased frying basket. Bake for 16-18 minutes, turning once. Serve the chops drizzled with mole sauce.

Nutrition Facts (per serving):
Calories: 328 | Carbohydrates: 12g | Protein: 22g | Fat: 20g | Fiber: 0.2g

Servings: 3 | 8 Minutes

217 Lamb Koftas Meatballs

Ingredients:
1 pound ground lamb
1 teaspoon ground cumin
1 teaspoon ground coriander
2 tablespoons chopped fresh mint
1 egg, beaten
½ teaspoon salt
freshly ground black pepper

Directions:
Combine all ingredients in a bowl and mix together well. Divide the mixture into 10 portions. Roll each portion into a ball and then by cupping the meatball in your hand, shape it into an oval.
Preheat the air fryer to 400°F.
Air-fry the koftas for 8 minutes.
Serve warm with the cucumber-yogurt dip.

Nutrition Facts (per serving):
Calories: 218 | Carbohydrates: 1g | Protein: 9g | Fat: 19g | Fiber: 0g

---

Servings: 3 | 15 Minutes

218 Lemon And Thyme Sea Bass

Ingredients:
8 oz sea bass, trimmed, peeled
4 lemon slices
1 tablespoon thyme
2 teaspoons sesame oil
1 teaspoon salt

Directions:
Fill the sea bass with lemon slices and rub with thyme, salt, and sesame oil. Then preheat the air fryer to 385°F and put the fish in the air fryer basket. Cook it for 12 minutes. Then flip the fish on another side and cook it for 3 minutes more.

Nutrition Facts (per serving):
Calories: 144 | Carbohydrates: 0.8g | Protein: 18.9g | Fat: 7.1g | Fiber: 0.2g

---

 Servings: 4   20 minutes

219 Crispy Fish Finger Sticks

Ingredients:
2 fresh white fish fillets, cut into 4 fingers each
1 egg
½ cup buttermilk
1 cup panko breadcrumbs
Salt and black pepper to taste
1 cup aioli (or garlic mayo)

Directions:
Preheat the air fryer to 380 F. In a bowl, beat the egg and buttermilk. On a plate, combine breadcrumbs, salt, and pepper. Dip each finger into the egg mixture, roll it up in the crumbs, and spritz it with cooking spray. Arrange on the greased frying basket and AirFry for 10 minutes, turning once. Serve with aioli.

Nutrition Facts (per serving):
Calories: 390 | Carbohydrates: 16g | Protein: 21g | Fat: 27g | Fiber: 1g

---

 Servings: 4   25 minutes

220 Bavarian-Style Crispy Pork Schnitzel

Ingredients:
4 pork chops, center-cut
1 egg, beaten
1 tsp chili powder
2 tbsp flour
2 tbsp sour cream
Salt and black pepper to taste
½ cup breadcrumbs
2 tbsp olive oil

Directions:
Preheat the air fryer to 380 F. Using a meat tenderizer, pound the chops until ¼-inch thickness. Whisk the egg and sour cream in a bowl. Mix the breadcrumbs with chili powder, salt, and pepper in another bowl. Coat the chops with flour, then egg mixture, and finally in breadcrumbs. Brush with olive oil and arrange them on the frying basket. AirFry for 13-15 minutes, turning once until golden brown. Serve.

Nutrition Facts (per serving):
Calories: 291 | Carbohydrates: 5g | Protein: 22g | Fat: 20g | Fiber: 0.5g

221 Ground Beef

Servings: 4 | **Time:** 9 Minutes

Ingredients:
- 1 pound 70/30 ground beef
- ¼ cup water
- 1 teaspoon salt
- ½ teaspoon ground black pepper
- 1 teaspoon garlic powder

Directions:
Preheat the air fryer to 400°F. In a medium bowl, mix beef with remaining ingredients. Place beef in a 6" round cake pan and press into an even layer. Place in the air fryer basket and set the timer to 10 minutes. After 5 minutes, open the air fryer and stir ground beef with a spatula. Return to the air fryer. After 2 more minutes, open the air fryer, remove the pan and drain any excess fat from the ground beef. Return to the air fryer for and cook 2 more minutes until beef is brown and no pink remains.

Nutrition Facts (per serving):
Calories: 228 | Carbohydrates: 0.4g | Protein: 9g | Fat: 20g | Fiber: 0g

222 Maple Butter Salmon

Servings: 4 | **Time:** 12 Minutes

Ingredients:
- 2 tablespoons salted butter, melted
- 1 teaspoon low-carb maple syrup
- 1 teaspoon yellow mustard
- 4 boneless, skinless salmon fillets
- ½ teaspoon salt

Directions:
In a small bowl, whisk together butter, syrup, and mustard. Brush ½ mixture over each fillet on both sides. Sprinkle fillets with salt on both sides. Place salmon into ungreased air fryer basket. Adjust the temperature to 400°F and set the timer for 12 minutes. Halfway through cooking, brush fillets on both sides with remaining syrup mixture. Salmon will easily flake and have an internal temperature of at least 145°F when done. Serve warm.

Nutrition Facts (per serving):
Calories: 284 | Carbohydrates: 1.1g | Protein: 25.6g | Fat: 19.2g | Fiber: 0.0g

223 Three Meat Cheesy Omelet

Servings: 2 | **Time:** 20 minutes

Ingredients:
- 1 beef sausage, chopped
- 4 slices prosciutto, chopped
- 3 oz salami, chopped
- 1 cup mozzarella cheese, grated
- 4 eggs
- 1 green onion, chopped
- 1 tbsp ketchup
- 1 tsp fresh parsley, chopped

Directions:
Preheat the air fryer to 350 F. Whisk the eggs with ketchup in a bowl. Stir in the green onion, mozzarella, salami, and prosciutto. AirFry the sausage in a greased baking pan inside the fryer for 2 minutes. Slide out and pour the egg mixture over. Bake for 8-10 more minutes until golden. Serve topped with parsley.

Nutrition Facts (per serving):
Calories: 330 | Carbohydrates: 2g | Protein: 23g | Fat: 25g | Fiber: 0g

224 Beef Koftas in Tomato Sauce

Servings: 4 | **Time:** 25 minutes

Ingredients:
- 1 lb ground beef
- 1 medium onion, chopped
- 1 egg
- 4 tbsp breadcrumbs
- 1 tbsp fresh parsley, chopped
- ½ tbsp thyme leaves, chopped
- 10 oz tomato sauce
- Salt and black pepper to taste

Directions:
Preheat the air fryer to 380 F. Mix all the ingredients, except for the tomato sauce, into a bowl. Shape the mixture into palm sized balls. Place the meatballs in the greased frying basket and AirFry for 12-14 minutes, shaking once. Pour the tomato sauce in a deep saucepan over medium heat and simmer for 2 minutes or until heated through. Add in the meatballs and stir with a wooden spoon to coat. Serve.

Nutrition Facts (per serving):
Calories: 263 | Carbohydrates: 3.5g | Protein: 19.5g | Fat: 18g | Fiber: 0.8g

Servings: 4 — 7 Minutes

225 Baked Chicken Nachos

Ingredients:
50 tortilla chips
2 cups shredded cooked chicken breast, divided
2 cups shredded Mexican-blend cheese, divided
½ cup sliced pickled jalapeño peppers, divided
½ cup diced red onion, divided

Directions:
Preheat the air fryer to 300°F.
Use foil to make a bowl shape that fits the shape of the air fryer basket. Place half tortilla chips in the bottom of foil bowl, then top with 1 cup chicken, 1 cup cheese, ¼ cup jalapeños, and ¼ cup onion. Repeat with remaining chips and toppings.
Place foil bowl in the air fryer basket and cook 7 minutes until cheese is melted and toppings heated through. Serve warm.

Nutrition Facts (per serving):
Calories: 225 | Carbohydrates: 2.9g | Protein: 10g | Fat: 19g | Fiber: 0.5g

Servings: 1 — 12 Minutes

226 Thyme Scallops

Ingredients:
1 lb. scallops
Salt and pepper
½ tbsp. butter
½ cup thyme, chopped

Directions:
Wash the scallops and dry them completely. Season with pepper and salt, then set aside while you prepare the pan.
Grease a foil pan in several spots with the butter and cover the bottom with the thyme. Place the scallops on top.
Pre-heat the fryer at 400°F and set the rack inside. Place the foil pan on the rack and allow to cook for seven minutes.
Take care when removing the pan from the fryer and transfer the scallops to a serving dish. Spoon any remaining butter in the pan over the fish and enjoy.

Nutrition Facts (per serving):
Calories: 138 | Carbohydrates: 1.2g | Protein: 13.5g | Fat: 8.2g | Fiber: 0.2g

 Servings: 1 20 minutes

227 Japanese-Style Omelet

Ingredients:
½ cup cubed tofu
3 whole eggs
Salt and black pepper to taste
¼ tsp ground coriander
¼ tsp cumin
1 tsp soy sauce
1 tbsp green onions, chopped
¼ onion, chopped

Directions:
In a bowl, mix eggs, onion, soy sauce, ground coriander, cumin, black pepper, and salt. Add in the tofu and pour the mixture into a greased baking pan. Place in the preheated air fryer and Bake for 8 minutes at 360 F. Remove, and let cool for 2 minutes. Sprinkle with green onions and serve.

Nutrition Facts (per serving):
Calories: 280 | Carbohydrates: 4g | Protein: 20g | Fat: 20g | Fiber: 1g

 Servings: 4 25 minutes

228 Beef Meatballs with Cranberry Sauce

Ingredients:
1 small onion, chopped
1 lb grounded beef
1 tbsp fresh parsley, chopped
½ tbsp fresh thyme leaves, chopped
1 whole egg, beaten
3 tbsp breadcrumbs
Salt and black pepper to taste
1 cup cranberry sauce

Directions:
Preheat the air fryer to 390 F. In a bowl, mix all the ingredients, except for the cranberry sauce. Roll the mixture into 10-12 balls. Place the balls in the greased frying basket and Bake in the fryer for 8 minutes. Place the cranberry sauce in a saucepan over medium heat and stir for 2-3 minutes until heated through. Pour the sauce over the meatballs and serve.

Nutrition Facts (per serving):
Calories: 338 | Carbohydrates: 10g | Protein: 19g | Fat: 22g | Fiber: 0.5g

Servings: 2   8 Minutes

229 Quick Chicken For Filling

Ingredients:
1 pound chicken tenders, skinless and boneless
½ teaspoon ground cumin
½ teaspoon garlic powder
cooking spray

Directions:
Sprinkle raw chicken tenders with seasonings. Spray air fryer basket lightly with cooking spray to prevent sticking. Place chicken in air fryer basket in single layer. Cook at 390°F for 4 minutes, turn chicken strips over, and cook for an additional 4 minutes. Test for doneness. Thick tenders may require an additional minute or two.

Nutrition Facts (per serving):
Calories: 216 | Carbohydrates: 0.3g | Protein: 10g | Fat: 18.5g | Fiber: 0g

 Servings: 2   15 Minutes

230 Timeless Garlic-lemon Scallops

Ingredients:
2 tbsp butter, melted
1 garlic clove, minced
1 tbsp lemon juice
1 lb jumbo sea scallops

Directions:
Preheat air fryer to 400°F. Whisk butter, garlic, and lemon juice in a bowl. Roll scallops in the mixture to coat all sides. Place scallops in the frying basket and Air Fry for 4 minutes, flipping once. Brush the tops of each scallop with butter mixture and cook for 4 more minutes, flipping once. Serve and enjoy!

Nutrition Facts (per serving):
Calories: 147 | Carbohydrates: 1.1g | Protein: 12.8g | Fat: 9.6g | Fiber: 0g

 Servings: 2   20 minutes

231 Ham & Cheddar Omelet

Ingredients:
4 eggs
3 tbsp cheddar cheese, grated
1 tsp soy sauce
½ cup ham, chopped

Directions:
Preheat the air fryer to 350 F. In a bowl, whisk the eggs with soy sauce. Fold in the chopped ham and mix well to combine. Spoon the egg mixture into a greased baking pan and pour into the frying basket. Bake for 6-8 minutes until golden on top. Sprinkle with the cheddar cheese and serve warm.

Nutrition Facts (per serving):
Calories: 220 | Carbohydrates: 1g | Protein: 19g | Fat: 15g | Fiber: 0g

 Servings: 4   25 minutes

232 South American Arepas with Cilantro Sauce

Ingredients:
1 ½ lb ground beef
1 Fresno chili pepper, chopped
2 tbsp fresh cilantro, chopped
Salt and black pepper to taste
4 cheese arepas (buns), halved
½ red onion, sliced
1 cup mayonnaise
2 tbsp fresh lime juice

Directions:
In a small bowl, mix the mayonnaise with lime juice and cilantro. Season with salt and set aside. Preheat the air fryer to 350 F. In a bowl, combine the ground beef, Fresno chili, salt, and black pepper. Mold the mixture into 4 patties. Spray them lightly on both sides with cooking spray and place in the frying basket. AirFry for 8 minutes, flip them, and cook for another 4-6 minutes or until browned and cooked through. Serve on cheese arepas with red onion and cilantro lime mayo sauce.

Nutrition Facts (per serving):
Calories: 935 | Carbohydrates: 15g | Protein: 25g | Fat: 83g | Fiber: 1g

Servings: 4   🕐 10 Minutes

233 Chicken Chunks

Ingredients:
1 pound chicken tenders cut in large chunks, about 1½ inches
salt and pepper
½ cup cornstarch
2 eggs, beaten
1 cup panko breadcrumbs
oil for misting or cooking spray

Directions:
Season chicken chunks to your liking with salt and pepper.
Dip chicken chunks in cornstarch. Then dip in egg and shake off excess. Then roll in panko crumbs to coat well.
Spray all sides of chicken chunks with oil or cooking spray.
Place chicken in air fryer basket in single layer and cook at 390°F for 5 minutes. Spray with oil, turn chunks over, and spray other side.
Cook for an additional 5 minutes or until chicken juices run clear and outside is golden brown.
Repeat steps 4 and 5 to cook remaining chicken.

Nutrition Facts (per serving):
Calories: 218 | Carbohydrates: 2.4g | Protein: 9g | Fat: 18.2g | Fiber: 0.2g

---

 Servings: 2   🕐 15 Minutes

234 Restaurant-style Flounder Cutlets

Ingredients:
1 egg
1 cup Pecorino Romano cheese, grated
Sea salt and white pepper, to taste
1/2 teaspoon cayenne pepper
1 teaspoon dried parsley flakes
2 flounder fillets

Directions:
To make a breading station, whisk the egg until frothy. In another bowl, mix Pecorino Romano cheese, and spices.
Dip the fish in the egg mixture and turn to coat evenly; then, dredge in the cracker crumb mixture, turning a couple of times to coat evenly.
Cook in the preheated Air Fryer at 390°F for 5 minutes; turn them over and cook another 5 minutes. Enjoy!

Nutrition Facts (per serving):
Calories: 182 | Carbohydrates: 1.9g | Protein: 15.2g | Fat: 12.4g | Fiber: 0g

---

 Servings: 2   20 minutes

235 Spanish Chorizo Frittata

Ingredients:
4 eggs
1 large potato, boiled and cubed
¼ cup Manchego cheese, grated
1 tbsp parsley, chopped
1 Spanish chorizo, chopped
½ small red onion, chopped
¼ tsp paprika
Salt and black pepper to taste

Directions:
Preheat the air fryer to 330 F. In a bowl, beat the eggs with paprika, salt, and pepper. Stir in all of the remaining ingredients, except for the parsley. Spread the egg batter on the greased baking pan and insert it into the air fryer. Bake for 8-10 minutes until the top is golden. Garnish with parsley to serve.

Nutrition Facts (per serving):
Calories: 360 | Carbohydrates: 14g | Protein: 20g | Fat: 26g | Fiber: 2g

---

 Servings: 4   25 minutes

236 Healthy Burgers

Ingredients:
1 ½ lb ground beef
½ tsp onion powder
Salt and black pepper to taste
½ tsp dried oregano
1 tbsp Worcestershire sauce
½ tsp garlic powder
1 tsp Maggi seasoning sauce
1 tbsp olive oil

Directions:
Preheat the air fryer to 350 F. In a bowl, combine Worcestershire and Maggi sauces, onion and garlic powders, oregano, salt, and pepper. Add in the ground beef and mix until well combined. Divide the meat mixture into 4 equal pieces and flatten to form patties. Brush with olive oil and place the patties in the frying basket. AirFry for 14-16 minutes, turning once halfway through. Serve immediately.

Nutrition Facts (per serving):
Calories: 364 | Carbohydrates: 0.3g | Protein: 24g | Fat: 30g | Fiber: 0g

Servings: 4 | 10 Minutes

237 Chicken Nuggets

Ingredients:
1 pound ground chicken breast
1 ½ teaspoons salt, divided
¾ teaspoon ground black pepper, divided
1 ½ cups plain bread crumbs, divided
2 large eggs

Directions:
Preheat the air fryer to 400°F.
In a large bowl, mix chicken, 1 teaspoon salt, ½ teaspoon pepper, and ½ cup bread crumbs.
In a small bowl, whisk eggs. In a separate medium bowl, mix remaining 1 cup bread crumbs with remaining ½ teaspoon salt and ¼ teaspoon pepper. Scoop 1 tablespoon chicken mixture and flatten it into a nugget shape.
Dip into eggs, shaking off excess before rolling in bread crumb mixture. Repeat with remaining chicken mixture to make twenty nuggets.
Place nuggets in the air fryer basket and spritz with cooking spray. Cook 10 minutes, turning halfway through cooking time, until internal temperature reaches 165°F. Serve warm.

Nutrition Facts (per serving):
Calories: 220 | Carbohydrates: 2.5g | Protein: 9g | Fat: 18.5g | Fiber: 0.2g

---

Servings: 2 | 12 Minutes

238 Italian Baked Cod

Ingredients:
4 cod fillets
2 tablespoons salted butter, melted
1 teaspoon Italian seasoning
¼ teaspoon salt
½ cup low-carb marinara sauce

Directions:
Place cod into an ungreased 6" round nonstick baking dish. Pour butter over cod and sprinkle with Italian seasoning and salt. Top with marinara.
Place dish into air fryer basket. Adjust the temperature to 350°F and set the timer for 12 minutes. Fillets will be lightly browned, easily flake, and have an internal temperature of at least 145°F when done. Serve warm.

Nutrition Facts (per serving):
Calories: 182 | Carbohydrates: 2.4g | Protein: 15.2g | Fat: 11.8g | Fiber: 0.3g

---

 Servings: 2 20 minutes

239 Air Fried Shirred Eggs

Ingredients:
2 tsp butter, melted
4 eggs
2 tbsp heavy cream
4 smoked ham slices
3 tbsp Parmesan cheese, grated
¼ tsp paprika
Salt and black pepper to taste
2 tsp fresh chives, chopped

Directions:
Preheat the air fryer to 320 F. Lightly grease 4 ramekins with butter. Line the bottom of each ramekin with a piece of smoked ham. Crack the eggs on top of the ham and season with salt and pepper. Drizzle with heavy cream and sprinkle with Parmesan cheese. AirFry for 10-12 minutes until the eggs are completely set. Garnish with paprika and fresh chives to serve.

Nutrition Facts (per serving):
Calories: 290 | Carbohydrates: 2g | Protein: 20g | Fat: 22g | Fiber: 0g

---

 Servings: 4 25 minutes

240 Homemade Hot Beef Satay

Ingredients:
2 lb flank steaks, cut into long strips
2 tbsp fish sauce
2 tbsp soy sauce
2 tbsp sugar
1 ½ tsp garlic powder
1 ½ tsp ground ginger
2 tsp hot sauce
2 tbsp fresh cilantro, chopped
½ cup roasted peanuts, chopped

Directions:
Preheat the air fryer to 400 F. In a Ziploc bag, add the beef strips, fish sauce, sugar, garlic powder, soy sauce, ginger, and hot sauce. Seal the bag and shake thoroughly.
Open the bag, remove the beef strips, shake off the excess marinade, and place in the frying basket in a single layer. Avoid overlapping. AirFry for 6 minutes, turn the beef, and cook further for 6 minutes. Dish the meat and garnish with roasted peanuts and freshly chopped cilantro.

Nutrition Facts (per serving):
Calories: 523 | Carbohydrates: 3.8g | Protein: 40g | Fat: 35g | Fiber: 0.8g

Servings: 2 — 7 Minutes

241 Tilapia Fish Fillets

Ingredients:
- 2 tilapia fillets
- 1 tsp old bay seasoning
- 1/2 tsp butter
- 1/4 tsp lemon pepper
- Pepper
- Salt

Directions:
Spray air fryer basket with cooking spray.
Place fish fillets into the air fryer basket and season with lemon pepper, old bay seasoning, pepper, and salt.
Spray fish fillets with cooking spray and cook at 400°F for 7 minutes.
Serve and enjoy.

Nutrition Facts (per serving):
Calories: 190 | Carbohydrates: 1g | Protein: 22g | Fat: 10g | Fiber: 0g

---

Servings: 4 — 12 Minutes

242 Fish Taco Bowl

Ingredients:
- 2 cups finely shredded cabbage
- ½ cup mayonnaise
- Juice of 1 medium lime, divided
- 4 boneless, skinless tilapia fillets
- 2 teaspoons chili powder
- 1 teaspoon salt
- ½ teaspoon ground black pepper

Directions:
In a large bowl, mix cabbage, mayonnaise, and half of lime juice to make a slaw. Cover and refrigerate while the fish cooks.
Preheat the air fryer to 400°F.
Sprinkle tilapia with chili powder, salt, and pepper. Spritz each side with cooking spray.
Place fillets in the air fryer basket and cook 12 minutes, turning halfway through cooking time, until fish is opaque, flakes easily, and reaches an internal temperature of 145°F.
Allow fish to cool 5 minutes before chopping into bite-sized pieces. To serve, place ½ cup slaw into each bowl and top with one-fourth of fish. Squeeze remaining lime juice over fish. Serve warm.

Nutrition Facts (per serving):
Calories: 186 | Carbohydrates: 3.1g | Protein: 20g | Fat: 10g | Fiber: 1.2g

---

Servings: 2 — 20 minutes

243 Prosciutto, Mozzarella & Eggs in a Cup

Ingredients:
- 4 prosciutto slices
- 2 eggs
- 4 tomato slices
- ¼ tsp balsamic vinegar
- 2 tbsp mozzarella cheese, grated
- ¼ tsp maple syrup
- 2 tbsp mayonnaise
- Salt and black pepper to taste

Directions:
Preheat the air fryer to 350 F. Grease 2 cups with cooking spray. Line the bottom and sides of each cup with prosciutto, patching up any holes using little pieces if necessary. Place the tomato slices on top and divide the mozzarella cheese between the cups. Crack the eggs over the mozzarella cheese and drizzle with maple syrup and balsamic vinegar. Season with salt and pepper. Bake in the fryer until the egg whites are just set, about 10-12 minutes. Top with mayonnaise and serve.

Nutrition Facts (per serving):
Calories: 250 | Carbohydrates: 3g | Protein: 14g | Fat: 20g | Fiber: 0.5g

---

Servings: 4 — 25 minutes

244 Garlic Steak with Mexican Salsa

Ingredients:
- 2 rib-eye steaks
- 1 tbsp olive oil
- Garlic salt and black pepper to taste
- ½ cup heavy cream
- 1 avocado, roughly chopped
- 7 oz canned sweetcorn
- ½ red onion, sliced
- 10 cherry tomatoes, quartered
- 2 tbsp fresh cilantro, chopped
- 1 green chili, minced
- 1 lime, zested and juiced
- ½ cup heavy cream

Directions:
Preheat your air fryer to 390 F. In a bowl, whisk the olive oil, garlic salt, and black pepper. Massage the mixture onto the rib-eye steaks to coat on all sides. Lay the steaks in the greased frying basket and AirFry for 16-18 minutes, turning once halfway through. Remove to a plate.
In a bowl, mix the avocado, corn, cherry tomatoes, red onion, cilantro, chili, lime juice, and lime zest. Season to taste. Serve the steaks with the Mexican salsa and a dollop of heavy cream on the side.

Nutrition Facts (per serving):
Calories: 1245 | Carbohydrates: 11g | Protein: 37.5g | Fat: 112g | Fiber: 4g

Servings: 4   8 Minutes

245 Blackened Red Snapper

Ingredients:

1½ teaspoons black pepper
¼ teaspoon thyme
¼ teaspoon garlic powder
⅛ teaspoon cayenne pepper
1 teaspoon olive oil
4 4-ounce red snapper fillet portions, skin on
4 thin slices lemon
cooking spray

Directions:

Mix the spices and oil together to make a paste. Rub into both sides of the fish.
Spray air fryer basket with nonstick cooking spray and lay snapper steaks in basket, skin-side down.
Place a lemon slice on each piece of fish.
Cook at 390°F for 8 minutes. The fish will not flake when done, but it should be white through the center.

Nutrition Facts (per serving):
Calories: 174 | Carbohydrates: 0.9g | Protein: 23.8g | Fat: 7.7g | Fiber: 0.3g

 Servings: 4   12 Minutes

246 Cod Nuggets

Ingredients:

2 boneless, skinless cod fillets
1 ½ teaspoons salt, divided
¾ teaspoon ground black pepper, divided
2 large eggs
1 cup plain bread crumbs

Directions:

Preheat the air fryer to 350°F.
Cut cod fillets into sixteen even-sized pieces. In a large bowl, add cod nuggets and sprinkle with 1 teaspoon salt and ½ teaspoon pepper.
In a small bowl, whisk eggs. In another small bowl, mix bread crumbs with remaining ½ teaspoon salt and ¼ teaspoon pepper.
One by one, dip nuggets in the eggs, shaking off excess before rolling in the bread crumb mixture. Repeat to make sixteen nuggets.
Place nuggets in the air fryer basket and spritz with cooking spray. Cook 12 minutes, turning halfway through cooking time. Nuggets will be done when golden brown and have an internal temperature of at least 145°F. Serve warm.

Nutrition Facts (per serving):
Calories: 210 | Carbohydrates: 6g | Protein: 19g | Fat: 11g | Fiber: 0.5g

 Servings: 6   20 minutes

247 Cheese & Ham Breakfast Egg Cups

Ingredients:

4 eggs, beaten
1 tbsp olive oil
½ cup Colby cheese, shredded
2 ¼ cups frozen hash browns, thawed
1 cup smoked ham, chopped
½ tsp Cajun seasoning

Directions:

Preheat the air fryer to 360 F. Gather 12 silicone muffin cups and coat with olive oil. Whisk the eggs, hash browns, smoked ham, Colby cheese, and Cajun seasoning in a large bowl and add a heaping spoonful into each muffin cup. Put the muffin cups in the frying basket and AirFry 8-10 minutes until golden brown and the center is set. Transfer to a wire rack to cool completely. Serve.

Nutrition Facts (per serving):
Calories: 177 | Carbohydrates: 7g | Protein: 10.5g | Fat: 12.5g | Fiber: 0.5g

 Servings: 4   25 minutes

248 Gorgonzola Rib Eye Steak

Ingredients:

1 ½ lb rib-eye steak
1 tsp garlic powder
1 cup heavy cream
1 cup gorgonzola cheese, crumbled
2 tbsp fresh chives, chopped
2 tbsp olive oil
Salt and black pepper to taste

Directions:

Preheat the air fryer to 400 F. In a bowl, combine olive oil, garlic powder, salt, and pepper. Rub the steak with the seasoning and place it in the frying basket. Bake for 14-16 minutes, flipping once.
Warm the heavy cream in a skillet over medium heat. Add the gorgonzola cheese and chives; stir until you obtain a smooth sauce, and the cheese is melted, 3 minutes. Drizzle the sauce over the steaks.

Nutrition Facts (per serving):
Calories: 635 | Carbohydrates: 3g | Protein: 28g | Fat: 58g | Fiber: 0g

Servings: 2 — 10 Minutes

249 Swordfish With Capers And Tomatoes

Ingredients:
2 1-inch thick swordfish steaks
A pinch of salt and black pepper
30 ounces tomatoes, chopped
2 tablespoons capers, drained
1 tablespoon red vinegar
2 tablespoons oregano, chopped

Directions:
In a pan that fits the air fryer, combine all the ingredients, toss, put the pan in the fryer and cook at 390ºF for 10 minutes, flipping the fish halfway. Divide the mix between plates and serve.

Nutrition Facts (per serving):
Calories: 199 | Carbohydrates: 2.6g | Protein: 14.2g | Fat: 14.8g | Fiber: 0.8g

---

Servings: 4 — 13 Minutes

250 Bacon-wrapped Cajun Scallops

Ingredients:
8 slices bacon
8 sea scallops, rinsed and patted dry
1 teaspoon Cajun seasoning
4 tablespoons salted butter, melted

Directions:
Preheat the air fryer to 375ºF.
Place bacon in the air fryer basket and cook 3 minutes. Remove bacon and wrap each scallop in one slice bacon before securing with a toothpick.
Sprinkle Cajun seasoning evenly over scallops. Spritz scallops lightly with cooking spray and place in the air fryer basket in a single layer. Cook 10 minutes, turning halfway through cooking time, until scallops are opaque and firm and internal temperature reaches at least 130ºF. Drizzle with butter. Serve warm.

Nutrition Facts (per serving):
Calories: 185 | Carbohydrates: 1g | Protein: 14g | Fat: 13g | Fiber: 0g

---

Servings: 2 — 20 minutes

251 Air Fried Sourdough Sandwiches

Ingredients:
4 slices sourdough bread
2 tbsp mayonnaise
2 slices ham
2 lettuce leaves
1 tomato, sliced
2 slices mozzarella cheese

Directions:
Preheat the air fryer to 350 F. On a clean working board, lay the bread slices and spread them with mayonnaise. Top 2 of the slices with ham, lettuce leaves, tomato slices, and mozzarella. Cover with the remaining bread slices to form two sandwiches. AirFry for 12 minutes, flipping once. Serve hot.

Nutrition Facts (per serving):
Calories: 455 | Carbohydrates: 40g | Protein: 19g | Fat: 22.5g | Fiber: 2.8g

---

Servings: 4 — 25 minutes

252 Chimichurri New York Steak

Ingredients:
½ cup chimichurri salsa
1 tbsp olive oil
1 ½ lb New York strip steak
1 tbsp smoked paprika
Salt and black pepper to taste
1 jar (16-oz) roasted peppers, sliced

Directions:
Preheat the air fryer to 380 F. Rub the steak with smoked paprika, salt, and black pepper. Drizzle with olive oil and Bake in the air fryer for 12-14 minutes, turning once halfway through. Transfer to a cutting board and let it sit for 5 minutes. Slice, drizzle with chimichurri salsa, and serve with roasted peppers.

Nutrition Facts (per serving):
Calories: 460 | Carbohydrates: 5g | Protein: 28g | Fat: 36g | Fiber: 1.5g

Servings: 4 | 7 Minutes

253 Crispy Parmesan Lobster Tails

Ingredients:
- 4 lobster tails
- 2 tablespoons salted butter, melted
- 1½ teaspoons Cajun seasoning, divided
- ¼ teaspoon salt
- ¼ teaspoon ground black pepper
- ¼ cup grated Parmesan cheese
- ½ ounce plain pork rinds, finely crushed

Directions:
Cut lobster tails open carefully with a pair of scissors and gently pull meat away from shells, resting meat on top of shells.
Brush lobster meat with butter and sprinkle with 1 teaspoon Cajun seasoning, ¼ teaspoon per tail.
In a small bowl, mix remaining Cajun seasoning, salt, pepper, Parmesan, and pork rinds. Gently press ¼ mixture onto meat on each lobster tail.
Carefully place tails into ungreased air fryer basket. Adjust the temperature to 400°F and set the timer for 7 minutes. Lobster tails will be crispy and golden on top and have an internal temperature of at least 145°F when done. Serve warm.

Nutrition Facts (per serving):
Calories: 176 | Carbohydrates: 1.3g | Protein: 15.6g | Fat: 11.6g | Fiber: 0.2g

---

Servings: 4 | 12 Minutes

254 Mediterranean-style Cod

Ingredients:
- 4 cod fillets
- 3 tablespoons fresh lemon juice
- 1 tablespoon olive oil
- ¼ teaspoon salt
- 6 cherry tomatoes, halved
- ¼ cup pitted and sliced kalamata olives

Directions:
Place cod into an ungreased 6" round nonstick baking dish. Pour lemon juice into dish and drizzle cod with olive oil. Sprinkle with salt. Place tomatoes and olives around baking dish in between fillets.
Place dish into air fryer basket. Adjust the temperature to 350°F and set the timer for 12 minutes, carefully turning cod halfway through cooking. Fillets will be lightly browned, easily flake, and have an internal temperature of at least 145°F when done. Serve warm.

Nutrition Facts (per serving):
Calories: 210 | Carbohydrates: 2g | Protein: 24g | Fat: 11g | Fiber: 0.5g

---

Servings: 6 | 20 minutes

255 Sausage & Egg Casserole

Ingredients:
- 2 tbsp olive oil
- 1 lb Italian sausages
- 6 eggs
- 1 red pepper, diced
- 1 green pepper, diced
- 1 yellow pepper, diced
- 1 sweet onion, diced
- 1 cup cheddar cheese, shredded
- Salt and black pepper to taste
- 2 tbsp fresh parsley, chopped

Directions:
Warm the olive oil in a skillet over medium heat. Add the sausages and brown them slightly, turning occasionally, about 5 minutes. Once done, drain any excess fat derived from cooking and set aside. Arrange the sausages on the bottom of a greased casserole dish that fits in your air fryer. Top with onion, red pepper, green pepper, and yellow pepper. Sprinkle with cheddar cheese on top.
In a bowl, beat the eggs with salt and pepper. Pour the mixture over the cheese. Place the casserole dish in the frying basket and Bake at 360 F for 15 minutes. Serve warm garnished with fresh parsley.

Nutrition Facts (per serving):
Calories: 413 | Carbohydrates: 7.8g | Protein: 19.7g | Fat: 32.7g | Fiber: 1.3g

---

Servings: 2 | 25 minutes

256 Parsley Crumbed Beef Strips

Ingredients:
- 2 tbsp vegetable oil
- ½ tsp fresh parsley, chopped
- 1 cup breadcrumbs
- 1 whole egg, whisked
- 1 thin beef sirloin steak, cut into strips
- 1 lemon, juiced

Directions:
Preheat the air fryer to 370 F. In a bowl, add breadcrumbs, parsley, and vegetable oil and stir well to get a loose mixture. Dip the beef in the egg, then coat in the crumbs mixture. Place the strips in the greased frying basket and AirFry for 14-16 minutes, flipping once. Serve with a drizzle of lemon juice.

Nutrition Facts (per serving):
Calories: 435 | Carbohydrates: 15g | Protein: 25g | Fat: 30g | Fiber: 1g

Servings: 3 — 10 Minutes

257 Simple Sesame Squid On The Grill

Ingredients:
1 ½ pounds squid, cleaned
2 tablespoon toasted sesame oil
Salt and pepper to taste

Directions:
Preheat the air fryer at 390ºF. Place the grill pan accessory in the air fryer. Season the squid with sesame oil, salt and pepper. Grill the squid for 10 minutes.

Nutrition Facts (per serving):
Calories: 142 | Carbohydrates: 1.2g | Protein: 17.8g | Fat: 7.4g | Fiber: 0g

---

Servings: 2 — 15 Minutes

258 Catalan Sardines With Romesco Sauce

Ingredients:
2 cans skinless, boneless sardines in oil, drained
½ cup warmed romesco sauce
½ cup bread crumbs

Directions:
Preheat air fryer to 350ºF. In a shallow dish, add bread crumbs. Roll in sardines to coat. Place sardines in the greased frying basket and Air Fry for 6 minutes, turning once. Serve with romesco sauce.

Nutrition Facts (per serving):
Calories: 280 | Carbohydrates: 9g | Protein: 19g | Fat: 18g | Fiber: 1g

---

Servings: 1 — 20 minutes

259 Grilled Tofu Sandwich with Cabbage

Ingredients:
2 slices of bread
1 tofu slice, 1-inch thick
¼ cup red cabbage, shredded
2 tsp olive oil
¼ tsp vinegar
Salt to taste

Directions:
Preheat the air fryer to 350 F. Add the bread slices to the frying basket and AirFry for 3 minutes; set aside. Brush the tofu with some olive oil and place in the air fryer. AirFry for 5 minutes on each side.
Mix the cabbage, remaining olive oil, and vinegar. Season with salt. Place the tofu on top of one bread slice, place the cabbage over, and top with the other bread slice. Serve with cream cheese-mustard dip.

Nutrition Facts (per serving):
Calories: 386 | Carbohydrates: 35.5g | Protein: 16.5g | Fat: 17g | Fiber: 3.5g

---

Servings: 4 — 25 minutes

260 Air Fried Beef with Veggies & Oyster Sauce

Ingredients:
1 lb circular beef steak, cut into strips
½ cauliflower head, cut into florets
2 carrots, sliced into rings
⅓ cup oyster sauce
2 tbsp sesame oil
⅓ cup sherry
1 tsp soy sauce
1 tsp white sugar
1 tsp cornstarch
1 tbsp olive oil
1 garlic clove, minced
2 tbsp pine nuts, toasted

Directions:
Preheat the air fryer to 390 F. In a bowl, mix all ingredients, except for the beef, cauliflower, and carrots. Add in the beef and stir to coat. Bake in the fryer for 14-16 minutes, shaking once or twice. Blanch the cauliflower and carrots in salted water in a pot over medium heat for 3-4 minutes. Drain and place on a serving plate. Top with pine nuts. When the beef is ready, place it on the side of the veggies and serve.

Nutrition Facts (per serving):
Calories: 410 | Carbohydrates: 17g | Protein: 30g | Fat: 25g | Fiber: 3g

Servings: 4 — 7 Minutes

261 Crab-stuffed Avocado Boats

Ingredients:
2 medium avocados, halved and pitted
8 ounces cooked crabmeat
¼ teaspoon Old Bay Seasoning
2 tablespoons peeled and diced yellow onion
2 tablespoons mayonnaise

Directions:
Scoop out avocado flesh in each avocado half, leaving ½" around edges to form a shell. Chop scooped-out avocado.
In a medium bowl, combine crabmeat, Old Bay Seasoning, onion, mayonnaise, and chopped avocado. Place ¼ mixture into each avocado shell. Place avocado boats into ungreased air fryer basket. Adjust the temperature to 350°F and set the timer for 7 minutes. Avocado will be browned on the top and mixture will be bubbling when done. Serve warm.

Nutrition Facts (per serving):
Calories: 179 | Carbohydrates: 2.4g | Protein: 10.6g | Fat: 14.2g | Fiber: 1.9g

---

Servings: 4 — 15 Minutes

262 Potato-crusted Cod

Ingredients:
4 boneless, skinless cod fillets
2 tablespoons olive oil
½ teaspoon salt, divided
1 teaspoon dried dill
2 cups mashed potato flakes

Directions:
Preheat the air fryer to 350°F.
Place cod fillets on a work surface and brush with oil. Sprinkle with ¼ teaspoon salt and dill.
In a large bowl, combine mashed potato flakes with remaining salt.
Roll each fillet in the potato mixture and spritz with cooking spray.
Place in the air fryer basket and cook 15 minutes, turning halfway through cooking time. Cod will be golden brown and have an internal temperature of at least 145°F when done. Serve warm.

Nutrition Facts (per serving):
Calories: 265 | Carbohydrates: 19g | Protein: 26g | Fat: 10g | Fiber: 1g

---

 Servings: 4 20 minutes

263 Air Fried Italian Calzone

Ingredients:
1 pizza dough
4 oz cheddar cheese, grated
1 oz mozzarella cheese, grated
1 oz bacon, diced
2 cups cooked turkey, shredded
1 egg, beaten
4 tbsp tomato paste
½ tsp dried basil
½ tsp dried oregano
Salt and black pepper to taste

Directions:
Preheat the air fryer to 350 F. Divide the pizza dough into 4 equal pieces, so you have the dough for 4 pizza crusts. Combine the tomato paste, basil, and oregano in a small bowl. Brush the mixture onto the crusts; make sure not to go all the way to avoid brushing near the edges of each crust.
Scatter half of the turkey on top and season with salt and black pepper. Top with bacon, mozzarella and cheddar cheeses. Brush the edges with the beaten egg. Fold the crusts and seal with a fork. Bake for 10-12 minutes until puffed and golden, turning it over halfway through cooking. Serve warm.

Nutrition Facts (per serving):
Calories: 442 | Carbohydrates: 26g | Protein: 30.8g | Fat: 21.3g | Fiber: 1.6g

---

 Servings: 2 25 minutes

264 Lamb Meatballs with Roasted Veggie Bake

Ingredients:
½ lb ground lamb
1 shallot, chopped
½ tsp garlic powder
1 egg, beaten
1 potato, chopped
¼ red onion, sliced
1 carrot, sliced diagonally
½ small beetroot, sliced
1 cup cherry tomatoes, halved
2 tbsp olive oil
Salt and black pepper to taste
Parmesan shavings

Directions:
Preheat the air fryer to 370 F. In a bowl, mix red onion, potato, cherry tomatoes, carrot, beetroot, salt, and olive oil. Transfer to the frying basket and Bake for 10 minutes, shaking once. In another bowl, mix the ground lamb, egg, shallot, garlic powder, salt, and black pepper. Shape the mixture into balls. Place them over the vegetables in the air fryer, and AirFry for 12-14 minutes, flipping once. Remove the dish and top with Parmesan shavings to serve.

Nutrition Facts (per serving):
Calories: 510 | Carbohydrates: 22g | Protein: 28g | Fat: 34g | Fiber: 4g

Servings: 4 | 10 Minutes

265 Cajun Lobster Tails

Ingredients:
4 lobster tails
2 tablespoons salted butter, melted
2 teaspoons lemon juice
1 tablespoon Cajun seasoning

Directions:
Preheat the air fryer to 400°F.
Carefully cut open lobster tails with kitchen scissors and pull back the shell a little to expose the meat. Drizzle butter and lemon juice over each tail, then sprinkle with Cajun seasoning.
Place tails in the air fryer basket and cook 10 minutes until lobster shells are bright red and internal temperature reaches at least 145°F. Serve warm.

Nutrition Facts (per serving):
Calories: 168 | Carbohydrates: 0.9g | Protein: 15.6g | Fat: 11.2g | Fiber: 0g

---

Servings: 4 | 12 Minutes

266 Salmon Patties

Ingredients:
1 pouch cooked salmon
6 tablespoons panko bread crumbs
½ cup mayonnaise
2 teaspoons Old Bay Seasoning

Directions:
Preheat the air fryer to 350°F.
In a large bowl, combine all ingredients. Divide mixture into four equal portions. Using your hands, form into patties and spritz with cooking spray. Place in the air fryer basket and cook 12 minutes, turning halfway through cooking time, until brown and firm. Serve warm.

Nutrition Facts (per serving):
Calories: 211 | Carbohydrates: 4.6g | Protein: 14.3g | Fat: 15.8g | Fiber: 0.3g

---

 Servings: 4 20 minutes

267 Italian Sausage Patties

Ingredients:
1 lb ground Italian sausage
¼ cup breadcrumbs
1 tsp red pepper flakes
Salt and black pepper to taste
¼ tsp garlic powder
1 egg, beaten

Directions:
Preheat the air fryer to 350 F. Thoroughly mix all the ingredients in a large bowl. Make balls out of the mixture using your hands. Flatten the balls to make the patties. Arrange them on the greased frying basket. Place them in the fryer and AirFry for 15 minutes, flipping once halfway through. Serve.

Nutrition Facts (per serving):
Calories: 347 | Carbohydrates: 6.5g | Protein: 16.4g | Fat: 26.8g | Fiber: 0.4g

---

 Servings: 4 25 minutes

268 Herby Roast Beef

Ingredients:
2 lb beef loin
Salt and black pepper to taste
½ tsp dried thyme
½ tsp dried rosemary
½ tsp dried oregano
½ tsp garlic powder
1 tsp onion powder
2 tbsp olive oil

Directions:
Preheat the air fryer to 380 F. In a bowl, combine all the ingredients, except for the beef. Rub the mixture onto the meat. Place it in the air fryer and Bake for 8-10 minutes. Turn the meat over and cook for 7-8 more minutes until well roasted. Let cool before slicing. Serve with steamed veggies if desired.

Nutrition Facts (per serving):
Calories: 525 | Carbohydrates: 1g | Protein: 44g | Fat: 38g | Fiber: 0g

Servings: 2 — 8 Minutes

269 Herbed Haddock

Ingredients:
- 2 haddock fillets
- 2 tablespoons pine nuts
- 3 tablespoons fresh basil, chopped
- 1 tablespoon Parmesan cheese, grated
- ½ cup extra-virgin olive oil
- Salt and black pepper, to taste

Directions:
Preheat the Air fryer to 355ºF and grease an Air fryer basket.
Coat the haddock fillets evenly with olive oil and season with salt and black pepper.
Place the haddock fillets in the Air fryer basket and cook for about 8 minutes.
Dish out the haddock fillets in serving plates. Meanwhile, put remaining ingredients in a food processor and pulse until smooth.
Top this cheese sauce over the haddock fillets and serve hot.

Nutrition Facts (per serving):
Calories: 195 | Carbohydrates: 1.1g | Protein: 13.2g | Fat: 15.4g | Fiber: 0.4g

---

Servings: 4 — 12 Minutes

270 Italian Shrimp

Ingredients:
- 1 pound shrimp, peeled and deveined
- A pinch of salt and black pepper
- 1 tablespoon sesame seeds, toasted
- ½ teaspoon Italian seasoning
- 1 tablespoon olive oil

Directions:
In a bowl, mix the shrimp with the rest of the ingredients and toss well. Put the shrimp in the air fryer's basket, cook at 370ºF for 12 minutes, divide into bowls and serve,

Nutrition Facts (per serving):
Calories: 178 | Carbohydrates: 1.2g | Protein: 22.6g | Fat: 9.1g | Fiber: 0.3g

---

 Servings: 12 20 minutes

271 Blueberry Oat Bars

Ingredients:
- 2 cups rolled oats
- ¼ cup ground almonds
- ¼ cup sugar
- 1 tsp baking powder
- ½ tsp ground cinnamon
- 2 eggs, lightly beaten
- ½ cup canola oil
- ½ cup milk
- 1 tsp vanilla extract
- 2 cups blueberries

Directions:
Spray a baking pan that fits in your air fryer with oil. In a bowl, add oats, almonds, sugar, baking powder, and cinnamon; stir well. In another bowl, whisk eggs, canola oil, milk, and vanilla. Stir the wet ingredients into the oat mixture. Fold in the blueberries. Pour the mixture into the pan and place it inside the fryer. Bake for 10 minutes. Remove to a wire rack to cool and then cut into 12 bars.

Nutrition Facts (per serving):
Calories: 194 | Carbohydrates: 18.1g | Protein: 3.4g | Fat: 12.3g | Fiber: 0.9g

---

Servings: 2 25 minutes

272 Beef Liver with Onions

Ingredients:
- 1 lb beef liver, sliced
- 2 onions, sliced
- 1 tbsp black truffle oil
- Salt and black pepper to taste
- 1 garlic clove, minced
- 1 tbsp fresh parsley, chopped

Directions:
Preheat the air fryer to 360 F. Season the liver with salt and pepper; brush with the oil. Spread the onion slices on a greased frying basket. Bake in the fryer for 5 minutes. Arrange the liver on top of the onions and Bake further for 12-14 minutes, turning once halfway through cooking. Serve with garlic and parsley.

Nutrition Facts (per serving):
Calories: 365 | Carbohydrates: 9g | Protein: 34g | Fat: 22g | Fiber: 1g

Servings: 2 | 8 Minutes

273 Spicy Prawns

Ingredients:
6 prawns
1/4 tsp pepper
1/2 tsp chili powder
1 tsp chili flakes
1/4 tsp salt

Directions:
Preheat the air fryer to 350ºF.
In a bowl, mix together spices add prawns.
Spray air fryer basket with cooking spray.
Transfer prawns into the air fryer basket and cook for 8 minutes.
Serve and enjoy.

Nutrition Facts (per serving):
Calories: 86 | Carbohydrates: 0.6g | Protein: 11.2g | Fat: 3.8g | Fiber: 0g

---

Servings: 4 | 15 Minutes

274 Air Fried Cod With Basil Vinaigrette

Ingredients:
¼ cup olive oil
4 cod fillets
A bunch of basil, torn
Juice from 1 lemon, freshly squeezed
Salt and pepper to taste

Directions:
Preheat the air fryer for 5 minutes.
Season the cod fillets with salt and pepper to taste.
Place in the air fryer and cook for 15 minutes at 350ºF.
Meanwhile, mix the rest of the ingredients in a bowl and toss to combine.
Serve the air fried cod with the basil vinaigrette.

Nutrition Facts (per serving):
Calories: 258 | Carbohydrates: 1.3g | Protein: 25.4g | Fat: 16.8g | Fiber: 0.3g

---

Servings: 4 | 20 minutes

275 Roasted Asparagus with Serrano Ham

Ingredients:
12 spears asparagus, trimmed
12 Serrano ham slices
¼ cup Parmesan cheese, grated
Salt and black pepper to taste

Directions:
Preheat the air fryer to 350 F. Season asparagus with salt and black pepper. Wrap each ham slice around each asparagus spear from one end to the other end to cover completely. Arrange them on the greased frying basket and AirFry for 10 minutes, shaking once or twice throughout cooking. When ready, scatter with Parmesan cheese and serve immediately.

Nutrition Facts (per serving):
Calories: 175 | Carbohydrates: 3.3g | Protein: 18.8g | Fat: 10.8g | Fiber: 1g

---

Servings: 4 | 25 minutes

276 African Minty Lamb Kofta

Ingredients:
1 lb ground lamb
1 tsp cumin
2 tbsp mint, chopped
1 tsp garlic powder
1 tsp onion powder
1 tbsp ras el hanout
½ tsp dried coriander
4 bamboo skewers
Salt and black pepper to taste

Directions:
In a bowl, mix ground lamb, cumin, garlic and onion powders, mint, ras el hanout, coriander, salt, and black pepper. Mold into sausage shapes and place onto skewers. Let sit for 15 minutes in the fridge.
Preheat the air fryer to 380 F. Grease the frying basket with cooking spray. Arrange the skewers in the basket and AirFry for 10-12 minutes, turning once halfway through. Serve with yogurt dip if desired.

Nutrition Facts (per serving):
Calories: 380 | Carbohydrates: 1g | Protein: 27g | Fat: 29g | Fiber: 0g

Servings: 2 | 10 Minutes

277 Crunchy And Buttery Cod With Ritz Cracker Crust

Ingredients:
- 4 tablespoons butter, melted
- 8 to 10 RITZ crackers, crushed into crumbs
- 2 cod fillets
- salt and freshly ground black pepper
- 1 lemon

Directions:
Preheat the air fryer to 380ºF.
Melt the butter in a small saucepan on the stovetop or in a microwavable dish in the microwave, and then transfer the butter to a shallow dish. Place the crushed RITZ crackers into a second shallow dish.
Season the fish fillets with salt and freshly ground black pepper. Dip them into the butter and then coat both sides with the RITZ crackers.
Place the fish into the air fryer basket and air-fry at 380ºF for 10 minutes, flipping the fish over halfway through the cooking time.
Serve with a wedge of lemon to squeeze over the top.

Nutrition Facts (per serving):
Calories: 192 | Carbohydrates: 3.2g | Protein: 13.5g | Fat: 13.8g | Fiber: 0.2g

---

Servings: 4 | 12 Minutes

278 Crab Cakes

Ingredients:
- 2 cans lump crabmeat, drained
- ½ cup plain bread crumbs
- ½ cup mayonnaise
- 1 ½ teaspoons Old Bay Seasoning
- Zest and juice of ½ medium lemon
- ½ teaspoon salt
- ½ teaspoon ground black pepper
- Cooking spray

Directions:
Preheat the air fryer to 375ºF.
In a large bowl, mix all ingredients.
Scoop ¼ cup mixture and form into a 4" patty. Repeat to make eight crab cakes. Spritz cakes with cooking spray.
Place in the air fryer basket and cook 12 minutes, turning halfway through cooking time, until edges are brown and center is firm. Serve warm.

Nutrition Facts (per serving):
Calories: 238 | Carbohydrates: 6.4g | Protein: 18.2g | Fat: 15.2g | Fiber: 0.5g

---

 Servings: 4 20 minutes

279 Korean Chili Chicken Wings

Ingredients:
- 8 chicken wings
- Salt to taste
- 1 tsp sesame oil
- Juice from half lemon
- ¼ cup sriracha chili sauce
- 1-inch piece ginger, grated
- 1 tsp garlic powder
- 1 tsp sesame seeds

Directions:
Preheat the air fryer to 370 F. Grease the air frying basket with cooking spray. In a bowl, mix salt, ginger, garlic, lemon juice, sesame oil, and chili sauce. Coat the wings in the mixture. Transfer the wings to the basket and AirFry for 15 minutes, flipping once. Sprinkle with sesame seeds and serve.

Nutrition Facts (per serving):
Calories: 343 | Carbohydrates: 5g | Protein: 32.5g | Fat: 22g | Fiber: 0.4g

---

 Servings: 4 25 minutes

280 Lamb Chops with Lemony Couscous

Ingredients:
- 4 lamb chops
- 2 tbsp olive oil
- 2 garlic cloves, minced
- Salt and black pepper to taste
- 2 tbsp fresh thyme, chopped
- 1 cup couscous
- 1 lemon, zested and juiced

Directions:
Preheat the air fryer to 400 F. Rub the lamb chops with olive oil, garlic, salt, and black pepper. Place them in the greased frying basket. AirFry for 14-16 minutes, turning once halfway through cooking.
Meanwhile, place the couscous in a heatproof bowl and pour over 1½ cups of salted boiling water. Cover and let it sit for 8-12 minutes until all the water is absorbed. Gently stir in the lemon juice and lemon zest and fresh thyme with a fork. Serve the lamb on a bed of couscous and enjoy!

Nutrition Facts (per serving):
Calories: 470 | Carbohydrates: 22g | Protein: 28g | Fat: 30g | Fiber: 2g

Servings: 4 | 10 Minutes

281 Lobster Tails

Ingredients:
- 4 lobster tails
- 2 tablespoons salted butter, melted
- 1 tablespoon finely minced garlic
- ¼ teaspoon salt
- ¼ teaspoon ground black pepper
- 2 tablespoons lemon juice

Directions:
Preheat the air fryer to 400°F.
Carefully cut open lobster tails with kitchen scissors and pull back the shell a little to expose the meat. Drizzle butter over each tail, then sprinkle with garlic, salt, and pepper.
Place tails in the air fryer basket and cook 10 minutes until lobster is firm and opaque and internal temperature reaches at least 145°F.
Drizzle lemon juice over lobster meat. Serve warm.

Nutrition Facts (per serving):
Calories: 154 | Carbohydrates: 1g | Protein: 14g | Fat: 10.5g | Fiber: 0g

---

Servings: 6 | 15 Minutes Per Batch

282 Snow Crab Legs

Ingredients:
- 8 pounds fresh shell-on snow crab legs
- 2 tablespoons olive oil
- 2 teaspoons Old Bay Seasoning
- 4 tablespoons salted butter, melted
- 2 teaspoons lemon juice

Directions:
Preheat the air fryer to 400°F.
Drizzle crab legs with oil and sprinkle with Old Bay. Place in the air fryer basket, working in batches as necessary. Cook 15 minutes, turning halfway through cooking time, until crab turns a bright red-orange.
In a small bowl, whisk together butter and lemon juice. Serve as a dipping sauce with warm crab legs.

Nutrition Facts (per serving):
Calories: 296 | Carbohydrates: 1.2g | Protein: 31.6g | Fat: 17.8g | Fiber: 0.1g

---

 Servings: 4 20 minutes

283 Air-Fried Chicken Thighs

Ingredients:
- 1 ½ lb chicken thighs
- 2 eggs, lightly beaten
- 1 cup seasoned breadcrumbs
- ½ tsp oregano
- Salt and black pepper to taste

Directions:
Preheat the air fryer to 390 F. Season the thighs with oregano, salt, and black pepper. In a bowl, add the beaten eggs. In a separate bowl, add the breadcrumbs. Dip the thighs in the egg wash. Then roll them in the breadcrumbs and press firmly, so the breadcrumbs stick well. Spray the thighs with cooking spray and arrange them in the frying basket in a single layer, skin-side up. AirFry for 12 minutes, turn the thighs over, and cook for 6-8 more minutes until crispy. Serve and enjoy!

Nutrition Facts (per serving):
Calories: 466 | Carbohydrates: 18.8g | Protein: 41.5g | Fat: 23.5g | Fiber: 1g

---

 Servings: 4 25 minutes

284 Easy Lamb Chop Bites

Ingredients:
- 1 lb lamb loin chops
- 1 egg
- ¼ cup buttermilk
- 1 cup corn flakes, crushed
- Salt and black pepper to taste

Directions:
In a bowl, whisk the egg with buttermilk. Add in the lamb and stir to coat. On a plate, spread the corn flakes and mix them with salt and pepper. Coat the lamb chops in the cornflakes and arrange them on the greased frying basket. AirFry for 12-16 minutes at 360 F, turning once halfway through. Serve.

Nutrition Facts (per serving):
Calories: 430 | Carbohydrates: 10g | Protein: 30g | Fat: 30g | Fiber: 1g

Servings: 4 | 10 Minutes

285 Outrageous Crispy Fried Salmon Skin

Ingredients:
- ½ pound salmon skin, patted dry
- 4 tablespoons coconut oil
- Salt and pepper to taste

Directions:
Preheat the air fryer for 5 minutes.
In a large bowl, combine everything and mix well.
Place in the fryer basket and close.
Cook for 10 minutes at 400°F.
Halfway through the cooking time, give a good shake to evenly cook the skin.

Nutrition Facts (per serving):
Calories: 202 | Carbohydrates: 0.5g | Protein: 8g | Fat: 19g | Fiber: 0g

---

Servings: 4 | 15 Minutes

286 Spinach And Artichoke-stuffed Peppers

Ingredients:
- 2 ounces cream cheese, softened
- ½ cup shredded mozzarella cheese
- ½ cup chopped fresh spinach leaves
- ¼ cup chopped canned artichoke hearts
- 2 medium green bell peppers, halved and seeded

Directions:
In a medium bowl, mix cream cheese, mozzarella, spinach, and artichokes. Spoon ¼ cheese mixture into each pepper half.
Place peppers into ungreased air fryer basket. Adjust the temperature to 320°F and set the timer for 15 minutes. Peppers will be tender and cheese will be bubbling and brown when done. Serve warm.

Nutrition Facts (per serving):
Calories: 139 | Carbohydrates: 5.1g | Protein: 5.8g | Fat: 10.3g | Fiber: 1.6g

---

Servings: 4 | 20 minutes

287 Chicken & Oat Croquettes

Ingredients:
- 1 lb ground chicken
- 2 eggs
- Salt and black pepper to taste
- 1 cup oats, crumbled
- ½ tsp garlic powder
- 1 tsp dried parsley

Directions:
Preheat the air fryer to 360 F. Mix the chicken with garlic, parsley, salt, and pepper. In a bowl, beat the eggs with a pinch of salt. In a third bowl, add the oats. Form croquettes out of the chicken mixture. Dip in the eggs and coat in the oats. AirFry them in the greased frying basket for 10 minutes, shaking once.

Nutrition Facts (per serving):
Calories: 290 | Carbohydrates: 9.5g | Protein: 27g | Fat: 16g | Fiber: 1.3g

---

Servings: 4 | 25 minutes

288 Lamb Taquitos

Ingredients:
- 1 lb lamb meat, sliced into strips
- 2 tbsp olive oil
- 2 tsp fresh cilantro, chopped
- 2 tsp fire-roasted green chilies
- 2 tbsp queso fresco, crumbled
- 4 corn tortillas

Directions:
Warm olive oil in a skillet over medium heat and stir-fry the lamb for 5-6 minutes. Remove and stir in green chilies. Preheat the air fryer to 400 F. Divide the mixture between tortillas and roll up them. Spritz with cooking spray and AirFry for 8 minutes, turning once. Top with queso fresco and cilantro to serve.

Nutrition Facts (per serving):
Calories: 430 | Carbohydrates: 18g | Protein: 28g | Fat: 28g | Fiber: 2g

Servings: 4 — 6 Minutes

289 Easy Lobster Tail With Salted Butetr

Ingredients:
- 2 tablespoons melted butter
- 4 lobster tails
- Salt and pepper to taste

Directions:
Preheat the air fryer to 390°F.
Place the grill pan accessory.
Cut the lobster through the tail section using a pair of kitchen scissors.
Brush the lobster tails with melted butter and season with salt and pepper to taste.
Place on the grill pan and cook for 6 minutes.

Nutrition Facts (per serving):
Calories: 198 | Carbohydrates: 0g | Protein: 17g | Fat: 14g | Fiber: 0g

---

Servings: 4 — 15 Minutes

290 Crispy Apple Fries With Caramel Sauce

Ingredients:
- 4 medium apples, cored
- ¼ tsp cinnamon
- ¼ tsp nutmeg
- 1 cup caramel sauce

Directions:
Preheat air fryer to 350°F. Slice the apples to a 1/3-inch thickness for a crunchy chip. Place in a large bowl and sprinkle with cinnamon and nutmeg. Place the slices in the air fryer basket. Bake for 6 minutes. Shake the basket, then cook for another 4 minutes or until crunchy. Serve drizzled with caramel sauce and enjoy!

Nutrition Facts (per serving):
Calories: 226 | Carbohydrates: 45.2g | Protein: 0.5g | Fat: 4.2g | Fiber: 3.6g

---

 Servings: 4 20 minutes

291 Mexican-Style Air Fryer Nachos

Ingredients:
- 8 corn tortillas, cut into wedges
- 1 tbsp olive oil
- ½ tsp ground cumin
- ½ tsp chili powder
- ½ tsp paprika
- ½ tsp cayenne pepper
- ½ tsp salt
- ½ tsp ground coriander

Directions:
Preheat the air fryer to 370 F. Brush the tortilla wedges with olive oil and arrange them in the frying basket in an even layer. Mix the spices thoroughly in a small bowl. Sprinkle the tortilla wedges with the spice mixture. AirFry for 2-3 minutes, shake the basket, and fry for another 2-3 minutes until crunchy and nicely browned. Serve the nachos immediately.

Nutrition Facts (per serving):
Calories: 150 | Carbohydrates: 20g | Protein: 2.5g | Fat: 6.5g | Fiber: 2.1g

---

 Servings: 4 25 minutes

292 One-Tray Parmesan Chicken Wings

Ingredients:
- 8 chicken wings
- 1 tsp Dijon mustard
- Salt and black pepper to taste
- 2 tbsp olive oil
- 4 tbsp Parmesan cheese, grated
- 2 tsp fresh parsley, chopped

Directions:
Preheat the air fryer to 380 F. Season the wings with salt and pepper. Brush them with mustard. Coat the chicken wings with 2 tbsp of Parmesan cheese, drizzle with olive oil, and place in the greased frying basket. AirFry for 14-16 minutes, turning once. When cooked, sprinkle with the remaining Parmesan cheese and top freshly chopped parsley.

Nutrition Facts (per serving):
Calories: 310 | Carbohydrates: 1g | Protein: 22g | Fat: 24g | Fiber: 0g

Servings: 3 | 7 Minutes

293 Lemon-roasted Salmon Fillets

Ingredients:
3 6-ounce skin-on salmon fillets
Olive oil spray
9 Very thin lemon slices
¾ teaspoon Ground black pepper
¼ teaspoon Table salt

Directions:
Preheat the air fryer to 400°F. Generously coat the skin of each of the fillets with olive oil spray. Set the fillets skin side down on your work surface. Place three overlapping lemon slices down the length of each salmon fillet. Sprinkle them with the pepper and salt. Coat lightly with olive oil spray. Use a nonstick-safe spatula to transfer the fillets one by one to the basket, leaving as much air space between them as possible. Air-fry undisturbed for 7 minutes, or until cooked through.
Use a nonstick-safe spatula to transfer the fillets to serving plates. Cool for only a minute or two before serving.

Nutrition Facts (per serving):
Calories: 215 | Carbohydrates: 1g | Protein: 20g | Fat: 14g | Fiber: 0g

Servings: 3 | 12 Minutes

294 Lemony Green Beans

Ingredients:
1 pound green beans, trimmed and halved
1 teaspoon butter, melted
1 tablespoon fresh lemon juice
¼ teaspoon garlic powder

Directions:
Preheat the Air fryer to 400°F and grease an Air fryer basket.
Mix all the ingredients in a bowl and toss to coat well. Arrange the green beans into the Air fryer basket and cook for about 12 minutes.
Dish out in a serving plate and serve hot.

Nutrition Facts (per serving):
Calories: Fifty-eight | Carbohydrates: 9.4g | Protein: 2.0g | Fat: 1.6g | Fiber: 3.4g

Servings: 4-6 | 20 minutes

295 Salmon Mini Tarts

Ingredients:
15 mini tart shells
4 eggs, lightly beaten
½ cup heavy cream
3 oz smoked salmon
6 oz cream cheese, divided into 15 pieces
2 tbsp fresh dill, chopped

Directions:
Mix together the eggs and heavy cream in a bowl. Arrange the tarts on a greased air fryer muffin tray. Pour the mixture into the tarts, about halfway up the side, and top with a piece of salmon and cheese. Bake in the fryer for 10 minutes at 340 F, regularly checking them to avoid overcooking. When ready, remove them from the tray and let cool. Sprinkle with freshly chopped dill and enjoy.

Nutrition Facts (per serving):
Calories: 105 | Carbohydrates: 4.5g | Protein: 5g | Fat: 8g | Fiber: 0.2g

Servings: 2 | 25 minutes

296 Spanish-Style Crusted Chicken Fingers

Ingredients:
2 chicken breasts, cut into strips
Salt and black pepper to taste
1 tsp garlic powder
3 tbsp cornstarch
4 tbsp breadcrumbs
4 tbsp Manchego cheese, grated
1 egg, beaten

Directions:
Combine salt, garlic, and black pepper in a bowl. Add in the chicken strips and stir to coat. Marinate for 1 hour in the fridge. Mix the breadcrumbs with Manchego cheese in another bowl.
Preheat the air fryer to 350 F. Remove the chicken from the fridge, lightly toss in cornstarch, dip in egg and coat the strips in the cheese mixture. Place them in the greased frying basket and AirFry for 14-16 minutes, shaking once, until nice and crispy. Serve with a side of vegetable fries. Yummy!

Nutrition Facts (per serving):
Calories: 370 | Carbohydrates: 15g | Protein: 38g | Fat: 18g | Fiber: 1g

Servings: 4 — 10 Minutes

297 Shrimp Burgers

Ingredients:
- 10 ounces medium shrimp, peeled and deveined
- ¼ cup mayonnaise
- ½ cup panko bread crumbs
- ½ teaspoon Old Bay Seasoning
- ¼ teaspoon salt
- ⅛ teaspoon ground black pepper
- 4 hamburger buns

Directions:
Preheat the air fryer to 400°F.
In a food processor, add shrimp and pulse four times until broken down.
Scoop shrimp into a large bowl and mix with mayonnaise, bread crumbs, Old Bay, salt, and pepper until well combined.
Separate mixture into four portions and form into patties. They will feel wet but should be able to hold their shape.
Place in the air fryer basket and cook 10 minutes, turning halfway through cooking time, until burgers are brown and internal temperature reaches at least 145°F. Serve warm on buns.

Nutrition Facts (per serving):
Calories: 228 | Carbohydrates: 6g | Protein: 17g | Fat: 14g | Fiber: 0.5g

---

Servings: 1 — 15 Minutes

298 Tortilla Pizza Margherita

Ingredients:
- 1 flour tortilla
- ¼ cup tomato sauce
- ⅓ cup grated mozzarella
- 3 basil leaves

Directions:
Preheat air fryer to 350°F. Put the tortilla in the greased basket and pour the sauce in the center. Spread across the whole tortilla. Sprinkle with cheese and Bake for 8-10 minutes or until crisp. Remove carefully and top with basil leaves. Serve hot.

Nutrition Facts (per serving):
Calories: 248 | Carbohydrates: 22.6g | Protein: 11.2g | Fat: 12.4g | Fiber: 1.6g

---

Servings: 4 — 20 minutes

299 Rich Cod Fingers

Ingredients:
- 2 cups flour
- Salt and black pepper to taste
- 1 tsp seafood seasoning
- 1 cup cornmeal
- 1 lb cod fillets, cut into fingers
- 2 tbsp milk
- 2 eggs, beaten
- 1 cup breadcrumbs

Directions:
Preheat the air fryer to 400 F. In a bowl, mix the eggs with milk, salt, and black pepper. In a separate bowl, mix the flour, cornmeal, and seafood seasoning. In a third bowl, pour the breadcrumbs.
Roll the cod fingers in the flour mixture, then dip in the egg mixture, and finally coat with the breadcrumbs.
Place the fingers in the frying basket and AirFry for 12-14 minutes, shaking once or twice. Serve hot.

Nutrition Facts (per serving):
Calories: 340 | Carbohydrates: 28g | Protein: 27g | Fat: 13g | Fiber: 1.6g

---

Servings: 4 — 25 minutes

300 Quinoa Chicken Nuggets

Ingredients:
- 2 chicken breasts, cut into large chunks
- ½ cup cooked quinoa, cooled
- 1 cup flour
- 2 eggs, beaten
- ½ tsp cayenne pepper
- Salt and black pepper to taste

Directions:
In a bowl, beat the egg with salt and black pepper. Spread the flour on a plate and mix in the cayenne pepper. Coat the chicken in the flour, then dip in the eggs, shake off, and coat in the quinoa. Press firmly so the quinoa sticks on the chunks. Spritz with cooking spray and AirFry the nuggets in the fryer for 14-16 minutes at 360 F, turning once halfway through cooking. Serve hot.

Nutrition Facts (per serving):
Calories: 320 | Carbohydrates: 20g | Protein: 30g | Fat: 12g | Fiber: 2g

301 Lime Bay Scallops

Servings: 4 | 10 Minutes

Ingredients:
- 2 tbsp butter, melted
- 1 lime, juiced
- ¼ tsp salt
- 1 lb bay scallops
- 2 tbsp chopped cilantro

Directions:
Preheat air fryer to 350°F. Combine all ingredients in a bowl, except for the cilantro. Place scallops in the frying basket and Air Fry for 5 minutes, tossing once. Serve immediately topped with cilantro.

Nutrition Facts (per serving):
Calories: 170 | Carbohydrates: 2g | Protein: 19g | Fat: 9g | Fiber: 0g

302 Caramelized Carrots

Servings: 3 | 15 Minutes

Ingredients:
- 1 small bag baby carrots
- ½ cup butter, melted
- ½ cup brown sugar

Directions:
Preheat the Air fryer to 400°F and grease an Air fryer basket.
Mix the butter and brown sugar in a bowl.
Add the carrots and toss to coat well.
Arrange the carrots in the Air fryer basket and cook for about 15 minutes.
Dish out and serve warm.

Nutrition Facts (per serving):
Calories: 243 | Carbohydrates: 24.8g | Protein: 0.7g | Fat: 16.5g | Fiber: 2.9g

303 Black Bean & Corn Flatbreads

Servings: 4 | 20 minutes

Ingredients:
- 4 flatbreads, warm
- 2 oz cream cheese, softened
- ¼ cup cheddar cheese, shredded
- ½ (15-oz) can corn, drained and rinsed
- ½ (15-oz) can black beans, drained and rinsed
- ¼ cup chunky salsa
- ½ tsp ground cumin
- ½ tsp paprika
- Salt and black pepper to taste
- 2 tbsp fresh cilantro, chopped

Directions:
Preheat the air fryer to 320 F. Add the black beans, corn, chunky salsa, cream cheese, cheddar cheese, cumin, paprika, salt, and pepper in a bowl. Mix well. Spread the mixture out on a baking dish and insert in the air fryer. AirFry for 9-11 minutes until heated through. Divide the mixture among the flatbreads. Top with cilantro and serve warm.

Nutrition Facts (per serving):
Calories: 310 | Carbohydrates: 34g | Protein: 9g | Fat: 15g | Fiber: 5g

304 San Antonio Taco Chicken Strips

Servings: 4 | 25 minutes

Ingredients:
- 3 mixed bell peppers, cut into chunks
- 1 red onion, sliced
- 1 lb chicken tenderloins, cut into strips
- 1 tbsp olive oil
- 2 tbsp cilantro, chopped
- 1 tbsp taco seasoning

Directions:
Preheat the air fryer to 375 F. Mix the strips, bell peppers, onion, olive oil, and taco seasoning in a large bowl and stir until the strips are coated. Place the strips and veggies in the greased fryer basket and AirFry for 7 minutes. Shake the basket, and cook for 5-8 more minutes, until the chicken is thoroughly cooked, and the veggies are starting to char. Serve topped with cilantro.

Nutrition Facts (per serving):
Calories: 260 | Carbohydrates: 10g | Protein: 30g | Fat: 11g | Fiber: 2g

Servings: 4 — 10 Minutes

305 Lemon Pepper-breaded Tilapia

Ingredients:
1 large egg
⅓ cup all-purpose flour
¼ cup grated Parmesan cheese
½ tablespoon lemon pepper seasoning
4 boneless, skinless tilapia fillets

Directions:
Preheat the air fryer to 375ºF.
In a medium bowl, whisk egg. On a large plate, mix flour, Parmesan, and lemon pepper seasoning. Pat tilapia dry. Dip each fillet into egg, gently shaking off excess. Press into flour mixture, then spritz both sides with cooking spray.
Place in the air fryer basket and cook 10 minutes, turning halfway through cooking, until fillets are golden and crispy and internal temperature reaches at least 145ºF. Serve warm.

Nutrition Facts (per serving):
Calories: 192 | Carbohydrates: 3g | Protein: 19g | Fat: 11g | Fiber: 0.5g

---

Servings: 2 — 15 Minutes

306 Broccoli Salad

Ingredients:
3 cups fresh broccoli florets
2 tbsp. coconut oil, melted
¼ cup sliced s
½ medium lemon, juiced

Directions:
Take a six-inch baking dish and fill with the broccoli florets. Pour the melted coconut oil over the broccoli and add in the sliced s. Toss together. Put the dish in the air fryer.
Cook at 380ºF for seven minutes, stirring at the halfway point.
Place the broccoli in a bowl and drizzle the lemon juice over it.

Nutrition Facts (per serving):
Calories: 134 | Carbohydrates: 6.4g | Protein: 2.9g | Fat: 10.6g | Fiber: 2.6g

---

 Servings: 2 20 minutes

307 Italian Pork Sausage Pizza

Ingredients:
1 piece pizza crust dough
½ tsp dried oregano
¼ cup tomato sauce
¼ cup mozzarella cheese, shredded
1 shallot, thinly sliced
1 Italian pork sausage, sliced
4 fresh basil leaves
4 black olives

Directions:
Preheat the air fryer to 390 F. Spread tomato sauce over the pizza dough and sprinkle with oregano. Top with mozzarella cheese, shallot, and pork sausage slices.
Place the pizza dough on the greased frying basket. Bake for 10 minutes until the crust is golden and the cheese is melted. Scatter over basil leaves and olives to serve.

Nutrition Facts (per serving):
Calories: 390 | Carbohydrates: 35g | Protein: 15g | Fat: 22g | Fiber: 2g

---

 Servings: 4 25 minutes

308 Crunchy Coconut Chicken Dippers

Ingredients:
2 cups coconut flakes
4 chicken breasts, cut into strips
½ cup cornstarch
Salt and black pepper to taste
2 eggs, beaten

Directions:
Preheat the air fryer to 400 F. Pulse the popcorn in a blender until crumbs-like texture. In a bowl, combine the cornflour, oregano, salt, and black pepper. In another bowl, beat the eggs with some salt.
In a third bowl, mix the breadcrumbs with the popcorn crumbs. Dip the chicken strips in the cornflour, then in the eggs, and then coat in the crumbs. Place in the greased frying basket. Drizzle with butter and AirFry for 12-14 minutes, shaking once or twice during cooking, until nice and crispy. Serve hot.

Nutrition Facts (per serving):
Calories: 430 | Carbohydrates: 18g | Protein: 36g | Fat: 24g | Fiber: 3g

Servings: 4 | 8 Minutes

309 Sea Scallops

Ingredients:
1½ pounds sea scallops
salt and pepper
2 eggs
½ cup flour
½ cup plain breadcrumbs
oil for misting or cooking spray

Directions:
Rinse scallops and remove the tough side muscle. Sprinkle to taste with salt and pepper.
Beat eggs together in a shallow dish. Place flour in a second shallow dish and breadcrumbs in a third.
Preheat air fryer to 390°F.
Dip scallops in flour, then eggs, and then roll in breadcrumbs. Mist with oil or cooking spray.
Place scallops in air fryer basket in a single layer, leaving some space between. You should be able to cook about a dozen at a time.
Cook at 390°F for 8 minutes, watching carefully so as not to overcook. Scallops are done when they turn opaque all the way through. They will feel slightly firm when pressed with tines of a fork.
Repeat step 6 to cook remaining scallops.

Nutrition Facts (per serving):
Calories: 198 | Carbohydrates: 4g | Protein: 23g | Fat: 9g | Fiber: 0.2g

---

Servings: 5 | 15 Minutes

310 Avocado Rolls

Ingredients:
10 egg roll wrappers
1 tomato, diced
¼ tsp pepper
½ tsp salt

Directions:
Place all filling ingredients in a bowl; mash with a fork until somewhat smooth. There should be chunks left. Divide the feeling between the egg wrappers. Wet your finger and brush along the edges, so the wrappers can seal well. Roll and seal the wrappers. Arrange them on a baking sheet lined dish, and place in the air fryer. Cook at 350°F for 5 minutes. Serve with sweet chili dipping and enjoy.

Nutrition Facts (per serving):
Calories: 211 | Carbohydrates: 20.6g | Protein: 4.2g | Fat: 13.4g | Fiber: 3.8g

---

Servings: 4 | 20 minutes

311 Delicious Chicken Tortillas

Ingredients:
1 cup cooked chicken, shredded
1 cup mozzarella cheese, shredded
¼ cup salsa
¼ cup Greek yogurt
Salt and black pepper to taste
8 flour tortillas

Directions:
In a bowl, mix the chicken, mozzarella, salsa, Greek yogurt, salt, and black pepper. Lay 2 tbsp of the mixture at the center of the tortillas. Roll tightly around the mixture. Spray the taquitos with cooking spray and arrange them in the frying basket. AirFry for 12-14 minutes at 380 F, turning once. Serve.

Nutrition Facts (per serving):
Calories: 360 | Carbohydrates: 32g | Protein: 22g | Fat: 16g | Fiber: 2g

---

Servings: 4 | 25 minutes

312 Popcorn Chicken Tenders

Ingredients:
1 lb chicken tenders, cut into strips
½ cup cooked popcorn
½ cup panko breadcrumbs
2 eggs
½ cup cornflour
½ tsp dried oregano
2 tbsp butter, melted
Salt and black pepper to taste

Directions:
Preheat the air fryer to 400 F. Pulse the popcorn in a blender until crumbs-like texture. In a bowl, combine the cornflour, oregano, salt, and black pepper. In another bowl, beat the eggs with some salt.
In a third bowl, mix the breadcrumbs with the popcorn crumbs. Dip the chicken strips in the cornflour, then in the eggs, and then coat in the crumbs. Place in the greased frying basket. Drizzle with butter and AirFry for 12-14 minutes, shaking once or twice during cooking, until nice and crispy. Serve hot.

Nutrition Facts (per serving):
Calories: 410 | Carbohydrates: 22g | Protein: 32g | Fat: 23g | Fiber: 2g

Servings: 4 | 10 Minutes

313 Shrimp Al Pesto

Ingredients:
1 lb peeled shrimp, deveined
¼ cup pesto sauce
1 lime, sliced
2 cups cooked farro

Directions:
Preheat air fryer to 360°F. Coat the shrimp with the pesto sauce in a bowl. Put the shrimp in a single layer in the frying basket. Put the lime slices over the shrimp and Roast for 5 minutes. Remove lime and discard. Serve the shrimp over a bed of farro pilaf. Enjoy!

Nutrition Facts (per serving):
Calories: 350 | Carbohydrates: 28g | Protein: 27g | Fat: 15g | Fiber: 4g

Servings: 4 | 15 Minutes

314 Effortless Mac `n´ Cheese

Ingredients:
1 cup heavy cream
1 cup milk
½ cup mozzarella cheese
2 tsp grated Parmesan cheese
16 oz cooked elbow macaroni

Directions:
Preheat air fryer to 400°F. Whisk the heavy cream, milk, mozzarella cheese, and Parmesan cheese until smooth in a bowl. Stir in the macaroni and pour into a baking dish. Cover with foil and Bake in the air fryer for 6 minutes. Remove foil and Bake until cooked through and bubbly, 3-5 minutes. Serve warm.

Nutrition Facts (per serving):
Calories: 412 | Carbohydrates: 39.6g | Protein: 13.2g | Fat: 23.4g | Fiber: 1.8g

 Servings: 4 20 minutes

315 Spanish Chorizo with Brussels Sprouts

Ingredients:
4 Spanish chorizo sausages, halved
1 lb Brussels sprouts, trimmed and halved
2 tbsp olive oil
Salt and black pepper to taste
1 tsp garlic puree
1 thyme sprig, chopped

Directions:
Preheat the air fryer to 390 F. In a bowl, mix olive oil, garlic puree, salt, and black pepper. Add the Brussels sprouts and toss to coat. Arrange chorizo and Brussels sprouts on the greased frying basket and AirFry for 11-14 minutes, tossing once halfway through cooking. Top with thyme to serve.

Nutrition Facts (per serving):
Calories: 360 | Carbohydrates: 9g | Protein: 14g | Fat: 30g | Fiber: 3.5g

 Servings: 4 25 minutes

316 Cajun Chicken Tenders

Ingredients:
1 lb chicken breasts, sliced
3 eggs
1 cup flour
2 tbsp olive oil
½ tbsp garlic powder
Salt and black pepper to taste
1 tbsp Cajun seasoning
¼ cup milk

Directions:
Sprinkle the chicken slices with garlic powder and Cajun seasoning. Pour the flour on a plate. In a bowl, whisk the eggs along with milk and olive oil. Season with salt and black pepper.
Preheat the air fryer to 370 F. Dip the chicken slices into the egg mixture, and then coat in the flour. Arrange them on the greased frying basket and AirFry for 12-14 minutes, flipping once until crispy.

Nutrition Facts (per serving):
Calories: 390 | Carbohydrates: 18g | Protein: 36g | Fat: 20g | Fiber: 1g

317 Tuna Cakes

Servings: 4 | 10 Minutes

Ingredients:
- 4 pouches tuna, drained
- 1 large egg, whisked
- 2 tablespoons peeled and chopped white onion
- ½ teaspoon Old Bay Seasoning

Directions:
In a large bowl, mix all ingredients together and form into four patties.
Place patties into ungreased air fryer basket. Adjust the temperature to 400°F and set the timer for 10 minutes. Patties will be browned and crispy when done. Let cool 5 minutes before serving.

Nutrition Facts (per serving):
Calories: 192 | Carbohydrates: 1.5g | Protein: 22.4g | Fat: 10.2g | Fiber: 0.2g

318 Garden Fresh Green Beans

Servings: 4 | 12 Minutes

Ingredients:
- 1 pound green beans, washed and trimmed
- 1 teaspoon butter, melted
- 1 tablespoon fresh lemon juice
- ¼ teaspoon garlic powder
- Salt and freshly ground pepper, to taste

Directions:
Preheat the Air fryer to 400°F and grease an Air fryer basket.
Put all the ingredients in a large bowl and transfer into the Air fryer basket.
Cook for about 8 minutes and dish out in a bowl to serve warm.

Nutrition Facts (per serving):
Calories: Fifty-six | Carbohydrates: 9.1g | Protein: 2.1g | Fat: 1.8g | Fiber: 3.2g

319 Plum & Pancetta Bombs

Servings: 4-6 | 20 minutes

Ingredients:
- 1 ¼ cups soft goat cheese, crumbled
- 1 tbsp fresh rosemary, finely chopped
- 1 cup almonds, chopped
- Salt and black pepper to taste
- 15 dried plums, soaked and chopped
- 15 pancetta slices

Directions:
Line the frying basket with baking paper. In a bowl, add goat cheese, rosemary, almonds, salt, black pepper, and plums; stir well. Roll into balls and wrap with a pancetta slice. Place them into the fryer and AirFry for 10 minutes at 400 F, shaking once. Let cool for a few minutes. Serve with toothpicks.

Nutrition Facts (per serving):
Calories: 120 | Carbohydrates: 5g | Protein: 5g | Fat: 9g | Fiber: 1g

320 Almond-Fried Crispy Chicken

Servings: 4 | 25 minutes

Ingredients:
- 4 chicken breasts, cubed
- 2 cups almond meal
- 3 whole eggs
- ½ cup cornstarch
- Salt and black pepper to taste
- ½ tsp cayenne pepper

Directions:
Preheat the air fryer to 350 F. In a bowl, mix the cornstarch, salt, black pepper, and cayenne pepper and toss in the chicken. In another bowl, beat the eggs. In a third bowl, pour the almond meal. Dredge the chicken in the eggs, then in almond meal. AirFry for 14-16 minutes, shaking once or twice. Serve.

Nutrition Facts (per serving):
Calories: 470 | Carbohydrates: 12g | Protein: 42g | Fat: 28g | Fiber: 3g

Servings: 2 | 8 Minutes

321 Garlic And Dill Salmon

Ingredients:
12 ounces salmon filets with skin
2 tablespoons melted butter
1 tablespoon extra-virgin olive oil
2 garlic cloves, minced
1 tablespoon fresh dill
½ teaspoon sea salt
½ lemon

Directions:
Pat the salmon dry with paper towels.
In a small bowl, mix together the melted butter, olive oil, garlic, and dill.
Sprinkle the top of the salmon with sea salt. Brush all sides of the salmon with the garlic and dill butter.
Preheat the air fryer to 350°F.
Place the salmon, skin side down, in the air fryer basket. Cook for 6 to 8 minutes, or until the fish flakes in the center.
Remove the salmon and plate on a serving platter. Squeeze fresh lemon over the top of the salmon. Serve immediately.

Nutrition Facts (per serving):
Calories: 384 | Carbohydrates: 1.1g | Protein: 28.7g | Fat: 29.5g | Fiber: 0.1g

---

Servings: 2 | 15 Minutes

322 Cauliflower Steak With Thick Sauce

Ingredients:
¼ cup almond milk
¼ teaspoon vegetable stock powder
1 cauliflower, sliced into two
1 tablespoon olive oil
2 tablespoons onion, chopped
salt and pepper to taste

Directions:
Soak the cauliflower in salted water or brine for at least 2 hours.
Preheat the air fryer to 400°F.
Rinse the cauliflower and place inside the air fryer and cook for 15 minutes.
Meanwhile, heat oil in a skillet over medium flame. Sauté the onions and stir until translucent. Add the vegetable stock powder and milk.
Bring to boil and adjust the heat to low.
Allow the sauce to reduce and season with salt and pepper.
Place cauliflower steak on a plate and pour over sauce.

Nutrition Facts (per serving):
Calories: 112 | Carbohydrates: 8.6g | Protein: 3.1g | Fat: 7.4g | Fiber: 3.4g

---

Servings: 4 | 20 minutes

323 Paprika Baked Parsnips

Ingredients:
½ tbsp paprika
1 lb parsnips, peeled and halved
4 tbsp avocado oil
2 tbsp fresh cilantro, chopped
2 tbsp Parmesan cheese, grated
1 tsp garlic powder
Salt and black pepper to taste

Directions:
Preheat the air fryer to 390 F.
In a bowl, mix paprika, avocado oil, garlic, salt, and black pepper. Toss in the parsnips to coat. Arrange them on the greased frying basket and Bake for 14-16 minutes, turning once halfway through cooking, until golden and crunchy. Remove and sprinkle with Parmesan cheese and cilantro. Serve.

Nutrition Facts (per serving):
Calories: 230 | Carbohydrates: 18g | Protein: 3.5g | Fat: 17g | Fiber: 5g

---

Servings: 4 | 25 minutes

324 Jerusalem Matzah & Chicken Schnitzels

Ingredients:
4 chicken breasts
1 cup panko breadcrumbs
2 tbsp Parmesan cheese, grated
6 sage leaves, chopped
½ cup fine matzah meal
2 beaten eggs

Directions:
Pound the chicken to ¼-inch thickness using a rolling pin. In a bowl, mix Parmesan cheese, sage, and breadcrumbs. Coat the chicken in matzah meal, dip it in the eggs, then coat in the crumbs' mixture. Preheat the air fryer to 390 F. Spritz the chicken breasts with cooking spray and AirFry them for 14-16 minutes, turning once halfway through, until golden and crispy. Serve warm.

Nutrition Facts (per serving):
Calories: 410 | Carbohydrates: 22g | Protein: 38g | Fat: 18g | Fiber: 1g

Servings: 4 — 8 Minutes

325 Bacon-wrapped Scallops

Ingredients:

16 large scallops
8 bacon strips
½ teaspoon black pepper
¼ teaspoon smoked paprika

Directions:

Pat the scallops dry with a paper towel. Slice each of the bacon strips in half. Wrap 1 bacon strip around 1 scallop and secure with a toothpick. Repeat with the remaining scallops. Season the scallops with pepper and paprika.
Preheat the air fryer to 350°F.
Place the bacon-wrapped scallops in the air fryer basket and cook for 4 minutes, shake the basket, cook another 3 minutes, shake the basket, and cook another 1 to 3 to minutes. When the bacon is crispy, the scallops should be cooked through and slightly firm, but not rubbery. Serve immediately.

Nutrition Facts (per serving):
Calories: 192 | Carbohydrates: 1.3g | Protein: 16.8g | Fat: 12.6g | Fiber: 0.2g

Servings: 4 — 12 Minutes

326 Cheddar Soufflés

Ingredients:

3 large eggs, whites and yolks separated
¼ teaspoon cream of tartar
½ cup shredded sharp Cheddar cheese
3 ounces cream cheese, softened

Directions:

In a large bowl, beat egg whites together with cream of tartar until soft peaks form, about 2 minutes.
In a separate medium bowl, beat egg yolks, Cheddar, and cream cheese together until frothy, about 1 minute. Add egg yolk mixture to whites, gently folding until combined.
Pour mixture evenly into four 4" ramekins greased with cooking spray. Place ramekins into air fryer basket. Adjust the temperature to 350°F and set the timer for 12 minutes. Eggs will be browned on the top and firm in the center when done. Serve warm.

Nutrition Facts (per serving):
Calories: 184 | Carbohydrates: 2g | Protein: 10g | Fat: 15g | Fiber: 0g

Servings: 2 — 20 minutes

327 Cheesy Mushrooms

Ingredients:

2 tbsp olive oil
Salt and black pepper to taste
10 button mushroom caps
2 tbsp mozzarella cheese, grated
2 tbsp cheddar cheese, grated
1 tsp Italian seasoning

Directions:

Preheat the air fryer to 390 F. In a bowl, mix olive oil, salt, black pepper, and Italian seasoning. Toss in the mushrooms to coat. Mix the cheeses in a separate bowl. Stuff the mushrooms with the cheese mixture and place them in the frying basket. Bake for 10-12 minutes until golden on top. Serve warm.

Nutrition Facts (per serving):
Calories: 170 | Carbohydrates: 3g | Protein: 5g | Fat: 15g | Fiber: 1g

Servings: 4 — 25 minutes

328 Sweet Curried Chicken Cutlets

Ingredients:

1 lb chicken breasts, halved crosswise
2 tbsp garlic mayonnaise
½ tsp chili powder
½ tsp curry powder
½ tsp brown sugar
2 tbsp soy sauce

Directions:

Put the chicken halves between 2 pieces of plastic wrap and gently pound them to ¼-inch thickness using a rolling pin. In a bowl, mix the chili powder, curry powder, brown sugar, and soy sauce. Add in the chicken and toss to coat. Cover with plastic wrap and refrigerate for 1 hour.
Preheat the air fryer to 350 F. Remove the chicken from the marinade and place it in the greased frying basket. AirFry for 8 minutes, flip, and cook further for 6-8 minutes until crispy. Serve with garlic mayo.

Nutrition Facts (per serving):
Calories: 280 | Carbohydrates: 4g | Protein: 32g | Fat: 14g | Fiber: 0g

Servings: 4 — 10 Minutes

329 Lemon Butter-dill Salmon

Ingredients:
4 skin-on salmon fillets
¾ teaspoon salt
½ teaspoon ground black pepper
1 medium lemon, halved
2 tablespoons salted butter, melted
1 teaspoon dried dill

Directions:
Preheat the air fryer to 375°F.
Sprinkle salmon with salt and pepper.
Juice half the lemon and slice the other half into ¼"-thick pieces. In a small bowl, combine juice with butter. Brush mixture over salmon.
Sprinkle dill evenly over salmon. Place lemon slices on top of salmon.
Place salmon in the air fryer basket and cook 10 minutes until salmon flakes easily and internal temperature reaches at least 145°F. Remove lemon slices before serving.

Nutrition Facts (per serving):
Calories: 294 | Carbohydrates: 1.0g | Protein: 25.8g | Fat: 20.6g | Fiber: 0.1g

---

Servings: 2 — 15 Minutes

330 Parsley Egg Scramble With Cottage Cheese

Ingredients:
1 tbsp cottage cheese, crumbled
4 eggs
Salt and pepper to taste
2 tsp heavy cream
1 tbsp chopped parsley

Directions:
Preheat air fryer to 400°F. Grease a baking pan with olive oil. Beat the eggs, salt, and pepper in a bowl. Pour it into the pan, place the pan in the frying basket, and Air Fry for 5 minutes. Using a silicone spatula, stir in heavy cream, cottage cheese, and half of parsley and Air Fry for another 2 minutes. Scatter with parsley to serve.

Nutrition Facts (per serving):
Calories: 163 | Carbohydrates: 1g | Protein: 12g | Fat: 12g | Fiber: 0g

---

Servings: 4 — 20 minutes

331 Walnut & Cheese Filled Mushrooms

Ingredients:
4 large portobello mushroom caps
⅓ cup walnuts, finely chopped
1 tbsp canola oil
½ cup mozzarella cheese, shredded
2 tbsp fresh parsley, chopped

Directions:
Preheat the air fryer to 350 F. Grease the frying basket with cooking spray.
Rub the mushrooms with canola oil and fill them with mozzarella cheese. Top with walnuts and arrange them in the greased frying basket. Bake for 10-12 minutes or until golden on top. Remove and let cool for a few minutes. Sprinkle with freshly chopped parsley and serve.

Nutrition Facts (per serving):
Calories: 210 | Carbohydrates: 5g | Protein: 8g | Fat: 18g | Fiber: 2g

---

Servings: 2 — 25 minutes

332 Lemony Chicken Breast

Ingredients:
1 chicken breast
2 lemon, juiced and rind reserved
1 tbsp chicken seasoning
1 tbsp garlic puree
Salt and black pepper to taste

Directions:
Preheat the air fryer to 350 F. Place a silver foil sheet on a flat surface. Add all seasonings along with the lemon rind. Lay the chicken breast onto a chopping board and trim any fat.
Season each side with the seasoning. Place in the silver foil sheet, seal, and flatten with a rolling pin. Place the breast in the frying basket and AirFry for 14-16 minutes, flipping once halfway through.

Nutrition Facts (per serving):
Calories: 120 | Carbohydrates: 1g | Protein: 26g | Fat: 1g | Fiber: 0g

Servings: 3 — 8 Minutes

333 Zesty Mahi Mahi

Ingredients:
1½ pounds Mahi Mahi fillets
1 lemon, cut into slices
1 tablespoon fresh dill, chopped
½ teaspoon red chili powder
Salt and ground black pepper, as required

Directions:
Preheat the Air fryer to 375°F and grease an Air fryer basket.
Season the Mahi Mahi fillets evenly with chili powder, salt, and black pepper.
Arrange the Mahi Mahi fillets into the Air fryer basket and top with the lemon slices.
Cook for about 8 minutes and dish out
Place the lemon slices over the salmon the salmon fillets in the serving plates.
Garnish with fresh dill and serve warm.

Nutrition Facts (per serving):
Calories: 186 | Carbohydrates: 1.1g | Protein: thirty.8g | Fat: 3.6g | Fiber: 0.2g

---

Servings: 4 — 15 Minutes

334 Parsley Omelet

Ingredients:
4 eggs, whisked
1 tablespoon parsley, chopped
½ teaspoons cheddar cheese, shredded
1 avocado, peeled, pitted and cubed
Cooking spray

Directions:
In a bowl, mix all the ingredients except the cooking spray and whisk well. Grease a baking pan that fits the Air Fryer with the cooking spray, pour the omelet mix, spread, introduce the pan in the machine and cook at 370°F for 15 minutes. Serve for breakfast.

Nutrition Facts (per serving):
Calories: 163 | Carbohydrates: 3g | Protein: 9g | Fat: 13g | Fiber: 2g

---

 Servings: 4 20 minutes

335 Chili Edamame

Ingredients:
1 (16-oz) bag frozen edamame in pods
1 red chili, finely chopped
1 tbsp olive oil
½ tsp garlic salt
½ tsp red pepper flakes
Black pepper to taste

Directions:
Preheat the air fryer to 380 F. In a mixing bowl, combine olive oil, garlic salt, red pepper flakes, and black pepper and mix well. Add in the edamame and toss to coat.
Transfer to the frying basket in a single layer and AirFry for 10 minutes, shaking once. Cook until lightly browned and just crispy. Work in batches if needed. Serve topped with the red chili.

Nutrition Facts (per serving):
Calories: 160 | Carbohydrates: 9g | Protein: 10g | Fat: 9g | Fiber: 4g

---

Servings: 4 25 minutes

336 Chicken Parmigiana with Fresh Rosemary

Ingredients:
1 lb chicken breasts, halved
1 cup seasoned breadcrumbs
½ cup Parmesan cheese, grated
Salt and black pepper to taste
2 eggs
2 sprigs rosemary, chopped

Directions:
Preheat the air fryer to 380 F. Put the chicken halves on a clean flat surface and cover with a clingfilm. Gently pound them to become thinner using a rolling pin. Beat the eggs in a bowl and season them with salt and black pepper. In a separate bowl, mix breadcrumbs with Parmesan cheese.
Dip the chicken in the eggs, then in the crumbs and spray with cooking spray. AirFry them for 6 minutes, flip and cook for 5-7 more minutes or until golden and crispy. Sprinkle with rosemary to serve.

Nutrition Facts (per serving):
Calories: 430 | Carbohydrates: 25g | Protein: 36g | Fat: 16g | Fiber: 1g

Servings: 3 — 10 Minutes

337 Tilapia Teriyaki

Ingredients:
4 tablespoons teriyaki sauce
1 tablespoon pineapple juice
1 pound tilapia fillets
cooking spray
6 ounces frozen mixed peppers with onions, thawed and drained
2 cups cooked rice

Directions:
Mix the teriyaki sauce and pineapple juice together in a small bowl.
Split tilapia fillets down the center lengthwise.
Brush all sides of fish with the sauce, spray air fryer basket with nonstick cooking spray, and place fish in the basket.
Stir the peppers and onions into the remaining sauce and spoon over the fish. Save any leftover sauce for drizzling over the fish when serving.
Cook at 360°F for 10 minutes, until fish flakes easily with a fork and is done in center.
Divide into 3 or 4 servings and serve each with approximately ½ cup cooked rice.

Nutrition Facts (per serving):
Calories: 328 | Carbohydrates: 26.7g | Protein: 27.1g | Fat: 11.2g | Fiber: 1.3g

Servings: 2 — 15 Minutes

338 Denver Eggs

Ingredients:
3 large eggs
1 tablespoon salted butter, melted
¼ cup seeded and chopped green bell pepper
2 tablespoons peeled and chopped yellow onion
¼ cup chopped cooked no-sugar-added ham
¼ teaspoon salt
¼ teaspoon ground black pepper

Directions:
Crack eggs into an ungreased 6" round nonstick baking dish. Mix in butter, bell pepper, onion, ham, salt, and black pepper.
Place dish into air fryer basket. Adjust the temperature to 320°F and set the timer for 15 minutes. The eggs will be fully cooked and firm in the middle when done.
Slice in half and serve warm on two medium plates.

Nutrition Facts (per serving):
Calories: 168 | Carbohydrates: 2g | Protein: 13g | Fat: 12g | Fiber: 0g

 Servings: 1 20 minutes

339 Easy Parmesan Sandwich

Ingredients:
4 tbsp Parmesan cheese, shredded
2 scallions
1 tbsp butter, softened
2 bread slices

Directions:
Preheat the air fryer to 360 F. Spread only one side of the bread slices with butter. Cover one of the buttered slices with Parmesan and scallions and top with the buttered side of the other slice to form a sandwich. Place in the frying basket and Bake for 10-12 minutes. Cut into 4 triangles and serve.

Nutrition Facts (per serving):
Calories: 310 | Carbohydrates: 24g | Protein: 10g | Fat: 19g | Fiber: 2g

 Servings: 4 25 minutes

340 Spinach Loaded Chicken Breasts

Ingredients:
1 cup spinach, chopped
4 tbsp cottage cheese, crumbled
2 chicken breasts
2 tbsp Italian seasoning
2 tbsp olive oil

Directions:
Preheat the air fryer to 390 F. Grease the basket with cooking spray. Mix spinach and cottage cheese in a bowl. Halve the breasts with a knife and flatten them with a meat mallet. Season with Italian seasoning. Divide the spinach/cheese mixture between the chicken pieces.
Roll them up to form cylinders and use toothpicks to secure them. Brush with olive oil and place them in the frying basket. Bake for 7-8 minutes, turn, and cook for 6 minutes or until golden brown. Serve.

Nutrition Facts (per serving):
Calories: 330 | Carbohydrates: 4g | Protein: 38g | Fat: 18g | Fiber: 2g

341 5-minute Shrimp

Servings: 4 | 5 Minutes

Ingredients:
- 1 pound medium shrimp, peeled and deveined
- 2 tablespoons salted butter, melted
- ¼ teaspoon salt
- ¼ teaspoon ground black pepper

Directions:
In a large bowl, toss shrimp in butter, then sprinkle with salt and pepper.
Place shrimp into ungreased air fryer basket. Adjust the temperature to 400°F and set the timer for 5 minutes, shaking the basket halfway through cooking. Shrimp will be opaque and pink when done. Serve warm.

Nutrition Facts (per serving):
Calories: 172 | Carbohydrates: 0.8g | Protein: 23.6g | Fat: 7.6g | Fiber: 0.1g

342 Tuna And Arugula Salad

Servings: 4 | 15 Minutes

Ingredients:
- ½ pound smoked tuna, flaked
- 1 cup arugula
- 2 spring onions, chopped
- 1 tablespoon olive oil
- A pinch of salt and black pepper

Directions:
In a bowl, all the ingredients except the oil and the arugula and whisk. Preheat the Air Fryer over 360°F, add the oil and grease it. Pour the tuna mix, stir well, and cook for 15 minutes. In a salad bowl, combine the arugula with the tuna mix, toss and serve for breakfast.

Nutrition Facts (per serving):
Calories: 120 | Carbohydrates: 1g | Protein: 15g | Fat: 6g | Fiber: 0g

343 Spicy Cheese Lings

Servings: 4 | 20 minutes

Ingredients:
- ½ cup grated cheddar cheese + extra for rolling
- 1 cup flour + extra for kneading
- ¼ tsp chili powder
- ½ tsp baking powder
- 3 tsp butter, melted
- A pinch of salt

Directions:
In a bowl, mix the cheese, flour, baking powder, chili powder, butter, and salt. Add some water and mix well to get a dough. Remove the dough onto a flat, floured surface. Using a rolling pin, roll out into a thin sheet and cut into lings' shape. Add the cheese lings to the greased frying basket and AirFry for 10-12 minutes at 350 F, flipping once halfway through. Serve with ketchup if desired.

Nutrition Facts (per serving):
Calories: 200 | Carbohydrates: 17g | Protein: 5g | Fat: 12g | Fiber: 1g

344 Chicken Breasts "En Papillote"

Servings: 4 | 25 minutes

Ingredients:
- 1 lb chicken breasts
- 2 tbsp butter, melted
- Salt and black pepper to taste
- ½ tsp dried marjoram

Directions:
Preheat the air fryer to 380 F. Place each chicken breast on a 12x12 inches aluminum foil wrap, and season with salt and pepper. Top with marjoram and butter. Wrap the foil around the breasts in a loose way to create a flow of air. Bake the in the fryer for 15 minutes. Unwrap, let cool slightly, and serve.

Nutrition Facts (per serving):
Calories: 250 | Carbohydrates: 0g | Protein: 30g | Fat: 14g | Fiber: 0g

345 Miso Fish

Servings: 2 | **Time:** 10 Minutes

Ingredients:
- 2 cod fish fillets
- 1 tbsp garlic, chopped
- 2 tsp swerve
- 2 tbsp miso

Directions:
Add all ingredients to the zip-lock bag. Shake well place in the refrigerator for overnight.
Place marinated fish fillets into the air fryer basket and cook at 350°F for 10 minutes.
Serve and enjoy.

Nutrition Facts (per serving):
Calories: 198 | Carbohydrates: 3.2g | Protein: 23.5g | Fat: 9.1g | Fiber: 0.3g

---

346 Bunless Breakfast Turkey Burgers

Servings: 4 | **Time:** 15 Minutes

Ingredients:
- 1 pound ground turkey breakfast sausage
- ½ teaspoon salt
- ¼ teaspoon ground black pepper
- ¼ cup seeded and chopped green bell pepper
- 2 tablespoons mayonnaise
- 1 medium avocado, peeled, pitted, and sliced

Directions:
In a large bowl, mix sausage with salt, black pepper, bell pepper, and mayonnaise. Form meat into four patties.
Place patties into ungreased air fryer basket. Adjust the temperature to 370°F and set the timer for 15 minutes, turning patties halfway through cooking. Burgers will be done when dark brown and they have an internal temperature of at least 165°F.
Serve burgers topped with avocado slices on four medium plates.

Nutrition Facts (per serving):
Calories: 265 | Carbohydrates: 3g | Protein: 16g | Fat: 21g | Fiber: 2g

---

347 Italian Pork Scallopini

Servings: 4 | **Time:** 20 minutes

Ingredients:
- 4 pork loin thin steaks
- Salt and black pepper to taste
- ¼ cup Parmesan cheese, grated
- 2 tbsp Italian breadcrumbs

Directions:
Preheat the air fryer to 390 F. Spritz the frying basket with cooking spray.
In a bowl, mix Italian breadcrumbs and Parmesan cheese. Season the pork steaks with salt and black pepper. Roll them in the breadcrumb mixture and spray them with cooking spray. Transfer to the frying basket and AirFry for 14-16 minutes, turning once halfway through. Serve immediately.

Nutrition Facts (per serving):
Calories: 211 | Carbohydrates: 1.5g | Protein: 21g | Fat: 12g | Fiber: 0g

---

348 Ham & Cheese Chicken Breasts

Servings: 4 | **Time:** 25 minutes

Ingredients:
- 4 chicken breasts
- 4 ham slices
- 4 Swiss cheese slices
- 3 tbsp all-purpose flour
- 4 tbsp butter
- ½ tbsp paprika
- 1 tbsp chicken bouillon granules
- ¼ cup dry white wine
- 1 cup heavy cream

Directions:
Preheat the air fryer to 380 F. Pound the chicken and put a slice of ham and cheese onto each one. Fold the edges over the filling and seal them with toothpicks. In a bowl, combine paprika and flour, and coat in the chicken. Transfer them to the greased frying basket and Bake for 15 minutes, turning once.
In a large skillet over medium heat, melt the butter and add the bouillon granules, wine, and heavy cream. Bring to a boil, reduce the heat to low, and simmer for 5 minutes. Serve the chicken with sauce

Nutrition Facts (per serving):
Calories: 620 | Carbohydrates: 10g | Protein: 45g | Fat: 42g | Fiber: 0g

Servings: 4 — 5 Minutes

349 Shrimp "scampi"

Ingredients:
1½ pounds Large shrimp, peeled and deveined
¼ cup Olive oil
2 tablespoons Minced garlic
1 teaspoon Dried oregano
Up to 1 teaspoon Red pepper flakes
½ teaspoon Table salt
2 tablespoons White balsamic vinegar

Directions:
Preheat the air fryer to 400°F.
Stir the shrimp, olive oil, garlic, oregano, red pepper flakes, and salt in a large bowl until the shrimp are well coated.
When the machine is at temperature, transfer the shrimp to the basket. They will overlap and even sit on top of each other. Air-fry for 5 minutes, tossing and rearranging the shrimp twice to make sure the covered surfaces are exposed, until pink and firm. Pour the contents of the basket into a serving bowl. Pour the vinegar over the shrimp while hot and toss to coat.

Nutrition Facts (per serving):
Calories: 236 | Carbohydrates: 2.5g | Protein: 26.7g | Fat: 13.6g | Fiber: 0.4g

---

Servings: 12 — 15 Minutes

350 Banana-nut Muffins

Ingredients:
1½ cups all-purpose flour
½ cup granulated sugar
1 teaspoon baking powder
½ cup salted butter, melted
1 large egg
2 medium bananas, peeled and mashed
½ cup chopped pecans

Directions:
Preheat the air fryer to 300°F.
In a large bowl, whisk together flour, sugar, and baking powder.
Add butter, egg, and bananas to dry mixture. Stir until well combined. Batter will be thick.
Gently fold in pecans. Divide batter evenly among twelve silicone or aluminum muffin cups, filling cups about halfway full.
Place cups in the air fryer basket, working in batches as necessary. Cook 15 minutes until muffin edges are brown and a toothpick inserted into the center comes out clean. Let cool 5 minutes before serving.

Nutrition Facts (per serving):
Calories: 200 | Carbohydrates: 24g | Protein: 3g | Fat: 11g | Fiber: 1g

---

 Servings: 4 20 minutes

351 Spicy Sweet Beef with Veggie Topping

Ingredients:
2 beef steaks, sliced into thin strips
2 garlic cloves, minced
2 tsp maple syrup
1 tsp oyster sauce
1 tsp cayenne pepper
½ tsp olive oil
Juice of 1 lime
Salt and black pepper to taste
1 cauliflower, cut into florets
2 carrots, cut into chunks
1 cup green peas

Directions:
Preheat the air fryer to 400 F. In a bowl, place the beef strips, garlic, maple syrup, oyster sauce, cayenne pepper, olive oil, lime juice, salt, and black pepper; stir to combine. Transfer the mixture to the frying basket. Top with the veggies. Transfer to the fryer and Bake for 12-14 minutes, shaking once.

Nutrition Facts (per serving):
Calories: 290 | Carbohydrates: 17g | Protein: 22g | Fat: 14g | Fiber: 5g

---

 Servings: 4 25 minutes

352 Restaurant-Style Chicken with Yogurt Sauce

Ingredients:
½ cup breadcrumbs
2 whole eggs, beaten
½ cup all-purpose flour
Salt and black pepper to taste
2 tbsp olive oil
1 ¼ lb chicken tenders
1 cup Greek yogurt
1 tbsp lemon juice
1 tbsp fresh dill, chopped

Directions:
Preheat the air fryer to 380 F. Pour the crumbs, eggs, and flour into 3 separate bowls. Season the tenders with salt and pepper and dredge them first in the flour, then in eggs, and finally in the crumbs. AirFry them in the greased frying basket for 10 minutes. Flip and cook for 5 more minutes or until golden. Mix the yogurt with lemon juice, dill, salt, and pepper until smooth. Serve with the tenders.

Nutrition Facts (per serving):
Calories: 410 | Carbohydrates: 22g | Protein: 38g | Fat: 16g | Fiber: 1g

Servings: 2 — 8 Minutes

353 Crunchy Coconut Shrimp

Ingredients:
8 ounces jumbo shrimp, peeled and deveined
2 tablespoons salted butter, melted
½ teaspoon Old Bay Seasoning
¼ cup unsweetened shredded coconut
¼ cup coconut flour

Directions:
In a large bowl, toss shrimp in butter and Old Bay Seasoning.
In a medium bowl, combine shredded coconut with coconut flour. Coat each piece of shrimp in coconut mixture.
Place shrimp into ungreased air fryer basket. Adjust the temperature to 400°F and set the timer for 8 minutes, gently turning shrimp halfway through cooking. Shrimp will be pink and C-shaped when done. Serve warm.

Nutrition Facts (per serving):
Calories: 284 | Carbohydrates: 6.1g | Protein: 22.8g | Fat: 19.2g | Fiber: 2.7g

Servings: 6 — 15 Minutes

354 Sausage-crusted Egg Cups

Ingredients:
12 ounces ground pork breakfast sausage
6 large eggs
½ teaspoon salt
¼ teaspoon ground black pepper
½ teaspoon crushed red pepper flakes

Directions:
Place sausage in six 4" ramekins greased with cooking oil. Press sausage down to cover bottom and about ½" up the sides of ramekins. Crack one egg into each ramekin and sprinkle evenly with salt, black pepper, and red pepper flakes.
Place ramekins into air fryer basket. Adjust the temperature to 350°F and set the timer for 15 minutes. Egg cups will be done when sausage is fully cooked to at least 145°F and the egg is firm. Serve warm.

Nutrition Facts (per serving):
Calories: 230 | Carbohydrates: 1g | Protein: 14g | Fat: 19g | Fiber: 0g

 Servings: 4 20 minutes

355 Thai Roasted Beef

Ingredients:
1 lb beef steak, sliced
Salt and black pepper to taste
2 tbsp soy sauce
1 tbsp fresh ginger, minced
2 chilies, seeded and chopped
2 garlic cloves, chopped
1 tsp brown sugar
Juice of 1 lime
2 tbsp mirin
1 tbsp fresh cilantro, chopped
1 tbsp fresh basil, chopped
2 tbsp sesame oil
2 tbsp fish sauce

Directions:
Place all ingredients, except for the beef, in a blender and process until smooth. Transfer to a zipper bag and add in the beef. Seal the bag, shake to combine, and refrigerate for 1 hour. Preheat the air fryer to 350 F. Place the marinated beef in the greased frying basket and AirFry for 12-14 minutes. Let sit for a couple of minutes before serving.

Nutrition Facts (per serving):
Calories: 355 | Carbohydrates: 6g | Protein: 27g | Fat: 25g | Fiber: 1g

 Servings: 4 25 minutes

356 Tasty Kiev-Style Chicken

Ingredients:
1 lb chicken breasts
4 tbsp butter, softened
1 tbsp fresh dill, chopped
2 garlic cloves, minced
1 tbsp lemon juice
Salt and black pepper to taste
1 cup plain flour
2 eggs, beaten in a bowl
1 cup panko breadcrumbs

Directions:
Preheat the air fryer to 390 F. In a bowl, mix butter, dill, garlic, lemon juice, salt, and pepper until a smooth paste is formed. Using a sharp knife, make a deep cut of each breast to create a large pocket.
Stuff with the butter mixture and secure with toothpicks. Coat the breasts in the flour, then dip in the eggs, and finally in the breadcrumbs. Place the chicken in the greased frying basket and Bake for 10 minutes. Turn over and cook for 5-7 more minutes or until golden. Serve sliced.

Nutrition Facts (per serving):
Calories: 460 | Carbohydrates: 28g | Protein: 36g | Fat: 22g | Fiber: 1g

Servings: 4 | 8 Minutes

357 Bell Peppers Cups

Ingredients:
- 8 mini red bell peppers, tops and seeds removed
- 1 teaspoon fresh parsley, chopped
- ¾ cup feta cheese, crumbled
- ½ tablespoon olive oil
- Freshly ground black pepper, to taste

Directions:
Preheat the Air fryer to 390°F and grease an Air fryer basket.
Mix feta cheese, parsley, olive oil and black pepper in a bowl.
Stuff the bell peppers with feta cheese mixture and arrange in the Air fryer basket.
Cook for about 8 minutes and dish out to serve hot.

Nutrition Facts (per serving):
Calories: 123 | Carbohydrates: 3.8g | Protein: 4.9g | Fat: 9.6g | Fiber: 1.0g

---

Servings: 4 | 15 Minutes

358 Cheesy Bell Pepper Eggs

Ingredients:
- 4 medium green bell peppers, tops removed, seeded
- 1 tablespoon coconut oil
- 3 ounces chopped cooked no-sugar-added ham
- ¼ cup peeled and chopped white onion
- 4 large eggs
- ½ teaspoon salt
- 1 cup shredded mild Cheddar cheese

Directions:
Place peppers upright into ungreased air fryer basket. Drizzle each pepper with coconut oil. Divide ham and onion evenly among peppers.
In a medium bowl, whisk eggs, then sprinkle with salt. Pour mixture evenly into each pepper. Top each with ¼ cup Cheddar.
Adjust the temperature to 320°F and set the timer for 15 minutes. Peppers will be tender and eggs will be firm when done.
Serve warm on four medium plates.

Nutrition Facts (per serving):
Calories: 255 | Carbohydrates: 5g | Protein: 19g | Fat: 18g | Fiber: 1g

---

Servings: 4 | 20 minutes

359 Bloody Mary Beef Steak with Avocado

Ingredients:
- 1 ½ lb flank steaks
- 2 tbsp tomato juice
- 1 lemon, juiced and zested
- 2 tbsp vodka
- 1 tsp Worcestershire sauce
- 1 tsp hot sauce
- Celery salt and black pepper to taste

Directions:
Combine tomato juice, vodka, Worcestershire sauce, hot sauce, lemon juice and zest, celery salt, and black pepper in a bowl. Add in the flank steaks and toss to coat. Marinate for 30 minutes.
Preheat the air fryer to 360 F. Remove the steaks from the marinade and place them in the greased frying basket. Bake for 14-16 minutes, turning once halfway through. Let them cool slightly before serving.

Nutrition Facts (per serving):
Calories: 330 | Carbohydrates: 1g | Protein: 30g | Fat: 22g | Fiber: 0g

---

Servings: 2 | 25 minutes

360 Rosemary & Oyster Chicken Breasts

Ingredients:
- 2 chicken breasts
- 1 tbsp ginger paste
- 1 tbsp soy sauce
- 1 tbsp olive oil
- 1 tbsp oyster sauce
- 2 fresh rosemary sprigs, chopped
- 1 tbsp brown sugar
- 2 lemon wedges

Directions:
Place the ginger paste, soy sauce, and olive oil in a mixing bowl and stir well. Coat in the chicken breasts. Cover the bowl with a lid and refrigerate for 30 minutes.
Preheat the air fryer to 370 F. Transfer the marinated chicken to a baking dish and Bake in the fryer for 6 minutes. Mix oyster sauce, rosemary, and brown sugar in a bowl. Pour the sauce over the chicken. Return to the air fryer and Bake for 8-10 minutes. Remove the rosemary and serve with lemon wedges.

Nutrition Facts (per serving):
Calories: 320 | Carbohydrates: 6g | Protein: 35g | Fat: 12g | Fiber: 0g

361 Healthy Apple-licious Chips

Servings: 1 — 6 Minutes

Ingredients:
½ teaspoon ground cumin
1 apple, cored and sliced thinly
1 tablespoon sugar
A pinch of salt

Directions:
Place all ingredients in a bowl and toss to coat everything.
Put the grill pan accessory in the air fryer and place the sliced apples on the grill pan.
Close the air fryer and cook for 6 minutes at 390°F.

Nutrition Facts (per serving):
Calories: 118 | Carbohydrates: 30.1g | Protein: 0.3g | Fat: 0.2g | Fiber: 3.9g

362 Roasted Peanuts

Servings: 1 — 14 Minutes

Ingredients:
2½ cups raw peanuts
1 tablespoon olive oil
Salt, as required

Directions:
Set the temperature of Air Fryer to 320°F.
Add the peanuts in an Air Fryer basket in a single layer.
Air Fry for about 9 minutes, tossing twice.
Remove the peanuts from Air Fryer basket and transfer into a bowl.
Add the oil, and salt and toss to coat well.
Return the nuts mixture into Air Fryer basket.
Air Fry for about 5 minutes.
Once done, transfer the hot nuts in a glass or steel bowl and serve.

Nutrition Facts (per serving):
Calories: 205 | Carbohydrates: 6g | Protein: 9g | Fat: 18g | Fiber: 3g

363 Wiener Beef Schnitzel

Servings: 1 — 20 minutes

Ingredients:
1 (½ inch thick) top sirloin steak
1 egg, beaten
2 oz panko breadcrumbs
2 tbsp flour, sifted
Lemon slices
¼ tsp garlic powder
1 parsley butter slice
Salt and black pepper to taste

Directions:
Preheat the air fryer to 350 F. Combine the breadcrumbs, garlic, salt, and pepper in a bowl. Dredge the steak in the flour, then dip in the egg, and finally toss it into the crumbs mixture. Place in the greased frying basket and AirFry for 12 minutes, turning once. Top with parsley butter and lemon slices.

Nutrition Facts (per serving):
Calories: 610 | Carbohydrates: 18g | Protein: 42g | Fat: 40g | Fiber: 1g

364 Chicken Thighs with Herby Tomatoes

Servings: 2 — 25 minutes

Ingredients:
2 chicken thighs
2 ripe tomatoes, sliced
¼ tsp red pepper flakes
2 cloves garlic, minced
¼ tbsp dried tarragon
¼ tbsp olive oil
Salt and black pepper to taste

Directions:
Preheat the air fryer to 390 F. Add the tomatoes, red pepper flakes, garlic, tarragon, and olive oil to a bowl. Mix well. Season the chicken with salt and pepper and place the thighs in the greased frying basket. Bake for 8-10 minutes, flipping once. Top with the tomato mixture and Bake for 5 more minutes.

Nutrition Facts (per serving):
Calories: 280 | Carbohydrates: 6g | Protein: 30g | Fat: 14g | Fiber: 2g

Servings: 4 | 8 Minutes

365 Caprese Eggplant Stacks

Ingredients:
1 medium eggplant, cut into 4 (½") slices
½ teaspoon salt
¼ teaspoon ground black pepper
4 (¼") slices tomato
2 ounces fresh mozzarella cheese, cut into 4 slices
1 tablespoon olive oil
¼ cup fresh basil, sliced

Directions:
Preheat the air fryer to 320°F.
In a 6" round pan, place eggplant slices. Sprinkle with salt and pepper. Top each with a tomato slice, then a mozzarella slice, and drizzle with oil.
Place in the air fryer basket and cook 8 minutes until eggplant is tender and cheese is melted. Garnish with fresh basil to serve.

Nutrition Facts (per serving):
Calories: 132 | Carbohydrates: 6.1g | Protein: 4.8g | Fat: 9.8g | Fiber: 2.9g

---

Servings: 2 | 15 Minutes

366 Spinach Dip

Ingredients:
8 ounces full-fat cream cheese, softened
½ cup mayonnaise
2 teaspoons minced garlic
1 cup grated Parmesan cheese
1 package frozen chopped spinach, thawed and drained

Directions:
Preheat the air fryer to 320°F.
In a large bowl, mix cream cheese, mayonnaise, garlic, and Parmesan.
Fold in spinach. Scrape mixture into a 6" round baking dish and place in the air fryer basket.
Cook 15 minutes until mixture is bubbling and top begins to turn brown. Serve warm.

Nutrition Facts (per serving):
Calories: 510 | Carbohydrates: 5g | Protein: 13g | Fat: 48g | Fiber: 2g

---

Servings: 4 | 20 minutes

367 Sweet & Sour Lamb Strips

Ingredients:
1 cup cornflour
1 tsp garlic powder
1 tsp allspice
Salt and black pepper to taste
2 eggs
1 lb lean lamb, cut into strips
For the sauce
6 tbsp ketchup
½ lemon, juiced
1 tsp honey
2 tbsp soy sauce

Directions:
Preheat the air fryer to 350 F. In a bowl, whisk all the sauce ingredients with ½ cup of water until smooth; reserve. In another bowl, mix the garlic powder, cornflour, allspice, salt, and black pepper.
In a third bowl, beat the eggs with a pinch of salt. Coat the lamb in the cornflour mixture, then dip in the eggs, then again in the cornflour mixture. Spray with cooking spray and place in the frying basket. AirFry for 14-16 minutes, shaking once halfway through. Serve drizzled with the prepared sauce.

Nutrition Facts (per serving):
Calories: 460 | Carbohydrates: 27g | Protein: 32g | Fat: 23g | Fiber: 1g

---

Servings: 4 | 25 minutes

368 Chicken Thighs with Parmesan Crust

Ingredients:
½ cup Italian breadcrumbs
2 tbsp Parmesan cheese, grated
1 tbsp butter, melted
4 chicken thighs
½ cup marinara sauce
½ cup sharp cheddar cheese, shredded

Directions:
Preheat the air fryer to 380 F. In a bowl, mix the breadcrumbs with cheddar cheese. Brush the thighs with butter. Dip each thigh into the crumbs mixture. Arrange them in the greased frying basket.
AirFry for 6-7 minutes, flip them over, top with shredded Parmesan cheese, and cook for another 4-6 minutes until crispy. Serve immediately with marinara sauce on the side.

Nutrition Facts (per serving):
Calories: 480 | Carbohydrates: 16g | Protein: 35g | Fat: 28g | Fiber: 2g

369 Breadcrumbs Stuffed Mushrooms

Servings: 4 | 10 Minutes

Ingredients:
- 1½ spelt bread slices
- 1 tablespoon flat-leaf parsley, finely chopped
- 16 small button mushrooms, stemmed and gills removed
- 1½ tablespoons olive oil
- 1 garlic clove, crushed
- Salt and black pepper, to taste

Directions:
Preheat the Air fryer to 390°F and grease an Air fryer basket.
Put the bread slices in a food processor and pulse until fine crumbs form.
Transfer the crumbs into a bowl and stir in the olive oil, garlic, parsley, salt, and black pepper.
Stuff the breadcrumbs mixture in each mushroom cap and arrange the mushrooms in the Air fryer basket. Cook for about 10 minutes and dish out in a bowl to serve warm.

Nutrition Facts (per serving):
Calories: 112 | Carbohydrates: 10.2g | Protein: 3.1g | Fat: 6.6g | Fiber: 2.0g

370 Savory Ranch Chicken Bites

Servings: 6 | 15 Minutes

Ingredients:
- 2 boneless, skinless chicken breasts, cut into 1" cubes
- 1 tablespoon coconut oil
- ½ teaspoon salt
- ¼ teaspoon ground black pepper
- ⅓ cup ranch dressing
- ½ cup shredded Colby cheese
- 4 slices cooked sugar-free bacon, crumbled

Directions:
Drizzle chicken with coconut oil. Sprinkle with salt and pepper, and place into an ungreased 6" round nonstick baking dish.
Place dish into air fryer basket. Adjust the temperature to 370°F and set the timer for 10 minutes, stirring chicken halfway through cooking.
When timer beeps, drizzle ranch dressing over chicken and top with Colby and bacon. Adjust the temperature to 400°F and set the timer for 5 minutes. When done, chicken will be browned and have an internal temperature of at least 165°F. Serve warm.

Nutrition Facts (per serving):
Calories: 240 | Carbohydrates: 1g | Protein: 21g | Fat: 16g | Fiber: 0g

371 Crispy Breaded Chicken Bites

Servings: 4 | 20 minutes

Ingredients:
- 4 chicken breasts, sliced
- 1 cup panko breadcrumbs
- ¼ cup grated Parmesan cheese
- 2 large eggs
- ¼ cup flour
- ½ cup ketchup

Directions:
Preheat the fryer to 360 F. In a bowl, mix Parmesan with breadcrumbs. Whisk the eggs in another bowl, and pour the flour in a third bowl. Dip the chicken slices into the flour, then into the eggs, and finally roll them in the cheese crumbs; press lightly to coat. Put the chicken in the greased frying basket and spritz with cooking oil. Bake for 14-16 minutes, flipping once until crispy. Serve with ketchup.

Nutrition Facts (per serving):
Calories: 410 | Carbohydrates: 24g | Protein: 38g | Fat: 18g | Fiber: 1g

372 Classic Buttermilk Chicken Thighs

Servings: 4 | 25 minutes

Ingredients:
- 1½ lb chicken thighs
- ½ tsp cayenne pepper
- Salt and black pepper to taste
- 1 cup flour
- ½ tsp paprika
- ½ tsp baking powder
- 2 cups buttermilk

Directions:
Place the chicken thighs in a bowl. Stir in cayenne, salt, black pepper, and buttermilk. Refrigerate for 2 hours. Preheat the air fryer to 350 F. In another bowl, mix flour, paprika, salt, and baking powder. Dredge the chicken thighs in the flour and then place them in the greased frying basket. Bake them for 16-18 minutes, flipping once halfway through cooking. Serve hot.

Nutrition Facts (per serving):
Calories: 470 | Carbohydrates: 30g | Protein: 35g | Fat: 22g | Fiber: 1g

Servings: 2 | 10 Minutes

373 Sweet And Sour Brussel Sprouts

Ingredients:
2 cups Brussels sprouts, trimmed and halved lengthwise
1 tablespoon balsamic vinegar
1 tablespoon maple syrup
Salt, as required

Directions:
Preheat the Air fryer to 400°F and grease an Air fryer basket.
Mix all the ingredients in a bowl and toss to coat well. Arrange the Brussel sprouts in the Air fryer basket and cook for about 10 minutes, shaking once halfway through.
Dish out in a bowl and serve hot.

Nutrition Facts (per serving):
Calories: 104 | Carbohydrates: 15.2g | Protein: 3.4g | Fat: 3.2g | Fiber: 4.6g

Servings: 1 | 15 Minutes

374 Roasted Chickpeas

Ingredients:
1 15-ounce can chickpeas, drained
2 teaspoons curry powder
¼ teaspoon salt
1 tablespoon olive oil

Directions:
Drain chickpeas thoroughly and spread in a single layer on paper towels. Cover with another paper towel and press gently to remove extra moisture. Don't press too hard or you'll crush the chickpeas.
Mix curry powder and salt together.
Place chickpeas in a medium bowl and sprinkle with seasonings. Stir well to coat.
Add olive oil and stir again to distribute oil.
Cook at 390°F for 15 minutes, stopping to shake basket about halfway through cooking time.
Cool completely and store in airtight container.

Nutrition Facts (per serving):
Calories: 360 | Carbohydrates: 35g | Protein: 12g | Fat: 18g | Fiber: 10g

Servings: 6 | 20 minutes

375 Spiced Chicken Tacos

Ingredients:
1 tbsp buffalo sauce
2 cups shredded cooked chicken
6 oz cream cheese, softened
2 oz sharp cheese, grated
1 tbsp olive oil
1 tsp ground cumin
½ tsp smoked paprika
12 flour tortillas

Directions:
Preheat air fryer to 360 F. Stir the cheeses and Buffalo sauce in a bowl, then add the chicken and stir some more. On a clean workspace, lay the tortillas and spoon 2-3 tablespoons of the chicken mixture at the center of each tortilla. Sprinkle with cumin and paprika. Roll them up and put them in the air fryer, seam side down. Spray each tortilla with olive oil and AirFry for 8-10 minutes or until golden and crisp.

Nutrition Facts (per serving):
Calories: 390 | Carbohydrates: 22g | Protein: 22g | Fat: 24g | Fiber: 1g

Servings: 4 | 25 minutes

376 Thai Chicken Satay

Ingredients:
1 lb chicken drumsticks
2 cloves garlic, minced
2 tbsp sesame oil
½ cup Thai peanut satay sauce
1 lime, zested and juiced
2 tbsp sesame seeds, toasted
4 scallions, chopped
1 red chili, sliced

Directions:
In a bowl, mix the satay sauce, sesame oil, garlic, lime zest, and lime juice. Add in the chicken and toss to coat. Place in the fridge for 2 hours to marinate. Preheat the air fryer to 380 F. Transfer the marinated chicken to the frying basket and AirFry for 18-20 minutes, flipping once halfway through. Garnish with sesame seeds, scallions, and red chili and serve.

Nutrition Facts (per serving):
Calories: 490 | Carbohydrates: 10g | Protein: 32g | Fat: 34g | Fiber: 2g

Servings: 4 8 Minutes

377 Strawberry Toast

Ingredients:
4 slices bread, ½-inch thick
butter-flavored cooking spray
1 cup sliced strawberries
1 teaspoon sugar

Directions:
Spray one side of each bread slice with butter-flavored cooking spray. Lay slices sprayed side down. Divide the strawberries among the bread slices. Sprinkle evenly with the sugar and place in the air fryer basket in a single layer.
Cook at 390°F for 8minutes. The bottom should look brown and crisp and the top should look glazed.

Nutrition Facts (per serving):
Calories: 79 | Carbohydrates: 16g | Protein: 2g | Fat: 1g | Fiber: 2g

Servings: 6 15 Minutes

378 Beef Taco-stuffed Meatballs

Ingredients:
4 ounces Colby jack cheese cut into ½" cubes
1 pound 80/20 ground beef
1 packet taco seasoning
½ cup bread crumbs

Directions:
Preheat the air fryer to 350°F. Chill cheese in the freezer 15 minutes.
In a large bowl, mix beef, taco seasoning, and bread crumbs. Roll mixture into balls, about 2" each, to make eighteen meatballs.
Remove cheese from freezer. Place one cube into each meatball by pressing gently into the center and shaping meat around cheese. Roll into a ball.
Spritz meatballs with cooking spray and place in the air fryer basket. Cook 15 minutes, shaking the basket three times during cooking, until meatballs are brown and internal temperature has reached at least 165°F. Serve warm.

Nutrition Facts (per serving):
Calories: 290 | Carbohydrates: 6g | Protein: 18g | Fat: 22g | Fiber: 0g

 Servings: 2   20 minutes

379 Rice Krispies Chicken Goujons

Ingredients:
2 chicken breasts, cut into strips
Salt and black pepper to taste
½ tsp dried tarragon
½ cup rice Krispies
1 egg, beaten
½ cup plain flour
1 tbsp butter, melted

Directions:
Preheat the air fryer to 390 F. Line the frying basket with baking paper. Season the chicken with salt and pepper. Roll the strips in flour, then dip in egg, and finally coat in the rice Krispies. Place the strips in the fryer, drizzle with butter, and AirFry for 12-14 minutes, shaking once. Top with tarragon to serve.

Nutrition Facts (per serving):
Calories: 360 | Carbohydrates: 22g | Protein: 36g | Fat: 14g | Fiber: 1g

 Servings: 4   25 minutes

380 Chicken Asian Lollipop

Ingredients:
1 lb mini chicken drumsticks
½ tbsp soy sauce
1 tbsp lime juice
Salt and black pepper to taste
1 tbsp cornstarch
1 garlic clove, minced
½ tbsp chili powder
½ tbsp garlic-ginger paste
1 tbsp plain vinegar
1 egg, beaten
1 tbsp flour
1 tbsp maple syrup

Directions:
Mix garlic-ginger paste, chili powder, maple syrup, soy sauce, vinegar, egg, garlic, salt, and black pepper in a bowl. Add the chicken and toss to coat. Mix cornstarch and flour in another bowl. Preheat the air fryer to 350 F. Roll the drumsticks into the flour mixture and AirFry in the greased frying basket for 5-7 minutes. Turn and cook for 5-7 more minutes or until golden. Serve drizzled with lime juice.

Nutrition Facts (per serving):
Calories: 380 | Carbohydrates: 12g | Protein: 30g | Fat: 20g | Fiber: 0g

Servings: 4 | 6 Minutes

381 Baked Eggs

Ingredients:
- 4 large eggs
- ⅛ teaspoon black pepper
- ⅛ teaspoon salt

Directions:
Preheat the air fryer to 330°F. Place 4 silicone muffin liners into the air fryer basket.
Crack 1 egg at a time into each silicone muffin liner. Sprinkle with black pepper and salt.
Bake for 6 minutes. Remove and let cool 2 minutes prior to serving.

Nutrition Facts (per serving):
Calories: 70 | Carbohydrates: 0g | Protein: 6g | Fat: 5g | Fiber: 0g

---

Servings: 4 | 15 Minutes

382 Wrapped Smokies In Bacon

Ingredients:
- 8 small smokies
- 8 bacon strips, sliced
- Salt and pepper to taste

Directions:
Preheat air fryer to 350°F. Wrap the bacon slices around smokies. Arrange the rolls, seam side down, on the greased frying basket. Sprinkle with salt and pepper and Air Fry for 5-8 minutes, turning once until the bacon is crisp and juicy around them. Serve and enjoy!

Nutrition Facts (per serving):
Calories: 290 | Carbohydrates: 1g | Protein: 10g | Fat: 26g | Fiber: 0g

---

Servings: 4 | 20 minutes

383 Crispy Chicken Tenders with Hot Aioli

Ingredients:
- 1 lb chicken breasts, cut into strips
- 4 tbsp olive oil
- 1 cup breadcrumbs
- Salt and black pepper to taste
- ½ tbsp garlic powder
- ½ tsp cayenne pepper
- ½ cup mayonnaise
- 2 tbsp lemon juice
- ½ tbsp ground chili

Directions:
Preheat the air fryer to 390 F. Mix the crumbs, salt, black pepper, garlic powder, and cayenne pepper in a bowl. Brush the strips with some olive oil. Coat them in the crumbs mixture and arrange them in the greased frying basket in an even layer. AirFry for 12-14 minutes, turning once halfway through. To prepare the hot aioli: add the mayo, lemon juice and ground chili in a small bowl and whisk to combine. Serve with the chicken tenders and enjoy!

Nutrition Facts (per serving):
Calories: 480 | Carbohydrates: 16g | Protein: 34g | Fat: 32g | Fiber: 1g

---

Servings: 4 | 25 minutes

384 Chipotle Buttered Turkey

Ingredients:
- 1 lb turkey breast, sliced
- 2 cups panko breadcrumbs
- Salt and chipotle powder to taste
- 1 stick butter, melted

Directions:
In a bowl, combine panko breadcrumbs and chipotle chili pepper. Sprinkle turkey with salt and brush with some butter. Coat the turkey with the crumbs mixture. Transfer to the frying basket and grease with some butter. AirFry for 10 minutes at 390 F. Flip the slices, drizzle with the remaining butter, and Bake for 4-7 more minutes, until nice and crispy. Serve and enjoy!

Nutrition Facts (per serving):
Calories: 438 | Carbohydrates: 18g | Protein: 31g | Fat: 26g | Fiber: 0.5g

385 Sweet Potato-cinnamon Toast

Servings: 6 | 8 Minutes

Ingredients:
1 small sweet potato, cut into ⅜-inch slices
oil for misting
ground cinnamon

Directions:
Preheat air fryer to 390°F.
Spray both sides of sweet potato slices with oil.
Sprinkle both sides with cinnamon to taste.
Place potato slices in air fryer basket in a single layer.
Cook for 4 minutes, turn, and cook for 4 more minutes or until potato slices are barely fork tender.

Nutrition Facts (per serving):
Calories: 21 | Carbohydrates: 5g | Protein: 0g | Fat: 0g | Fiber: 1g

386 Buffalo Cauliflower Wings

Servings: 4 | 14 Minutes

Ingredients:
1 cauliflower head, cut into florets
1 tbsp butter, melted
1/2 cup buffalo sauce
Pepper
Salt

Directions:
Spray air fryer basket with cooking spray.
In a bowl, mix together buffalo sauce, butter, pepper, and salt.
Add cauliflower florets into the air fryer basket and cook at 400 °F for 7 minutes.
Transfer cauliflower florets into the buffalo sauce mixture and toss well.
Again, add cauliflower florets into the air fryer basket and cook for 7 minutes more at 400 °F.
Serve and enjoy.

Nutrition Facts (per serving):
Calories: 90 | Carbohydrates: 7g | Protein: 2g | Fat: 6g | Fiber: 3g

387 Chicken Fillets with Sweet Chili Adobo

Servings: 4 | 20 minutes

Ingredients:
2 chicken breasts, halved
Salt and black pepper to taste
¼ cup sweet chili sauce
1 tsp turmeric

Directions:
Preheat the air fryer to 390 F. In a bowl, place the sweet chili sauce, salt, black pepper, and turmeric; mix well. Lightly brush the chicken with the mixture and place them in the greased frying basket. AirFry for 12-14 minutes, turning once halfway through. Serve with a side of steamed greens if desired.

Nutrition Facts (per serving):
Calories: 210 | Carbohydrates: 7g | Protein: 28g | Fat: 7g | Fiber: 0g

388 Crab Fritters with Sweet Chili Sauce

Servings: 4 | 25 minutes

Ingredients:
1 lb jumbo crabmeat
1 lime, zested and juiced
1 tsp ginger paste
1 tsp garlic puree
1 tbsp fresh cilantro, chopped
1 red chili, roughly chopped
1 egg
¼ cup panko breadcrumbs
1 tsp soy sauce sauce
3 tbsp sweet chili sauce

Directions:
Preheat the air fryer to 400 F. In a bowl, mix crabmeat, lime zest, egg, ginger paste, and garlic puree. Form small cakes out of the mixture and dredge them in the breadcrumbs. Place in the greased frying basket and AirFry for 14-16 minutes, shaking once until golden brown. In a small bowl, mix the sweet chili sauce with lime juice and soy sauce. Serve the fritters topped with cilantro and the chili sauce.

Nutrition Facts (per serving):
Calories: 167 | Carbohydrates: 13g | Protein: 23g | Fat: 2.6g | Fiber: 0.4g

Servings: 1　　🕐　7 Minutes

389 Hole In One

Ingredients:
1 slice bread
1 teaspoon soft butter
1 egg
salt and pepper
1 tablespoon shredded Cheddar cheese
2 teaspoons diced ham

Directions:
Place a 6 x 6-inch baking dish inside air fryer basket and preheat fryer to 330°F.
Using a 2½-inch-diameter biscuit cutter, cut a hole in center of bread slice.
Spread softened butter on both sides of bread.
Lay bread slice in baking dish and crack egg into the hole. Sprinkle egg with salt and pepper to taste. Cook for 5 minutes.
Turn toast over and top it with shredded cheese and diced ham.
Cook for 2 more minutes or until yolk is done to your liking.

Nutrition Facts (per serving):
Calories: 207 | Carbohydrates: 7g | Protein: 11g | Fat: 15g | Fiber: 0g

 Servings: 4　　🕐　15 Minutes

390 Asian Five-spice Wings

Ingredients:
2 pounds chicken wings
½ cup Asian-style salad dressing
2 tablespoons Chinese five-spice powder

Directions:
Cut off wing tips and discard or freeze for stock. Cut remaining wing pieces in two at the joint.
Place wing pieces in a large sealable plastic bag. Pour in the Asian dressing, seal bag, and massage the marinade into the wings until well coated. Refrigerate for at least an hour.
Remove wings from bag, drain off excess marinade, and place wings in air fryer basket.
Cook at 360°F for 15 minutes or until juices run clear. About halfway through cooking time, shake the basket or stir wings for more even cooking.
Transfer cooked wings to plate in a single layer. Sprinkle half of the Chinese five-spice powder on the wings, turn, and sprinkle other side with remaining seasoning.

Nutrition Facts (per serving):
Calories: 320 | Carbohydrates: 5g | Protein: 26g | Fat: 22g | Fiber: 1g

 Servings: 4　　🕐　20 minutes

391 Greek Chicken Gyros

Ingredients:
2 chicken breasts, cut into strips
Salt and black pepper to taste
1 cup flour
1 egg, beaten
½ cup breadcrumbs
4 flatbreads
2 cups white cabbage, shredded
3 tbsp Greek yogurt dressing

Directions:
Preheat the air fryer to 380 F. Season the chicken with salt and black pepper. Pour the breadcrumbs in one bowl, the flour in another, and the egg in a third bowl. Dredge the strips in flour, then in the egg, and finally in the crumbs. Spray with cooking oil and transfer to the fryer. AirFry for 12-14 minutes, flipping once halfway through. Serve the "pitas" filled with the strips, cabbage, and yogurt dressing.

Nutrition Facts (per serving):
Calories: 380 | Carbohydrates: 38g | Protein: 28g | Fat: 10g | Fiber: 4g

 Servings: 4　　🕐　25 minutes

392 Cod Cornflake Nuggets with Avocado Dip

Ingredients:
1 ¼ lb cod fillets, cut into 4 chunks each
½ cup flour
2 eggs, beaten
1 cup cornflakes
1 tbsp olive oil
Salt and black pepper to taste
1 avocado, chopped
1 lime, juiced

Directions:
Mash the avocado with a fork in a small bowl. Stir in the lime juice and salt and set aside. Pour the olive oil and cornflakes in a food processor and process until crumbed.
Season the fish with salt and pepper. Preheat the air fryer to 350 F. Place flour, eggs and cornflakes in 3 separate bowls. Coat the fish in flour, dip in the eggs, then coat in the cornflakes. AirFry in the greased frying basket for 14-16 minutes, shaking once or twice, until golden. Serve with the avocado dip.

Nutrition Facts (per serving):
Calories: 333 | Carbohydrates: 20.8g | Protein: 34.5g | Fat: 12.9g | Fiber: 2.9g

Servings: 2 — 10 Minutes

393 Pizza Eggs

Ingredients:
1 cup shredded mozzarella cheese
7 slices pepperoni, chopped
1 large egg, whisked
¼ teaspoon dried oregano
¼ teaspoon dried parsley
¼ teaspoon garlic powder
¼ teaspoon salt

Directions:
Place mozzarella in a single layer on the bottom of an ungreased 6" round nonstick baking dish. Scatter pepperoni over cheese, then pour egg evenly around baking dish.
Sprinkle with remaining ingredients and place into air fryer basket. Adjust the temperature to 330°F and set the timer for 10 minutes. When cheese is brown and egg is set, dish will be done.
Let cool in dish 5 minutes before serving.

Nutrition Facts (per serving):
Calories: 248 | Carbohydrates: 2g | Protein: 18g | Fat: 19g | Fiber: 0g

---

Servings: 4 — 12 Minutes

394 Bacon-wrapped Jalapeño Poppers

Ingredients:
3 ounces full-fat cream cheese
½ cup shredded sharp Cheddar cheese
¼ teaspoon garlic powder
6 jalapeño peppers, trimmed and halved lengthwise, seeded and membranes removed
12 slices bacon

Directions:
Preheat the air fryer to 400°F.
In a large microwave-safe bowl, place cream cheese, Cheddar, and garlic powder. Microwave 20 seconds until softened and stir. Spoon cheese mixture into hollow jalapeño halves.
Wrap a bacon slice around each jalapeño half, completely covering pepper.
Place in the air fryer basket and cook 12 minutes, turning halfway through cooking time. Serve warm.

Nutrition Facts (per serving):
Calories: 275 | Carbohydrates: 3g | Protein: 10g | Fat: 25g | Fiber: <1g

---

Servings: 4 — 20 minutes

395 Swiss-Style Breaded Chicken

Ingredients:
½ cup seasoned breadcrumbs
¼ cup Gruyere cheese, grated
1 lb chicken breasts
½ cup flour
2 eggs, beaten
Salt and black pepper to taste
4 lemon slices

Directions:
Preheat the air fryer to 370 F. Spray the frying basket with cooking spray.
Mix the breadcrumbs with Gruyere cheese in a bowl, beat the eggs in another bowl, and pour the flour into a third bowl. Toss the chicken in the flour, then in the eggs, and finally in the breadcrumbs mixture.
Place in the frying basket and AirFry for 12-14 minutes. Turn the chicken over at the 6-minute mark. Once golden brown, remove to a plate and serve topped with lemon slices.

Nutrition Facts (per serving):
Calories: 400 | Carbohydrates: 20g | Protein: 38g | Fat: 18g | Fiber: 1g

---

Servings: 2 — 25 minutes

396 Gourmet Black Cod with Fennel & Pecans

Ingredients:
2 black cod fillets
Salt and black pepper to taste
1 small fennel bulb, sliced
½ cup pecans
2 tsp white balsamic vinegar
2 tbsp olive oil

Directions:
Preheat the air fryer to 400 F. Season the fillets with salt and pepper and drizzle with some olive oil. Place in them the frying basket and AirFry for 10-12 minutes, flipping once, or until golden brown.
Meanwhile, warm the remaining olive oil in a skillet over medium heat. Stir-fry the fennel for 5 minutes. Add in the pecans and cook for 3-4 minutes until toasted. Drizzle with the balsamic vinegar and season with salt and pepper. Stir well and remove from heat. Pour the mixture over the black cod and serve.

Nutrition Facts (per serving):
Calories: 582 | Carbohydrates: 10g | Protein: 22.5g | Fat: 54.5g | Fiber: 5.5g

397 Ham And Egg Toast Cups

Servings: 2 — 5 Minutes

Ingredients:
- 2 eggs
- 2 slices of ham
- 2 tablespoons butter
- Cheddar cheese, for topping
- Salt, to taste
- Black pepper, to taste

Directions:
Preheat the Air fryer to 400°F and grease both ramekins with melted butter.
Place each ham slice in the greased ramekins and crack each egg over ham slices.
Sprinkle with salt, black pepper and cheddar cheese and transfer into the Air fryer basket.
Cook for about 5 minutes and remove the ramekins from the basket.
Serve warm.

Nutrition Facts (per serving):
Calories: 245 | Carbohydrates: 1g | Protein: 13g | Fat: 21g | Fiber: 0g

398 Bacon-y Cauliflower Skewers

Servings: 4 — 12 Minutes

Ingredients:
- 4 slices sugar-free bacon, cut into thirds
- ¼ medium yellow onion, peeled and cut into 1" pieces
- 4 ounces cauliflower florets
- 1½ tablespoons olive oil
- ¼ teaspoon salt
- ¼ teaspoon garlic powder

Directions:
Place 1 piece bacon and 2 pieces onion on a 6" skewer. Add a second piece bacon, and 2 cauliflower florets, followed by another piece of bacon onto skewer. Repeat with remaining ingredients and three additional skewers to make four total skewers. Drizzle skewers with olive oil, then sprinkle with salt and garlic powder. Place skewers into ungreased air fryer basket. Adjust the temperature to 375°F and set the timer for 12 minutes, turning the skewers halfway through cooking. When done, vegetables will be tender and bacon will be crispy. Serve warm.

Nutrition Facts (per serving):
Calories: 120 | Carbohydrates: 3g | Protein: 3g | Fat: 10g | Fiber: 1g

399 Chicken Breasts with Avocado-Mango Salsa

Servings: 2 — 20 minutes

Ingredients:
- ½ lb chicken breasts, sliced
- 2 tbsp olive oil
- ½ tsp cayenne pepper powder
- Salt and black pepper to taste
- 1 mango, chopped
- 1 avocado, chopped
- 1 red pepper, chopped
- 1 tbsp balsamic vinegar

Directions:
In a bowl, mix the olive oil, cayenne pepper, salt, and black pepper. Add in the breasts, toss to coat, and marinate for 1 hour. Preheat the air fryer to 360 F. Place the chicken in the frying basket and AirFry for 12-14 minutes, flipping once. Meanwhile, mix the avocado, mango, red pepper, balsamic vinegar, and salt in a large bowl. Spoon the salsa over the chicken slices and serve.

Nutrition Facts (per serving):
Calories: 520 | Carbohydrates: 20g | Protein: 30g | Fat: 35g | Fiber: 8g

400 Pistachio-Crusted Salmon Fillets

Servings: 2 — 25 minutes

Ingredients:
- 2 salmon fillets
- 1 tsp yellow mustard
- 4 tbsp pistachios, chopped
- Salt and black pepper to taste
- 1 tsp garlic powder
- 2 tsp lemon juice
- 2 tbsp Parmesan cheese, grated
- 1 tsp olive oil

Directions:
Preheat the air fryer to 350 F. Whisk together the mustard, olive oil, lemon juice, salt, black pepper, and garlic powder in a bowl. Rub the mustard mixture evenly onto the salmon fillets.
Lay the fillets on the greased frying basket, skin side down and spread the pistachios and Parmesan cheese all over; press down gently to make a crust. Bake the salmon for 12-15 minutes until golden.

Nutrition Facts (per serving):
Calories: 364 | Carbohydrates: 6.4g | Protein: 30.3g | Fat: 24.9g | Fiber: 1.7g

Servings: 4 — 8 Minutes

401 Zucchini And Spring Onions Cakes

Ingredients:
8 ounces zucchinis, chopped
2 spring onions, chopped
2 eggs, whisked
Salt and black pepper to the taste
¼ teaspoon sweet paprika, chopped
Cooking spray

Directions:
In a bowl, mix all the ingredients except the cooking spray, stir well and shape medium fritters out of this mix. Put the basket in the Air Fryer, add the fritters inside, grease them with cooking spray and cook at 400ºF for 8 minutes. Divide the fritters between plates and serve for breakfast.

Nutrition Facts (per serving):
Calories: 49 | Carbohydrates: 2g | Protein: 4g | Fat: 3g | Fiber: 1g

---

Servings: 3 — 12 Minutes

402 Halloumi Fries

Ingredients:
1½ tablespoons Olive oil
1½ teaspoons Minced garlic
⅛ teaspoon Dried oregano
⅛ teaspoon Dried thyme
⅛ teaspoon Table salt
⅛ teaspoon Ground black pepper
¾ pound Halloumi

Directions:
Preheat the air fryer to 400ºF.
Whisk the oil, garlic, oregano, thyme, salt, and pepper in a medium bowl.
Lay the piece of halloumi flat on a cutting board. Slice it widthwise into ½-inch-thick sticks. Cut each stick lengthwise into ½-inch-thick batons.
Put these batons into the olive oil mixture. Toss gently but well to coat.
Place the batons in the basket in a single layer. Air-fry undisturbed for 12 minutes, or until lightly browned, particularly at the edges.
Dump the fries out onto a wire rack. They may need a little coaxing with a nonstick-safe spatula to come free. Cool for a couple of minutes before serving hot.

Nutrition Facts (per serving):
Calories: 320 | Carbohydrates: 2g | Protein: 20g | Fat: 26g | Fiber: 0g

---

 Servings: 2 20 minutes

403 French-Style Sweet Chicken Breasts

Ingredients:
1 tsp yellow mustard
1 tbsp apricot jam
2 garlic cloves, minced
Salt and black pepper to taste
1 lb chicken breasts
3 tbsp butter, melted

Directions:
Preheat the air fryer to 360 F. In a bowl, mix together mustard, butter, garlic, apricot jam, black pepper, and salt. Rub the chicken with the mixture and place them in the greased frying basket. AirFry for 10 minutes, flip, and cook them for 5-6 more minutes or until golden and crispy. Slice before serving.

Nutrition Facts (per serving):
Calories: 320 | Carbohydrates: 4g | Protein: 30g | Fat: 18g | Fiber: 0g

---

 Servings: 2 25 minutes

404 Salmon Fillets with Broccoli

Ingredients:
2 salmon fillets
2 tsp olive oil
Juice of 1 lime
1 tsp red chili flakes (optional)
Salt and black pepper to taste
5 oz broccoli florets, steamed

Directions:
In a bowl, add 1 tbsp of olive oil, lime juice, salt, and pepper and rub the mixture onto the fillets. Transfer to them to the frying basket. Drizzle the florets with the remaining olive oil and arrange them around the salmon. Bake in the preheated at 340 F air fryer for 14 minutes or until the salmon is fork-tender and crispy on top. Sprinkle the fillets with red chili flakes (optional) and serve with broccoli.

Nutrition Facts (per serving):
Calories: 299 | Carbohydrates: 6.5g | Protein: 27g | Fat: 18.5g | Fiber: 2g

Servings: 8 | 5 Minutes

405 Maple-bacon Doughnuts

Ingredients:
1 can refrigerated biscuit dough, separated
1 cup confectioners' sugar
¼ cup heavy cream
1 teaspoon maple extract
6 slices bacon, cooked and crumbled

Directions:
Preheat the air fryer to 350°F.
Place biscuits in the air fryer basket and cook 5 minutes, turning halfway through cooking time, until golden brown. Let cool 5 minutes.
In a medium bowl, whisk together confectioners' sugar, cream, and maple extract until smooth.
Dip top of each doughnut into glaze and set aside to set for 5 minutes. Top with crumbled bacon and serve immediately.

Nutrition Facts (per serving):
Calories: 287 | Carbohydrates: 30g | Protein: 5g | Fat: 17g | Fiber: 0g

---

Servings: 8 | 12 Minutes

406 Italian Dip

Ingredients:
8 oz cream cheese, softened
1 cup mozzarella cheese, shredded
½ cup roasted red peppers
⅓ cup basil pesto
¼ cup parmesan cheese, grated

Directions:
Add parmesan cheese and cream cheese into the food processor and process until smooth.
Transfer cheese mixture into the air fryer pan and spread evenly.
Pour basil pesto on top of cheese layer.
Sprinkle roasted pepper on top of basil pesto layer.
Sprinkle mozzarella cheese on top of pepper layer and place dish in air fryer basket.
Cook dip at 250°F for 12 minutes.
Serve and enjoy.

Nutrition Facts (per serving):
Calories: 210 | Carbohydrates: 3g | Protein: 6g | Fat: 20g | Fiber: <1g

---

 Servings: 4 20 minutes

407 French-Style Chicken Thighs

Ingredients:
1 tbsp herbs de Provence
1 lb bone-in, skinless chicken thighs
Salt and black pepper to taste
2 garlic cloves, minced
½ cup honey
¼ cup Dijon mustard
2 tbsp butter

Directions:
Preheat the air fryer to 390 F. In a bowl, mix herbs de Provence, salt, and pepper. Rub onto the chicken thighs. Transfer to the greased frying basket and Bake for 15 minutes, flipping once, until golden. Meanwhile, melt butter in a saucepan over medium heat. Stir in honey, mustard, and garlic; cook until reduced to a thick consistency, 3 minutes. Serve the chicken drizzled with the honey-mustard sauce.

Nutrition Facts (per serving):
Calories: 400 | Carbohydrates: 10g | Protein: 30g | Fat: 25g | Fiber: 0g

---

 Servings: 4 25 minutes

408 Smoked Trout Frittata

Ingredients:
2 tbsp olive oil
1 onion, sliced
1 egg, beaten
6 tbsp crème fraiche
½ tbsp horseradish sauce
1 cup smoked trout, diced
2 tbsp fresh dill, chopped

Directions:
Preheat the fryer to 350 F. Heat olive oil in a pan over medium heat and sauté the onion, 3 minutes. In a bowl, mix the egg with crème fraiche and horseradish sauce. Add the onion, dill, and trout; mix well. Pour the mixture into a greased baking dish and Bake inside the fryer for 14 minutes or until golden.

Nutrition Facts (per serving):
Calories: 217 | Carbohydrates: 3.85g | Protein: 8.8g | Fat: 18g | Fiber: 0.4g

Servings: 4 | 7 Minutes

409 Cinnamon Granola

Ingredients:
2 cups shelled pecans, chopped
1 cup unsweetened coconut flakes
1 cup slivered almonds
2 tablespoons granular erythritol
1 teaspoon ground cinnamon

Directions:
In a large bowl, mix all ingredients. Place mixture into an ungreased 6" round nonstick baking dish. Place dish into air fryer basket. Adjust the temperature to 320°F and set the timer for 7 minutes, stirring halfway through cooking.
Let cool in dish 10 minutes before serving. Store in airtight container at room temperature up to 5 days.

Nutrition Facts (per serving):
Calories: 535 | Carbohydrates: 10g | Protein: 9g | Fat: 52g | Fiber: 6g

---

Servings: 4 | 12 Minutes

410 Delicious Cheeseburgers

Ingredients:
1 lb ground beef
4 cheddar cheese slices
1/2 tsp Italian seasoning
Pepper
Salt
Cooking spray

Directions:
Spray air fryer basket with cooking spray.
In a bowl, mix together ground beef, Italian seasoning, pepper, and salt.
Make four equal shapes of patties from meat mixture and place into the air fryer basket.
Cook at 375°F for 5 minutes. Turn patties to another side and cook for 5 minutes more.
Place cheese slices on top of each patty and cook for 2 minutes more.
Serve and enjoy.

Nutrition Facts (per serving):
Calories: 330 | Carbohydrates: 1g | Protein: 23g | Fat: 26g | Fiber: 0g

---

 Servings: 4   20 minutes

411 Air Fried Chicken Bowl with Black Beans

Ingredients:
4 chicken breasts, cubed
1 can sweet corn
1 can black beans, rinsed and drained
1 cup red and green peppers, stripes, cooked
2 tbsp vegetable oil
1 tsp chili powder

Directions:
Preheat the air fryer to 380 F. Sprinkle the chicken with salt, black pepper, and a bit of oil. Place in the greased frying basket and AirFry for 14-16 minutes until golden and crispy. Meanwhile, in a deep skillet, pour the remaining oil and stir in chili powder, corn, peppers, and beans. Add a little bit of hot water and stir-fry for 3 minutes. Transfer the veggies to a serving platter and top with the fried chicken.

Nutrition Facts (per serving):
Calories: 400 | Carbohydrates: 32g | Protein: 35g | Fat: 14g | Fiber: 8g

---

Servings: 2 25 minutes

412 Baked Trout en Papillote with Herbs

Ingredients:
2 whole trouts, scaled and cleaned
¼ bulb fennel, sliced
½ brown onion, sliced
1 tbsp fresh parsley, chopped
1 tbsp fresh dill, chopped
1 tbsp olive oil
1 lemon, sliced
Garlic salt and black pepper to taste

Directions:
In a bowl, whisk the olive oil, brown onion, parsley, dill, fennel, garlic salt, and pepper.
Preheat the air fryer to 350 F. Open the cavity of the fish and fill with the spicy mixture. Wrap the fish completely in parchment paper and then in foil. Place the fish in the frying basket and Bake for 15 minutes. Remove the foil and paper. Top with lemon slices and serve warm.

Nutrition Facts (per serving):
Calories: 246 | Carbohydrates: 1.6g | Protein: 30.2g | Fat: 14.1g | Fiber: 0.2g

Servings: 6 — 10 Minutes

413 Sweet And Spicy Breakfast Sausage

Ingredients:

1 pound 84% lean ground pork
2 tablespoons brown sugar
1 teaspoon salt
½ teaspoon ground black pepper
½ teaspoon garlic powder
½ teaspoon dried fennel
½ teaspoon crushed red pepper flakes

Directions:

Preheat the air fryer to 400°F.
In a large bowl, mix all ingredients until well combined. Divide mixture into eight portions and form into patties.
Spritz patties with cooking spray and place in the air fryer basket. Cook 10 minutes until patties are brown and internal temperature reaches at least 145°F. Serve warm.

Nutrition Facts (per serving):
Calories: 247 | Carbohydrates: 2g | Protein: 18g | Fat: 18g | Fiber: 0g

 Servings: 4 — 15 Minutes

414 Stuffed Peppers

Ingredients:

½ pound cooked Italian sausage, drained
1 can diced tomatoes and green chilies, drained
2 teaspoons Italian seasoning
1 teaspoon salt
4 large green bell peppers, trimmed and seeded
1 cup shredded Italian-blend cheese
Cooking spray

Directions:

Preheat the air fryer to 320°F.
In a large bowl, mix sausage, tomatoes and chilies, Italian seasoning, and salt.
Spoon one-fourth of meat mixture into each pepper. Sprinkle ¼ cup cheese on top of each pepper. Spritz peppers with cooking spray and place in the air fryer basket.
Cook 15 minutes until peppers are tender and cheese is melted and bubbling. Serve warm.

Nutrition Facts (per serving):
Calories: 290 | Carbohydrates: 10g | Protein: 15g | Fat: 21g | Fiber: 3g

 Servings: 4 20 minutes

415 Creamy Onion Chicken

Ingredients:

4 chicken breasts, cubed
1½ cups onion soup mix
1 cup mushroom soup
½ cup heavy cream

Directions:

Preheat the fryer to 400 F. Warm the soup, soup mix, and the heavy cream in a pan over low heat for 1 minute. Pour over the chicken in a bowl, and let sit for 25 minutes. Remove the chicken to the greased frying basket and AirFry for 15 minutes, shaking once. Drizzle with the remaining sauce to serve.

Nutrition Facts (per serving):
Calories: 430 | Carbohydrates: 8g | Protein: 38g | Fat: 26g | Fiber: 1g

 Servings: 2 25 minutes

416 Golden Batter Fried Catfish Fillets

Ingredients:

4 catfish fillets, cut into strips
½ cup polenta
½ cup flour
¼ tsp cayenne pepper
1 tbsp fresh parsley, chopped
Salt and black pepper to taste
1 tsp onion powder
1 (7-oz) bottle club soda
1 lemon, sliced

Directions:

Preheat the fryer to 400 F. Sift the flour into a large bowl. Add in the onion powder, salt, black pepper, and cayenne pepper and stir to combine. Pour in the soda and whisk until a smooth batter is formed.
Lightly spray the fish with cooking spray. Dip the fish strips into the batter, then into the polenta. Put the fillets in the lightly greased frying basket and AirFry for 6-7 minutes. Flip or shake and cook further for 4-5 minutes or until brown and crispy. Garnish with parsley and lemon slices and serve.

Nutrition Facts (per serving):
Calories: 485 | Carbohydrates: 56.2g | Protein: 43.8g | Fat: 7.4g | Fiber: 3.5g

Servings: 4 | 7 Minutes

417 Seasoned Herbed Sourdough Croutons

Ingredients:
4 cups cubed sourdough bread, 1-inch cubes
1 tablespoon olive oil
1 teaspoon fresh thyme leaves
¼ – ½ teaspoon salt
freshly ground black pepper

Directions:
Combine all ingredients in a bowl and taste to make sure it is seasoned to your liking.
Preheat the air fryer to 400°F.
Toss the bread cubes into the air fryer and air-fry for 7 minutes, shaking the basket once or twice while they cook.
Serve warm or store in an airtight container.

Nutrition Facts (per serving):
Calories: 180 | Carbohydrates: 27g | Protein: 5g | Fat: 5g | Fiber: 2g

---

Servings: 4 | 15 Minutes

418 Bacon And Blue Cheese Burgers

Ingredients:
1 pound 70/30 ground beef
6 slices cooked sugar-free bacon, finely chopped
½ cup crumbled blue cheese
¼ cup peeled and chopped yellow onion
½ teaspoon salt
¼ teaspoon ground black pepper

Directions:
In a large bowl, mix ground beef, bacon, blue cheese, and onion. Separate into four sections and shape each section into a patty. Sprinkle with salt and pepper. Place patties into ungreased air fryer basket. Adjust the temperature to 350°F and set the timer for 15 minutes, turning patties halfway through cooking. Burgers will be done when internal temperature is at least 150°F for medium and 180°F for well. Serve warm.

Nutrition Facts (per serving):
Calories: 430 | Carbohydrates: 2g | Protein: 24g | Fat: 36g | Fiber: 0g

---

 Servings: 2 20 minutes

419 Cheesy Marinara Chicken

Ingredients:
2 chicken fillets, ½-inch thick
2 eggs, beaten
½ cup breadcrumbs
2 tbsp marinara sauce
2 tbsp Grana Padano cheese, grated
2 mozzarella cheese slices
Salt and black pepper to taste

Directions:
Season the chicken with salt and black pepper. Dip the fillets in the eggs, then in the crumbs, and arrange them in the greased frying basket. AirFry for 7-8 minutes at 400 F. Turn, top with marinara sauce, Grana Padano and mozzarella cheeses, and bake further for 5-6 more minutes. Serve warm.

Nutrition Facts (per serving):
Calories: 470 | Carbohydrates: 18g | Protein: 48g | Fat: 22g | Fiber: 2g

---

 Servings: 4 25 minutes

420 Ale-Battered Fish with Tartar Sauce

Ingredients:
4 lemon wedges
2 eggs
1 cup ale beer
1 cup flour
Salt and black pepper to taste
4 white fish fillets
½ cup light mayonnaise
½ cup Greek yogurt
2 dill pickles, chopped
1 tbsp capers
1 tbsp fresh dill, roughly chopped
Lemon wedges to serve

Directions:
Preheat the air fryer to 390 F. Beat the eggs in a bowl along with the ale beer, salt, and pepper. Dredge the fillets in the flour and shake off the excess. Dip them into the egg mixture and then in the flour again. Spray with cooking spray and place in the frying basket. AirFry for 10-12 minutes, turning once.
In a bowl, mix the mayonnaise, Greek yogurt, capers, salt, and dill pickles. Sprinkle the fish with a little bit of dill and serve with the sauce and some freshly cut lemon wedges on the side.

Nutrition Facts (per serving):
Calories: 375 | Carbohydrates: 29g | Protein: 31.1g | Fat: 13g | Fiber: 0.9g

Servings: 4 | 10 Minutes

421 Bagels

Ingredients:
1 cup self-rising flour
1 cup plain full-fat Greek yogurt
2 tablespoons granulated sugar
1 large egg, whisked

Directions:
Preheat the air fryer to 320°F.
In a large bowl, mix flour, yogurt, and sugar together until a ball of dough forms.
Turn dough out onto a lightly floured surface. Knead dough for 3 minutes, then form into a smooth ball. Cut dough into four sections. Roll each piece into an 8" rope, then shape into a circular bagel shape. Brush top and bottom of each bagel with egg.
Place in the air fryer basket and cook 10 minutes, turning halfway through cooking time to ensure even browning. Let cool 5 minutes before serving.

Nutrition Facts (per serving):
Calories: 170 | Carbohydrates: 23g | Protein: 8g | Fat: 4g | Fiber: 1g

---

Servings: 4 | 15 Minutes

422 Bacon Blue Cheese Burger

Ingredients:
1 pound ground sirloin
½ cup crumbled blue cheese
8 slices bacon, cooked and crumbled
1 teaspoon Worcestershire sauce
1 teaspoon salt
½ teaspoon ground black pepper
4 pretzel buns
Cooking spray

Directions:
Preheat the air fryer to 370°F.
In a large bowl, mix sirloin, cheese, bacon, and Worcestershire until well combined.
Form into four patties and sprinkle each side with salt and pepper. Spritz with cooking spray and place in the air fryer basket.
Cook 15 minutes, turning halfway through cooking time, until internal temperature reaches at least 160°F for well-done. Place on pretzel buns to serve.

Nutrition Facts (per serving):
Calories: 570 | Carbohydrates: 30g | Protein: 35g | Fat: 35g | Fiber: 1g

---

Servings: 2 | 20 minutes

423 Garlicky Chicken Cubes On A Green Bed

Ingredients:
1 chicken breast, cut into cubes
2 tbsp olive oil
1 garlic clove, minced
½ cup baby spinach
½ cup romaine lettuce, shredded
3 large kale leaves, chopped
1 tsp balsamic vinegar
Salt and black pepper to taste

Directions:
Preheat the air fryer to 390 F. In a bowl, add the chicken, 1 tbsp of olive oil, garlic, salt, and pepper; mix well. Pour the mixture into a baking dish that fits in the fryer. Bake for 14 minutes, shaking once. In a bowl, mix the greens, 1 tbsp of olive oil, and vinegar. Place the cooked chicken on top and serve.

Nutrition Facts (per serving):
Calories: 320 | Carbohydrates: 5g | Protein: 35g | Fat: 18g | Fiber: 3g

---

Servings: 4 | 25 minutes

424 Air Fried Tilapia Bites

Ingredients:
1 lb tilapia fillets, cut into chunks
½ cup cornflakes
1 cup flour
2 eggs, beaten
Salt to taste
Lemon wedges for serving

Directions:
Preheat the fryer to 390 F. Pour the flour, eggs, and cornflakes each into 3 different bowls. Salt the fish and dip first in the flour, then in the eggs, and finally in the cornflakes. Put in the greased frying basket and AirFry for 6 minutes. Shake or flip, and cook for 5 more minutes or until crispy. Serve with lemon.

Nutrition Facts (per serving):
Calories: 259 | Carbohydrates: 26.8g | Protein: 29.3g | Fat: 4.8g | Fiber: 0.8g

Servings: 4 — 10 Minutes

425 Spinach Spread

Ingredients:
2 tablespoons coconut cream
3 cups spinach leaves
2 tablespoons cilantro
2 tablespoons bacon, cooked and crumbled
Salt and black pepper to the taste

Directions:
In a pan that fits the air fryer, combine all the ingredients except the bacon, put the pan in the machine and cook at 360°F for 10 minutes. Transfer to a blender, pulse well, divide into bowls and serve with bacon sprinkled on top.

Nutrition Facts (per serving):
Calories: 60 | Carbohydrates: 2g | Protein: 2g | Fat: 5g | Fiber: 1g

---

Servings: 6 — 15 Minutes

426 Jumbo Italian Meatballs

Ingredients:
1 pound 80/20 ground beef
⅓ cup Italian bread crumbs
1 large egg
2 teaspoons Italian seasoning
¼ cup grated Parmesan cheese
1 teaspoon salt
½ teaspoon ground black pepper

Directions:
Preheat the air fryer to 400°F.
In a large bowl, mix all the ingredients. Roll mixture into balls, about 3" each, making twelve total. Place meatballs in the air fryer basket and cook 15 minutes, shaking the basket twice during cooking, until meatballs are brown on the outside and internal temperature reaches at least 160°F. Serve warm.

Nutrition Facts (per serving):
Calories: 270 | Carbohydrates: 3g | Protein: 18g | Fat: 20g | Fiber: 0g

---

 Servings: 4 20 minutes

427 Thyme Fried Chicken Legs

Ingredients:
4 chicken legs
½ lemon, juiced
1 tbsp garlic powder
½ tsp dried thyme
⅓ cup olive oil
Salt and black pepper to taste

Directions:
Preheat the fryer to 350 F. In a bowl, mix olive oil, thyme, garlic, lemon juice, salt, and pepper. Brush the chicken legs with most of the mixture and arrange them in the frying basket. Bake the legs in the air fryer for 8 minutes, flip the legs and brush again. Bake for 6 more minutes or until crispy. Serve.

Nutrition Facts (per serving):
Calories: 420 | Carbohydrates: 0g | Protein: 30g | Fat: 35g | Fiber: 0g

---

 Servings: 4 25 minutes

428 Sesame Halibut Fillets

Ingredients:
1 lb halibut fillets
4 biscuits, crumbled
3 tbsp flour
1 egg, beaten
Salt and black pepper to taste
¼ tsp dried rosemary
3 tbsp olive oil
2 tbsp sesame seeds

Directions:
Preheat the air fryer to 390 F.
In a bowl, combine flour, black pepper, and salt. In another bowl, combine sesame seeds, crumbled biscuits, olive oil, and rosemary. Dip the fish fillets into the flour mixture first, then into the beaten egg. Finally, coat them in the sesame/biscuit mixture. Arrange them on the greased frying basket and AirFry for 8 minutes. Flip the fillets and cook for 4-5 more minutes or until golden. Serve immediately.

Nutrition Facts (per serving):
Calories: 660 | Carbohydrates: 27g | Protein: 54.8g | Fat: 38.4g | Fiber: 1.3g

Servings: 2 | 9 Minutes

429 Easy Egg Bites

Ingredients:
- 2 large eggs
- ¼ cup full-fat cottage cheese
- ¼ cup shredded sharp Cheddar cheese
- ¼ teaspoon salt
- ⅛ teaspoon ground black pepper
- 6 tablespoons diced cooked ham

Directions:
Preheat the air fryer to 300°F. Spray six silicone muffin cups with cooking spray.
In a blender, place eggs, cottage cheese, Cheddar, salt, and pepper. Pulse five times until smooth and frothy. Place 1 tablespoon ham in the bottom of each prepared baking cup, then divide egg mixture among cups.
Place in the air fryer basket and cook 9 minutes until egg bites are firm in the center. Carefully remove cups from air fryer basket and cool 3 minutes before serving. Serve warm.

Nutrition Facts (per serving):
Calories: 235 | Carbohydrates: 2g | Protein: 20g | Fat: 16g | Fiber: 0g

---

Servings: 4 | 15 Minutes

430 Pesto Coated Rack Of Lamb

Ingredients:
- ½ bunch fresh mint
- 1 rack of lamb
- 1 garlic clove
- ¼ cup extra-virgin olive oil
- ½ tablespoon honey
- Salt and black pepper, to taste

Directions:
Preheat the Air fryer to 200°F and grease an Air fryer basket.
Put the mint, garlic, oil, honey, salt, and black pepper in a blender and pulse until smooth to make pesto.
Coat the rack of lamb with this pesto on both sides and arrange in the Air fryer basket.
Cook for about 15 minutes and cut the rack into individual chops to serve.

Nutrition Facts (per serving):
Calories: 450 | Carbohydrates: 2g | Protein: 28g | Fat: 36g | Fiber: <1g

---

Servings: 2 | 20 minutes

431 Thyme Turkey Nuggets

Ingredients:
- ½ lb ground turkey
- 1 egg, beaten
- 1 cup breadcrumbs
- ½ tsp dried thyme
- ½ tsp fresh parsley, chopped
- Salt and black pepper to taste

Directions:
Preheat the air fryer to 350 F. In a bowl, mix ground turkey, thyme, parsley, salt, and pepper. Shape the mixture into nuggets. Dip them in the egg, and then in the breadcrumbs. Place the nuggets in the frying basket, spray with cooking spray and AirFry for 12-14 minutes, flipping once. Serve with garlic mayo.

Nutrition Facts (per serving):
Calories: 426 | Carbohydrates: 40g | Protein: 31g | Fat: 14g | Fiber: 2g

---

Servings: 4 | 25 minutes

432 Peach Salsa & Beer Halibut Tacos

Ingredients:
- 4 corn tortillas
- 1 lb halibut fillets, sliced into strips
- 2 tbsp olive oil
- 1 ½ cups flour
- 1 (12-oz) can beer
- A pinch of salt
- 4 tbsp peach salsa
- 4 tsp fresh cilantro, chopped
- 1 tsp baking powder

Directions:
Preheat the fryer to 390 F. In a bowl, mix flour, baking powder, and salt. Pour in 1-2 oz of beer, enough to form a batter-like consistency. Save the rest of the beer to gulp with the tacos. Dip the fish strips into the beer batter. Arrange them in the greased frying basket and AirFry them for 8-10 minutes, shaking or flipping once. Spread the peach salsa on the tortillas. Serve topped with the strips and cilantro.

Nutrition Facts (per serving):
Calories: 443 | Carbohydrates: 51g | Protein: 29.9g | Fat: 10.5g | Fiber: 2.3g

Servings: 2 — 10 Minutes

433 Bacon & Hot Dogs Omelet

Ingredients:
4 eggs
1 bacon slice, chopped
2 hot dogs, chopped
2 small onions, chopped

Directions:
Set the temperature of Air Fryer to 320°F.
In an Air Fryer baking pan, crack the eggs and beat them well.
Now, add in the remaining ingredients and gently, stir to combine.
Air Fry for about 10 minutes.
Serve hot.

Nutrition Facts (per serving):
Calories: 320 | Carbohydrates: 4g | Protein: 20g | Fat: 25g | Fiber: 1g

Servings: 1 — 15 Minutes

434 Bjorn's Beef Steak

Ingredients:
1 steak, 1-inch thick
1 tbsp. olive oil
Black pepper to taste
Sea salt to taste

Directions:
Place the baking tray inside the Air Fryer and pre-heat for about 5 minutes at 390°F.
Brush or spray both sides of the steak with the oil. Season both sides with salt and pepper.
Take care when placing the steak in the baking tray and allow to cook for 3 minutes. Flip the meat over, and cook for an additional 3 minutes.
Take it out of the fryer and allow to sit for roughly 3 minutes before serving.

Nutrition Facts (per serving):
Calories: 500 | Carbohydrates: 0g | Protein: 46g | Fat: 34g | Fiber: 0g

Servings: 4 — 20 minutes

435 Old Bay Crab Sticks with Garlic Mayo

Ingredients:
1 lb crab sticks
1 tbsp old bay seasoning
⅓ cup panko breadcrumbs
2 eggs
½ cup mayonnaise
2 garlic cloves, minced
1 lime, juiced
1 cup flour

Directions:
Preheat the air fryer to 390 F. Beat the eggs in a bowl. In another bowl, mix the breadcrumbs with old bay seasoning. Pour the flour into a third bowl. Dip the sticks in the flour, then in the eggs, and finally in the breadcrumbs. Spray with cooking spray and AirFry for 12-14 minutes, flipping once, until golden. Mix the mayonnaise with garlic and lime juice. Serve as a dip along with crab sticks.

Nutrition Facts (per serving):
Calories: 567 | Carbohydrates: 48g | Protein: 17g | Fat: 31g | Fiber: 1g

Servings: 4 — 25 minutes

436 Brussels Sprouts with Garlic Aioli

Ingredients:
3 garlic cloves, minced
1 lb Brussels sprouts, trimmed and halved
Salt and black pepper to taste
2 tbsp olive oil
2 tsp lemon juice
¾ cup mayonnaise

Directions:
Place a pot with water over medium heat; bring to a boil. Blanch in the sprouts for 3 minutes; drain. Preheat the air fryer to 350 F. Drizzle the Brussels sprouts with olive oil and season to taste. Pour them into the frying basket and AirFry for 5 minutes, shaking once. In a bowl, whisk the mayonnaise, garlic, lemon juice, salt and black pepper to taste, to make aioli. Serve the sprouts with aioli.

Nutrition Facts (per serving):
Calories: 260 | Carbohydrates: 8g | Protein: 3g | Fat: 24g | Fiber: 3g

Servings: 6 | 8 Minutes

437 Peppered Maple Bacon Knots

Ingredients:
1 pound maple smoked center-cut bacon
¼ cup maple syrup
¼ cup brown sugar
coarsely cracked black peppercorns

Directions:
Tie each bacon strip in a loose knot and place them on a baking sheet.
Combine the maple syrup and brown sugar in a bowl. Brush each knot generously with this mixture and sprinkle with coarsely cracked black pepper.
Preheat the air fryer to 390°F.
Air-fry the bacon knots in batches. Place one layer of knots in the air fryer basket and air-fry for 5 minutes. Turn the bacon knots over and air-fry for an additional 3 minutes.
Serve warm.

Nutrition Facts (per serving):
Calories: 340 | Carbohydrates: 9g | Protein: 11g | Fat: 28g | Fiber: 0g

---

Servings: 4 | 12 Minutes

438 Bacon And Cheese-stuffed Pork Chops

Ingredients:
½ ounce plain pork rinds, finely crushed
½ cup shredded sharp Cheddar cheese
4 slices cooked sugar-free bacon, crumbled
4 boneless pork chops
½ teaspoon salt
¼ teaspoon ground black pepper

Directions:
In a small bowl, mix pork rinds, Cheddar, and bacon. Make a 3" slit in the side of each pork chop and stuff with ¼ pork rind mixture. Sprinkle each side of pork chops with salt and pepper.
Place pork chops into ungreased air fryer basket, stuffed side up. Adjust the temperature to 400°F and set the timer for 12 minutes. Pork chops will be browned and have an internal temperature of at least 145°F when done. Serve warm.

Nutrition Facts (per serving):
Calories: 360 | Carbohydrates: 1g | Protein: 35g | Fat: 23g | Fiber: 0g

---

Servings: 4 | 20 minutes

439 Sesame Prawns with Firecracker Sauce

Ingredients:
1 lb tiger prawns, peeled
Salt and black pepper to taste
2 eggs
½ cup flour
¼ cup sesame seeds
¾ cup seasoned breadcrumbs
Firecracker sauce
⅓ cup sour cream
2 tbsp buffalo sauce
¼ cup spicy ketchup
1 green onion, chopped

Directions:
Preheat the air fryer to 390 F. In a bowl, beat the eggs with a pinch of salt. In another bowl, mix the breadcrumbs with sesame seeds. In a third bowl, mix flour with salt and pepper. Dip the prawns in the flour, then in the eggs, and finally in the crumbs. Spray with cooking spray.
AirFry for 10-12 minutes, flipping once. Meanwhile, in a bowl mix all sauce ingredients, except for the green onion. Serve the prawns with firecracker sauce and scatter with freshly chopped green onions.

Nutrition Facts (per serving):
Calories: 376 | Carbohydrates: 35g | Protein: 28g | Fat: 13.5g | Fiber: 2g

---

Servings: 4 | 25 minutes

440 Zucchini Fries with Tabasco Dip

Ingredients:
2 zucchinis, sliced
2 egg whites
½ cup seasoned breadcrumbs
2 tbsp Parmesan cheese, grated
¼ tsp garlic powder
Salt and black pepper to taste
1 cup mayonnaise
¼ cup heavy cream
1 tbsp Tabasco sauce
1 tsp lime juice

Directions:
Preheat the air fryer to 400 F. In a bowl, beat egg whites with salt and black pepper. In another bowl, mix garlic powder, Parmesan cheese, and breadcrumbs. Dip zucchini strips in the egg whites, then in the crumbs and spray them with cooking oil. AirFry them for 13-15 minutes, turning once.
Meanwhile, in a bowl, mix mayonnaise, heavy cream, Tabasco sauce, and lime juice. Serve as a dip for the strips.

Nutrition Facts (per serving):
Calories: 250 | Carbohydrates: 8g | Protein: 4g | Fat: 23g | Fiber: 1g

Servings: 2 — 6 Minutes

441 Scrambled Eggs

Ingredients:
- 4 eggs
- 1/4 tsp garlic powder
- 1/4 tsp onion powder
- 1 tbsp parmesan cheese
- Pepper
- Salt

Directions:
Whisk eggs with garlic powder, onion powder, parmesan cheese, pepper, and salt. Pour egg mixture into the air fryer baking dish. Place dish in the air fryer and cook at 360°F for 2 minutes. Stir quickly and cook for 3-4 minutes more. Stir well and serve.

Nutrition Facts (per serving):
Calories: 155 | Carbohydrates: 1g | Protein: 12g | Fat: 11g | Fiber: 0g

---

Servings: 4 — 12 Minutes

442 Air Fried Thyme Garlic Lamb Chops

Ingredients:
- 4 lamb chops
- 4 garlic cloves, minced
- 3 tbsp olive oil
- 1 tbsp dried thyme
- Pepper
- Salt

Directions:
Preheat the air fryer to 390°F.
Season lamb chops with pepper and salt.
In a small bowl, mix together thyme, oil, and garlic and rub over lamb chops.
Place lamb chops into the air fryer and cook for 12 minutes. Turn halfway through.
Serve and enjoy.

Nutrition Facts (per serving):
Calories: 340 | Carbohydrates: 0g | Protein: 25g | Fat: 26g | Fiber: 0g

---

 Servings: 4   20 minutes

443 Ale-Battered Scampi with Tartare Sauce

Ingredients:
- 1 lb prawns, peeled and deveined
- 1 cup plain flour
- 1 cup ale beer
- Salt and black pepper to taste
- Tartare sauce:
- ½ cup mayonnaise
- 2 tbsp capers, roughly chopped
- 2 tbsp fresh dill, chopped
- 1 pickled cucumber, finely chopped
- 2 tsp lemon juice
- ½ tsp Worcestershire sauce

Directions:
Preheat the air fryer to 380 F. In a bowl, mix all sauce ingredients and keep in the fridge. Mix flour, ale beer, salt, and pepper in a large bowl. Dip in the prawns and place them in the greased frying basket. AirFry for 10-12 minutes, turning them once halfway through cooking. Serve with the tartare sauce.

Nutrition Facts (per serving):
Calories: 435 | Carbohydrates: 25g | Protein: 23g | Fat: 24.8g | Fiber: 1g

---

Servings: 4 25 minutes

444 Parmesan Zucchini Boats

Ingredients:
- 4 small zucchinis, cut lengthwise
- ½ cup Parmesan cheese, grated
- ½ cup breadcrumbs
- ¼ cup melted butter
- ¼ cup fresh parsley, chopped
- 4 garlic cloves, minced
- Salt and black pepper to taste

Directions:
Preheat the air fryer to 370 F. Scoop out the insides of the zucchini halves with a spoon. In a bowl, mix breadcrumbs, garlic, and parsley. Season with salt and pepper and stir in the zucchini flesh. Spoon the mixture into the zucchini "boats" and sprinkle with Parmesan cheese. Drizzle with melted butter. Arrange the boats on the greased frying basket and Bake for 12 minutes or until the cheese is golden.

Nutrition Facts (per serving):
Calories: 220 | Carbohydrates: 10g | Protein: 6g | Fat: 18g | Fiber: 2g

Servings: 2 | 10 Minutes

445 Creamy Parsley Soufflé

Ingredients:
- 2 eggs
- 1 tablespoon fresh parsley, chopped
- 1 fresh red chili pepper, chopped
- 2 tablespoons light cream
- Salt, to taste

Directions:
Preheat the Air fryer to 390°F and grease 2 soufflé dishes.
Mix together all the ingredients in a bowl until well combined.
Transfer the mixture into prepared soufflé dishes and place in the Air fryer.
Cook for about 10 minutes and dish out to serve warm.

Nutrition Facts (per serving):
Calories: 120 | Carbohydrates: 1g | Protein: 9g | Fat: 9g | Fiber: 0g

---

Servings: 4 | 12 Minutes

446 Parmesan-crusted Pork Chops

Ingredients:
- 1 large egg
- ½ cup grated Parmesan cheese
- 4 boneless pork chops
- ½ teaspoon salt
- ¼ teaspoon ground black pepper

Directions:
Whisk egg in a medium bowl and place Parmesan in a separate medium bowl.
Sprinkle pork chops on both sides with salt and pepper. Dip each pork chop into egg, then press both sides into Parmesan.
Place pork chops into ungreased air fryer basket. Adjust the temperature to 400°F and set the timer for 12 minutes, turning chops halfway through cooking.
Pork chops will be golden and have an internal temperature of at least 145°F when done. Serve warm.

Nutrition Facts (per serving):
Calories: 290 | Carbohydrates: 1g | Protein: 30g | Fat: 18g | Fiber: 0g

---

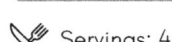
Servings: 4 | 20 minutes

447 Louisiana-Style Shrimp

Ingredients:
- 1 lb shrimp, peeled and deveined
- 2 eggs
- 1 cup flour
- 1 cup breadcrumbs
- 2 tbsp Cajun seasoning
- Salt and black pepper to taste
- 1 lemon, cut into wedges

Directions:
Preheat the air fryer to 390 F. Spray the basket with cooking oil. Beat the eggs in a bowl and season to taste. In a separate bowl, mix the crumbs and Cajun seasoning. In a third bowl, pour the flour. Dip the shrimp in flour, then in the eggs, and finally in the crumbs. AirFry the shrimp in the greased frying basket for 5 minutes. Flip and cook for 3-5 more minutes until crispy. Serve with lemon wedges.

Nutrition Facts (per serving):
Calories: 339 | Carbohydrates: 42g | Protein: 29g | Fat: 5.3g | Fiber: 1.5g

---

Servings: 4 | 25 minutes

448 Aunt's Roasted Carrots with Cilantro Sauce

Ingredients:
- ¼ cup olive oil
- 2 shallots, cut into wedges
- 4 carrots, halved lengthways
- 4 garlic cloves, lightly crushed
- ¼ tsp nutmeg
- ¼ tsp allspice
- ¼ cup cilantro, chopped
- ¼ lime, zested and juiced
- 1 tbsp Parmesan cheese, grated
- 1 tbsp pine nuts

Directions:
Preheat the air fryer to 370 F. Coat the carrots and shallots with allspice, nutmeg, and some olive oil. Put in the frying basket. Sprinkle with garlic and Bake for 15-20 minutes, shaking halfway through.
In a food processor, blitz the remaining olive oil, cilantro, lime zest and juice, Parmesan cheese, and pine nuts until the mixture forms a paste. Remove and serve on the side of the roasted veggies.

Nutrition Facts (per serving):
Calories: 210 | Carbohydrates: 10g | Protein: 2g | Fat: 18g | Fiber: 3g

Servings: 2 — 5 Minutes

449 Bacon Eggs

Ingredients:
2 eggs, hard-boiled, peeled
4 bacon slices
½ teaspoon avocado oil
1 teaspoon mustard

Directions:
Preheat the air fryer to 400°F. Then sprinkle the air fryer basket with avocado oil and place the bacon slices inside. Flatten them in one layer and cook for 2 minutes from each side. After this, cool the bacon to the room temperature. Wrap every egg into 2 bacon slices. Secure the eggs with toothpicks and place them in the air fryer. Cook the wrapped eggs for 1 minute at 400°F.

Nutrition Facts (per serving):
Calories: 230 | Carbohydrates: 0g | Protein: 12g | Fat: 20g | Fiber: 0g

---

Servings: 4 — 15 minutes

450 Avocado Egg Rolls

Ingredients:
2 ripe avocados, roughly chopped
8 egg roll wrappers
1 tomato, peeled and chopped
Salt and black pepper to taste

Directions:
Place the avocados, tomato, salt, and black pepper in a bowl. Mash with a fork until somewhat smooth. Divide the mixture between the egg wrappers. Fold the edges in and over the filling, roll up tightly, and seal the wrappers with a bit of water. Arrange them on the greased frying basket. Spray the rolls with cooking spray and Bake for 10 minutes at 350 F, turning halfway through until crispy and golden.

Nutrition Facts (per serving):
Calories: 215 | Carbohydrates: 20g | Protein: 4g | Fat: 14g | Fiber: 5g

---

 Servings: 4 20 minutes

451 Spicy Shrimp with Coconut-Avocado Dip

Ingredients:
1 ¼ lb tiger shrimp, peeled and deveined
2 garlic cloves, minced
¼ tsp red chili flakes
1 lime, juiced and zested
Salt to taste
1 tbsp fresh cilantro, chopped
1 large avocado, pitted
¼ cup coconut cream
2 tbsp olive oil

Directions:
Blend avocado, lime juice, coconut cream, cilantro, olive oil, and salt in a food processor until smooth. Transfer to a bowl, cover, and keep in the fridge until ready to use.
Preheat the air fryer to 390 F. In a bowl, place garlic, chili flakes, lime zest, and salt and add in the shrimp; toss to coat. Place them in the greased frying basket and AirFry for 8-10 minutes, turning them once halfway through cooking, until entirely pink. Serve with the chilled avocado dip.

Nutrition Facts (per serving):
Calories: 316 | Carbohydrates: 7g | Protein: 26g | Fat: 20.8g | Fiber: 3.5g

---

 Servings: 2 25 minutes

452 Tasty Balsamic Beets

Ingredients:
2 beets, cubed
⅓ cup balsamic vinegar
2 tbsp olive oil
1 tbsp honey
Salt and black pepper to taste
2 springs rosemary, chopped

Directions:
Preheat the air fryer to 400 F. In a bowl, mix beets, olive oil, rosemary, black pepper, and salt and toss to coat. AirFry the beets in the frying basket for 13-15 minutes, shaking once halfway through. Meanwhile, pour the vinegar and honey into a pan over medium heat. Bring to a boil and cook until reduced by half. Drizzle the beets with balsamic sauce and serve.

Nutrition Facts (per serving):
Calories: 170 | Carbohydrates: 18g | Protein: 2g | Fat: 10g | Fiber: 3g

Servings: 4 | 5 Minutes

453 Tuscan Toast

Ingredients:
¼ cup butter
½ teaspoon lemon juice
½ clove garlic
½ teaspoon dried parsley flakes
4 slices Italian bread, 1-inch thick

Directions:
Place butter, lemon juice, garlic, and parsley in a food processor. Process about 1 minute, or until garlic is pulverized and ingredients are well blended. Spread garlic butter on both sides of bread slices. Place bread slices upright in air fryer basket. Cook at 390°F for 5 minutes or until toasty brown.

Nutrition Facts (per serving):
Calories: 230 | Carbohydrates: 23g | Protein: 4g | Fat: 14g | Fiber: 1g

---

Servings: 4 | 15 minutes

454 Hot Air Fried Green Tomatoes

Ingredients:
8 green tomato slices
2 egg whites
½ cup flour
1 cup breadcrumbs
1 tsp cayenne pepper
½ tsp mustard powder
Salt and black pepper to taste

Directions:
Preheat the air fryer to 390 F. In a bowl, beat the egg whites with a pinch of salt. In a separate bowl, mix the flour, mustard powder, cayenne pepper, salt, and black pepper. Add the breadcrumbs to a third bowl. Dredge the tomato slices in the flour mixture, then in the egg whites, and finally in the crumbs. Spray with oil and arrange in the greased frying basket. AirFry for 8 minutes, turning once. Serve warm.

Nutrition Facts (per serving):
Calories: 155 | Carbohydrates: 24g | Protein: 5g | Fat: 3g | Fiber: 2g

---

Servings: 4 | 20 minutes

455 Rosemary Cashew Shrimp

Ingredients:
3 oz cashews, chopped
1 tbsp fresh rosemary, chopped
1 lb shrimp
1 garlic clove, minced
1 tbsp breadcrumbs
1 egg, beaten
1 tbsp olive oil
Salt and black pepper to taste

Directions:
Preheat the air fryer to 390 F. Whisk oil with garlic, salt, and pepper and brush the shrimp with the mixture. Mix rosemary, cashews, and breadcrumbs in a bowl. Dip the shrimp in the egg and coat in the crumbs. Place in the greased frying basket and AirFry for 4-6 minutes. Turn the shrimp and fry for 4-6 more minutes or until golden and crispy. Cover with a foil and let sit for a few minutes before serving.

Nutrition Facts (per serving):
Calories: 276 | Carbohydrates: 8g | Protein: 25g | Fat: 16g | Fiber: 0.8g

---

Servings: 4 | 25 minutes

456 Chili Corn on the Cob

Ingredients:
4 ears of sweet corn, shucked
1 clove garlic, minced
1 green chili, minced
1 lemon, zested
2 tbsp olive oil
2 tbsp butter, melted
Fine salt to taste

Directions:
Preheat the air fryer to 380 F. In a bowl, mix olive oil, garlic, lemon zest, and green chili. Rub the mixture on all sides of the corn ears. Place the ears in the greased frying basket (work in batches). AirFry for 14-16 minutes, turning once, until lightly browned. Remove to a platter and drizzle with melted butter. Scatter with salt and serve.

Nutrition Facts (per serving):
Calories: 180 | Carbohydrates: 22g | Protein: 3g | Fat: 10g | Fiber: 2g

Servings: 2 | 7 Minutes

457 Country Gravy

Ingredients:
- ¼ pound pork sausage, casings removed
- 1 tablespoon butter
- 2 tablespoons flour
- 2 cups whole milk
- ½ teaspoon salt
- freshly ground black pepper
- 1 teaspoon fresh thyme leaves

Directions:
Preheat a saucepan over medium heat. Add and brown the sausage, crumbling it into small pieces as it cooks. Add the butter and flour, stirring well to combine. Continue to cook for 2 minutes, stirring constantly.
Slowly pour in the milk, whisking as you do, and bring the mixture to a boil to thicken. Season with salt and freshly ground black pepper, lower the heat and simmer until the sauce has thickened to your desired consistency – about 5 minutes. Stir in the fresh thyme, season to taste and serve hot.

Nutrition Facts (per serving):
Calories: 370 | Carbohydrates: 14g | Protein: 13g | Fat: 30g | Fiber: 0g

---

Servings: 4 | 15 minutes

458 Mediterranean Bruschetta

Ingredients:
- 8 french baguette slices
- 2 tbsp olive oil
- 2 garlic cloves, haled
- 1 cup mozzarella cheese, grated
- 1 tsp fresh basil, chopped
- 1 cup mixed cherry tomatoes, quartered

Directions:
Brush the bread with olive oil and rub with garlic. Scatter mozzarella cheese on top. Arrange the slices in the frying basket and Bake for 8-10 minutes at 360 F. Top with cherry tomatoes and basil to serve.

Nutrition Facts (per serving):
Calories: 250 | Carbohydrates: 20g | Protein: 9g | Fat: 15g | Fiber: 1g

---

Servings: 4 | 20 minutes

459 Herbed Garlic Lobster

Ingredients:
- 4 oz lobster tails, halved
- 1 garlic clove, minced
- 2 tbsp butter, melted
- Salt and black pepper to taste
- ½ tbsp lemon juice
- 1 tbsp fresh parsley, chopped
- 1 tbsp fresh dill, chopped
- 1 tbsp fresh thyme, chopped

Directions:
Whisk the garlic, butter, lemon juice, salt, and pepper in a bowl until well mixed. Clean the skin of the lobster and cover it with the mixture. Preheat the air fryer to 380 F. Place the lobster in the greased frying basket and AirFry for 10 minutes, turning once. Serve sprinkled with parsley, thyme, and dill.

Nutrition Facts (per serving):
Calories: 77 | Carbohydrates: 0.5g | Protein: 5.4g | Fat: 5.8g | Fiber: 0.1g

---

Servings: 4 | 25 minutes

460 Parmesan Broccoli Bites

Ingredients:
- 1 small head broccoli
- 3 eggs
- 1 carrot, shredded
- ½ cup roasted red pepper, chopped
- Salt and black pepper to taste
- 2 tbsp Parmesan cheese, grated

Directions:
Blanch the broccoli in salted boiling water for 4-5 minutes until just tender. Drain and let cool slightly. Preheat the air fryer to 340 F. In a bowl, mix all the remaining ingredients. Cut the cooled broccoli into florets and mix in the egg mixture. Spoon the mixture into greased muffin cups and place in the air fryer. Bake for 12-14 minutes or until set and just turning golden. Let cool completely before serving.

Nutrition Facts (per serving):
Calories: 120 | Carbohydrates: 5g | Protein: 8g | Fat: 7g | Fiber: 2g

461 Carrot Chips

Servings: 4 | 10 Minutes

Ingredients:
1 pound carrots, thinly sliced
2 tablespoons extra-virgin olive oil
¼ teaspoon garlic powder
¼ teaspoon black pepper
½ teaspoon salt

Directions:
Preheat the air fryer to 390°F.
In a medium bowl, toss the carrot slices with the olive oil, garlic powder, pepper, and salt.
Liberally spray the air fryer basket with olive oil mist. Place the carrot slices in the air fryer basket. To allow for even cooking, don't overlap the carrots; cook in batches if necessary.
Cook for 5 minutes, shake the basket, and cook another 5 minutes.
Remove from the basket and serve warm. Repeat with the remaining carrot slices until they're all cooked.

Nutrition Facts (per serving):
Calories: 110 | Carbohydrates: 13g | Protein: 1g | Fat: 7g | Fiber: 4g

462 "Bikini" Ham & Cheese Sandwich

Servings: 1 | 15 minutes

Ingredients:
2 tbsp butter
2 slices bread
2 slices cheddar cheese
1 slice ham

Directions:
Preheat the air fryer to 370 F. Spread 1 tsp of butter on the outside of each of the bread slices. Place the cheese on the inside of one bread slice. Top with ham and the other cheese slice. Close with the second bread slice. AirFry for 8 minutes, flipping once halfway through. Cut diagonally and serve.

Nutrition Facts (per serving):
Calories: 490 | Carbohydrates: 28g | Protein: 19g | Fat: 33g | Fiber: 2g

463 Cod Fillets with Ginger-Cilantro Sauce

Servings: 4 | 20 minutes

Ingredients:
1 lb cod fillets
2 tbsp fresh cilantro, chopped
Salt to taste
4 green onions, chopped
1 cup water
1 tbsp ginger paste
5 tbsp light soy sauce
2 tbsp olive oil
1 tsp soy sauce
2 cubes rock sugar

Directions:
Preheat the air fryer to 360 F. Season the fillets with salt and drizzle with olive oil. Place in the frying basket and AirFry for 14-16 minutes, turning once. Meanwhile, heat the remaining oil in a pan over medium heat. Stir-fry the remaining ingredients for 5 minutes. Pour the sauce over the fish to serve.

Nutrition Facts (per serving):
Calories: 184 | Carbohydrates: 5g | Protein: 24g | Fat: 7.5g | Fiber: 0.3g

464 Indian Aloo Tikki

Servings: 2 | 25 minutes

Ingredients:
4 boiled potatoes, shredded
3 tbsp lemon juice
1 roasted bell pepper, chopped
Salt to taste
2 onions, chopped
¼ cup fennel, chopped
5 tbsp flour
2 tbsp ginger-garlic paste
1 tbsp mint leaves, chopped
1 tbsp fresh cilantro, chopped

Directions:
Preheat the air fryer to 360 F. In a bowl, mix cilantro, mint, fennel, ginger-garlic paste, flour, salt, and lemon juice. Add in the potatoes, bell pepper, and onions, and mix to combine. Make balls from the mixture and flatten them to form patties. Place them into the greased frying basket and AirFry them for 14-16 minutes, flipping once. Serve with mint chutney if desired.

Nutrition Facts (per serving):
Calories: 360 | Carbohydrates: 68g | Protein: 6g | Fat: 6g | Fiber: 8g

Servings: 8 — 10 Minutes

465 Cheesy Tortellini Bites

Ingredients:
1 large egg
½ teaspoon black pepper
½ teaspoon garlic powder
1 teaspoon Italian seasoning
12 ounces frozen cheese tortellini
½ cup panko breadcrumbs

Directions:
Preheat the air fryer to 380°F.
Spray the air fryer basket with an olive-oil-based spray.
In a medium bowl, whisk the egg with the pepper, garlic powder, and Italian seasoning.
Dip the tortellini in the egg batter and then coat with the breadcrumbs. Place each tortellini in the basket, trying not to overlap them. You may need to cook in batches to ensure the even crisp all around.
Bake for 5 minutes, shake the basket, and bake another 5 minutes.
Remove and let cool 5 minutes. Serve with marinara sauce, ranch, or your favorite dressing.

Nutrition Facts (per serving):
Calories: 190 | Carbohydrates: 25g | Protein: 8g | Fat: 6g | Fiber: 2g

---

Servings: 2 — 15 minutes

466 Easy Salmon Fillets

Ingredients:
2 salmon fillets
1 tbsp olive oil
Salt to taste
1 lemon, cut into wedges

Directions:
Preheat the air fryer to 380 F. Brush the salmon with olive oil and season with salt. Place the fillets in the greased frying basket and Bake for 8 minutes until tender, turning once. Serve with lemon wedges.

Nutrition Facts (per serving):
Calories: 360 | Carbohydrates: 1g | Protein: 34g | Fat: 24g | Fiber: 0g

---

 Servings: 4 20 minutes

467 American Panko Fish Nuggets

Ingredients:
1 lb white fish fillets
1 lemon, juiced
Salt and black pepper to taste
1 tsp dried dill
4 tbsp mayonnaise
2 eggs, beaten
1 tbsp garlic powder
1 cup breadcrumbs
1 tsp paprika

Directions:
Preheat the air fryer to 400 F. Season the fish with salt and black pepper. In a bowl, mix the beaten eggs, lemon juice, and mayonnaise. In a separate bowl, mix the crumbs, paprika, dill, and garlic.
Dredge the fillets in the eggs and then in the crumbs. Place them in the greased frying basket and AirFry for 14-16 minutes, flipping once halfway through cooking. Serve with tomato chutney if desired.

Nutrition Facts (per serving):
Calories: 345 | Carbohydrates: 20g | Protein: 29g | Fat: 16.4g | Fiber: 0.7g

---

 Servings: 4 25 minutes

468 Charred Broccolini with Lemon-Caper Sauce

Ingredients:
1 lb broccolini
2 tbsp olive oil
2 garlic cloves, sliced
½ tsp red chili flakes
2 tsp lemon juice
2 tbsp capers
Salt and black pepper to taste
1 tbsp fresh parsley, chopped

Directions:
Preheat the air fryer to 380 F. Season the broccolini with salt and black pepper. Place them in the frying basket and drizzle with some olive oil. AirFry until tender and charred, 8-10 minutes.
Meanwhile, warm the remaining oil in a pan and sauté the garlic for 35 seconds; remove from heat. Stir in lemon juice, capers, and chili flakes. Pour the sauce over the broccolini and top with parsley.

Nutrition Facts (per serving):
Calories: 100 | Carbohydrates: 7g | Protein: 4g | Fat: 7g | Fiber: 4g

469 Cheese Rounds

Servings: 4 | 6 Minutes

Ingredients:
1 cup Cheddar cheese, shredded

Directions:
Preheat the air fryer to 400°F. Then line the air fryer basket with baking paper. Sprinkle the cheese on the baking paper in the shape of small rounds. Cook them for 6 minutes or until the cheese is melted and starts to be crispy.

Nutrition Facts (per serving):
Calories: 115 | Carbohydrates: 1g | Protein: 7g | Fat: 9g | Fiber: 0g

470 Raspberry & Vanilla Pancakes

Servings: 4 | 15 minutes

Ingredients:
1 ½ cups all-purpose flour
1 cup milk
3 eggs, beaten
1 tsp baking powder
2 tbsp brown sugar
1 tsp vanilla extract
½ cup frozen raspberries, thawed
2 tbsp maple syrup

Directions:
Preheat the air fryer to 370 F. In a bowl, mix the flour, baking powder, milk, eggs, vanilla, and brown sugar. Gently stir in the raspberries to avoid coloring the batter. Working in batches, drop the batter into a greased baking pan using a spoon. Bake for 6-8 minutes, flipping once. Repeat the process with the remaining batter. Serve the pancakes with maple syrup.

Nutrition Facts (per serving):
Calories: 250 | Carbohydrates: 38g | Protein: 7g | Fat: 7g | Fiber: 2g

471 Golden Cod Fish Fillets

Servings: 4 | 20 minutes

Ingredients:
1 cup breadcrumbs
2 tbsp olive oil
2 eggs, beaten
4 cod fillets
A pinch of salt
1 cup flour

Directions:
Preheat the air fryer to 390 F. Mix the crumbs, olive oil, and salt in a bowl. In another bowl, beat the eggs. Put the flour into a third bowl. Toss the cod fillets in the flour, then in the eggs, and finally in the crumbs mixture. Place them in the greased frying basket and AirFry for 10 minutes. At the 6-minute mark, quickly turn the fillets. Remove to a plate and serve with dill-yogurt sauce if desired.

Nutrition Facts (per serving):
Calories: 400 | Carbohydrates: 41g | Protein: 32g | Fat: 11.8g | Fiber: 1.3g

472 Tomato Sandwiches with Feta & Pesto

Servings: 2 | 25 minutes

Ingredients:
1 heirloom tomato
1 (4-oz) block feta cheese
1 small red onion, thinly sliced
1 garlic clove
Salt to taste
2 tsp + ¼ cup olive oil
1 ½ tbsp pine nuts, toasted
2 tbsp fresh parsley, chopped
¼ cup Parmesan cheese, grated
¼ cup fresh basil, chopped

Directions:
Add basil, pine nuts, garlic, Parmesan cheese, and salt to a food processor. Pulse while slowly adding ¼ cup of olive oil. Preheat the air fryer to 390 F. Slice feta cheese and the tomato into ½-inch slices.
Spread the obtained pesto sauce on the tomato slices. Top with feta cheese and onion and drizzle with olive oil. Place the tomato in the greased frying basket and Bake for 6-8 minutes. Remove to a serving platter, sprinkle lightly with salt, and top with fresh parsley. Serve chilled.

Nutrition Facts (per serving):
Calories: 450 | Carbohydrates: 8g | Protein: 18g | Fat: 38g | Fiber: 3g

Servings: 6 | 6 Minutes

473 Bacon Candy

Ingredients:
1½ tablespoons Honey
1 teaspoon White wine vinegar
3 Extra thick-cut bacon strips, halved widthwise (gluten-free, if a concern)
½ teaspoon Ground black pepper

Directions:
Preheat the air fryer to 350°F.
Whisk the honey and vinegar in a small bowl until incorporated.
When the machine is at temperature, remove the basket. Lay the bacon strip halves in the basket in one layer. Brush the tops with the honey mixture; sprinkle each bacon strip evenly with black pepper. Return the basket to the machine and air-fry undisturbed for 6 minutes, or until the bacon is crunchy. Or a little less time if you prefer bacon that's still pliable, an extra minute if you want the bacon super crunchy. Take care that the honey coating doesn't burn. Remove the basket from the machine and set aside for 5 minutes. Use kitchen tongs to transfer the bacon strips to a serving plate.

Nutrition Facts (per serving):
Calories: 95 | Carbohydrates: 3g | Protein: 3g | Fat: 8g | Fiber: 0g

---

Servings: 2 | 15 minutes

474 Cinnamon French Toast Sticks

Ingredients:
4 white bread slices, cut them into strips
2 eggs
1 ½ tbsp butter
¼ tsp cinnamon powder + some for dusting
¼ nutmeg powder
¼ clove powder
2 tbsp brown sugar
1 tbsp icing sugar

Directions:
Preheat the air fryer to 350 F. In a bowl, add the eggs, brown sugar, clove powder, nutmeg powder, and cinnamon powder. Beat the mixture using a whisk until well combined. Dip the strips into the egg mixture. Arrange them on the greased frying basket and spritz with cooking spray. Bake for 2 minutes. Flip the toasts and cook for 3 more minutes. Dust the toasts with cinnamon and icing sugar to serve.

Nutrition Facts (per serving):
Calories: 330 | Carbohydrates: 32g | Protein: 9g | Fat: 18g | Fiber: 1g

---

Servings: 4 20 minutes

475 Cod Finger Pesto Sandwich

Ingredients:
4 cod fillets
4 bread rolls
1 cup breadcrumbs
4 tbsp pesto sauce
4 lettuce leaves
Salt and black pepper to taste

Directions:
Preheat the air fryer to 370 F. Season the fillets with salt and black pepper and coat them in breadcrumbs. Arrange them on the greased frying basket and Bake for 13-15 minutes, flipping once.
Cut the bread rolls in half. Divide lettuce leaves between the bottom halves and place the fillets over. Spread the pesto sauce on top of the fillets and cover with the remaining halves. Serve warm.

Nutrition Facts (per serving):
Calories: 437 | Carbohydrates: 50g | Protein: 32g | Fat: 12g | Fiber: 1.9g

---

Servings: 1 25 minutes

476 Vegetable Tortilla Pizza

Ingredients:
¼ tbsp tomato paste
1 tbsp cheddar cheese, grated
1 tbsp mozzarella cheese, grated
1 tbsp canned sweet corn
4 zucchini slices
4 eggplant slices
4 red onion rings
½ green bell pepper, chopped
1 large tortilla
A few fresh basil leaves, chopped

Directions:
Preheat the air fryer to 350 F. Spread the tomato paste on the tortilla. Arrange zucchini and eggplant slices first, then green bell peppers and onion rings. Sprinkle the corn all over. Top with cheddar and mozzarella cheeses. Place the pizza in the frying basket and Bake in the fryer for 10-12 minutes until nice and lightly browned on top. Sprinkle with freshly chopped basil leaves and serve.

Nutrition Facts (per serving):
Calories: 350 | Carbohydrates: 35g | Protein: 18g | Fat: 12g | Fiber: 6g

Servings: 2 | 10 Minutes

477 Fried Kale Chips

Ingredients:
1 head kale, torn into 1 ½-inch pieces
1 tbsp. olive oil
1 tsp. soy sauce

Directions:
Wash and dry the kale pieces.
Transfer the kale to a bowl and coat with the soy sauce and oil.
Place it in the Air Fryer and cook at 400°F for 3 minutes, tossing it halfway through the cooking process.

Nutrition Facts (per serving):
Calories: 90 | Carbohydrates: 7g | Protein: 3g | Fat: 6g | Fiber: 2g

---

Servings: 1 | 15 minutes

478 Masala Omelet The Indian Way

Ingredients:
1 garlic clove, crushed
1 green onion
½ chili powder
½ tsp garam masala
2 eggs
1 tbsp olive oil
1 tbsp fresh cilantro, chopped
Salt and black pepper to taste

Directions:
Preheat the air fryer to 360 F. In a bowl, whisk the eggs with salt and black pepper. Add in the green onion, garlic, chili powder, and garam masala; stir well. Transfer to a greased baking pan. Bake in the fryer for 8 minutes until the top is golden and the eggs are set. Scatter with fresh cilantro and serve.

Nutrition Facts (per serving):
Calories: 210 | Carbohydrates: 2g | Protein: 12g | Fat: 18g | Fiber: 0g

---

Servings: 4 | 20 minutes

479 Korean Kimchi-Spiced Salmon

Ingredients:
2 tbsp soy sauce
2 tbsp sesame oil
2 tbsp mirin
1 tbsp ginger puree
1 tsp kimchi spice
1 tsp sriracha sauce
2 lb salmon fillets
1 lime, cut into wedges

Directions:
Preheat the air fryer to 350 F. Grease the frying basket with cooking spray. In a bowl, mix together soy sauce, mirin, ginger puree, kimchi spice, and sriracha sauce. Add the salmon and toss to coat.
Place the fillets in the frying basket and drizzle with sesame oil. Bake for 10-12 minutes, flipping once halfway through. Garnish with lime wedges and serve.

Nutrition Facts (per serving):
Calories: 546 | Carbohydrates: 3.3g | Protein: 50.7g | Fat: 34.8g | Fiber: 0g

---

Servings: 4 | 25 minutes

480 Baked Mediterranean Shakshuka

Ingredients:
1 onion, sliced
2 garlic cloves, minced
2 tbsp olive oil
1 tsp ground cumin
2 tsp paprika
¼ tsp chili powder
1 red bell pepper, seeded and diced
2 (14.5-oz) cans tomatoes, diced
4 eggs
2 tbsp fresh parsley, chopped
4 tbsp feta cheese, crumbled
Salt and black pepper to taste

Directions:
Preheat the air fryer to 390 F. Heat olive oil in a skillet over medium heat and sauté bell pepper, onion, and garlic for 5 minutes until tender. Stir in paprika, parsley, chili, cumin, salt, and pepper and pour in the tomatoes. Simmer for 10 minutes; transfer to a baking dish. Crack in the eggs. Bake in the air fryer for 12-15 minutes or until the egg whites are set but the yolks are still runny. Top with feta to serve.

Nutrition Facts (per serving):
Calories: 300 | Carbohydrates: 18g | Protein: 20g | Fat: 18g | Fiber: 5g

Servings: 4 — 8 Minutes

481 Garlic-cream Cheese Wontons

Ingredients:
- 6 ounces full-fat cream cheese, softened
- 1 teaspoon garlic powder
- 12 wonton wrappers
- ¼ cup water

Directions:
Preheat the air fryer to 375°F.
In a medium bowl, mix cream cheese and garlic powder until smooth.
For each wonton, place 1 tablespoon cream cheese mixture in center of a wonton wrapper.
Brush edges of wonton with water to help it seal. Fold wonton to form a triangle. Spritz both sides with cooking spray. Repeat with remaining wontons and cream cheese mixture.
Place wontons in the air fryer basket. Cook 8 minutes, turning halfway through cooking time, until golden brown and crispy. Serve warm.

Nutrition Facts (per serving):
Calories: 185 | Carbohydrates: 17g | Protein: 4g | Fat: 11g | Fiber: 0g

---

Servings: 2 — 15 minutes

482 Baked Kale Omelet

Ingredients:
- 5 eggs
- 3 tbsp cottage cheese, crumbled
- 1 cup kale, chopped
- ½ tbsp fresh basil, chopped
- ½ tbsp fresh parsley, chopped
- Salt and black pepper to taste

Directions:
Beat the eggs, salt, and black pepper in a bowl. Stir in the rest of the ingredients. Pour the mixture into a greased baking pan and fit in the air fryer. Bake for 10 minutes at 330 F until slightly golden and set.

Nutrition Facts (per serving):
Calories: 190 | Carbohydrates: 2g | Protein: 14g | Fat: 13g | Fiber: 1g

---

Servings: 4 — 20 minutes

483 Easy Salmon with Greek Sauce

Ingredients:
- 1 lb salmon fillets
- Salt and black pepper to taste
- 2 tsp olive oil
- 2 tbsp fresh dill, chopped
- 1 cup sour cream
- 1 cup Greek yogurt

Directions:
In a bowl, mix the sour cream, Greek yogurt, dill, and salt. Keep in the fridge until ready to use. Preheat the air fryer to 340 F. Drizzle the fillets with olive oil and sprinkle with salt and pepper. Place the fish in the frying basket and Bake for 10-12 minutes, flipping once. Serve drizzled with the Greek sauce.

Nutrition Facts (per serving):
Calories: 403 | Carbohydrates: 4.6g | Protein: 31.8g | Fat: 29.5g | Fiber: 0g

---

Servings: 4 — 25 minutes

484 Traditional Swedish Meatballs

Ingredients:
- 1 lb ground pork
- 1 tbsp fresh dill, chopped
- ½ tsp nutmeg
- ⅓ cup seasoned breadcrumbs
- 1 egg, beaten
- Salt and white pepper to taste
- 2 tbsp butter
- ⅓ cup sour cream
- 2 tbsp flour

Directions:
Preheat the air fryer to 360 F. In a bowl, combine the ground pork, dill, nutmeg, breadcrumbs, egg, salt, and pepper and mix well. Shape the mixture into small balls. AirFry them in the greased frying basket for 12-14 minutes, flipping once.
Meanwhile, melt butter in a saucepan over medium heat and stir in the flour until lightly browned, about 2 minutes. Gradually pour 1 cup of water and whisk until the sauce thickens. Stir in sour cream and cook for 1 minute. Pour the sauce over the meatballs to serve.

Nutrition Facts (per serving):
Calories: 430 | Carbohydrates: 7g | Protein: 23g | Fat: 34g | Fiber: 0.5g

Servings: 4 | 5 Minutes

485 Croutons

Ingredients:

4 slices sourdough bread, diced into small cubes
2 tablespoons salted butter, melted
1 teaspoon chopped fresh parsley
2 tablespoons grated Parmesan cheese

Directions:

Preheat the air fryer to 400°F. Place bread cubes in a large bowl. Pour butter over bread cubes. Add parsley and Parmesan. Toss bread cubes until evenly coated. Place bread cubes in the air fryer basket in a single layer. Cook 5 minutes until well toasted. Serve cooled for maximum crunch.

Nutrition Facts (per serving):
Calories: 160 | Carbohydrates: 16g | Protein: 4g | Fat: 9g | Fiber: 1g

---

Servings: 2 | 15 minutes

486 Vienna Sausage & Cherry Tomato Frittata

Ingredients:

2 Vienna sausages, sliced
Salt and black pepper to taste
1 tbsp fresh parsley, chopped
½ cup milk
4 eggs
½ tsp red pepper flakes, crushed
4 cherry tomatoes, halved
2 tbsp Parmesan cheese, shredded

Directions:

Preheat the air fryer to 360 F. In a bowl, whisk the eggs and milk. Stir in the Parmesan cheese, red pepper flakes, salt, parsley, and black pepper. Add the mixture to a lightly greased baking pan and top with sausage slices and cherry tomatoes. Bake in the fryer for 8 minutes until the eggs are set. Serve hot.

Nutrition Facts (per serving):
Calories: 250 | Carbohydrates: 3g | Protein: 17g | Fat: 18g | Fiber: 0.5g

---

Servings: 4 | 20 minutes

487 Wild Salmon with Creamy Parsley Sauce

Ingredients:

4 Alaskan wild salmon fillets
2 tsp olive oil
Salt and black pepper to taste
½ cup heavy cream
½ cup milk
2 tbsp fresh parsley, chopped

Directions:

Preheat the air fryer to 380 F. Drizzle the fillets with olive oil and season with salt and black pepper. Place in them in the frying basket and Bake for 14-16 minutes, turning once, until tender and crispy. In a bowl, mix the milk, parsley, salt, and heavy cream. Serve the salmon with the sauce and enjoy!

Nutrition Facts (per serving):
Calories: 299 | Carbohydrates: 6.5g | Protein: 27g | Fat: 18.5g | Fiber: 2g

---

Servings: 4 | 25 minutes

488 Serbian Pork Skewers with Yogurt Sauce

Ingredients:

1 lb pork sausage meat
Salt and black pepper to taste
1 onion, chopped
½ tsp garlic puree
1 tsp ground cumin
1 cup Greek yogurt
2 tbsp walnuts, finely chopped
1 tbsp fresh dill, chopped

Directions:

Preheat the air fryer to 340 F. In a bowl, mix the sausage meat, onion, garlic puree, ground cumin, salt, and pepper. Knead until everything is well incorporated. Form patties out the mixture, about ½ inch thick, and thread them onto flat skewers. Lay them on the greased frying basket.
AirFry for 14-16 minutes, turning them over once or twice until golden. Whisk the yogurt, walnuts, garlic, dill, and salt in a small bowl to obtain a sauce. Serve the skewers with the yogurt sauce.

Nutrition Facts (per serving):
Calories: 410 | Carbohydrates: 6g | Protein: 22g | Fat: 33g | Fiber: 1g

Servings: 36   10 Minutes

489 Mini Greek Meatballs

Ingredients:
- 1 cup fresh spinach leaves
- ¼ cup peeled and diced red onion
- ½ cup crumbled feta cheese
- 1 pound 85/15 ground turkey
- ½ teaspoon salt
- ½ teaspoon ground cumin
- ¼ teaspoon ground black pepper

Directions:
Place spinach, onion, and feta in a food processor, and pulse ten times until spinach is chopped. Scoop into a large bowl.
Add turkey to bowl and sprinkle with salt, cumin, and pepper. Mix until fully combined. Roll mixture into thirty-six meatballs.
Place meatballs into ungreased air fryer basket, working in batches if needed. Adjust the temperature to 350ºF and set the timer for 10 minutes, shaking basket twice during cooking. Meatballs will be browned and have an internal temperature of at least 165ºF when done. Serve warm.

Nutrition Facts (per serving):
Calories: 45 | Carbohydrates: 0g | Protein: 4g | Fat: 3g | Fiber: 0g

---

Servings: 2   15 minutes

490 Buttered Eggs in Hole

Ingredients:
- 2 bread slices
- 2 eggs
- Salt and black pepper to taste
- 1 tbsp butter, softened

Directions:
Preheat the air fryer to 360 F. Place a heatproof pan in the frying basket and brush with butter. Make a hole in the middle of the bread slices with a bread knife and place in the heatproof pan in 2 batches. Crack an egg into the center of each hole; adjust the seasoning. Bake in the air fryer for 4 minutes. Turn the bread with a spatula and cook for another 4 minutes. Serve warm.

Nutrition Facts (per serving):
Calories: 215 | Carbohydrates: 12g | Protein: 7g | Fat: 15g | Fiber: 1g

---

Servings: 4   20 minutes

491 Sweet Caribbean Salmon Fillets

Ingredients:
- 4 salmon fillets
- ½ tsp brown sugar
- 1 tbsp Cajun seasoning
- 1 lemon, zested and juiced
- 1 tbsp fresh parsley, chopped
- 2 tbsp mango salsa

Directions:
Preheat the air fryer to 350 F. In a bowl, mix the sugar, Cajun seasoning, lemon juice and zest, and coat the salmon in the mixture. Line the frying basket with parchment paper and grease it with oil. Place in the fish and Bake for 11-13 minutes, turning once. Top with parsley and mango salsa to serve.

Nutrition Facts (per serving):
Calories: 487 | Carbohydrates: 2.3g | Protein: 39g | Fat: 35g | Fiber: 0g

---

Servings: 4   25 minutes

492 Pork Chops with Mustard-Apricot Glaze

Ingredients:
- 4 pork chops, ½-inch thick
- Salt and black pepper to taste
- 1 tbsp apricot jam
- 1 ½ tbsp minced, finely chopped
- 2 tbsp wholegrain mustard

Directions:
In a bowl, add apricot jam, garlic, mustard, salt, and black pepper; mix well. Add the pork chops and toss to coat. Place the chops in the greased frying basket and Bake for 10 minutes at 350 F. Turn the chops with a spatula and cook further for 6-8 minutes until golden and crispy. Once ready, remove the chops to a serving platter and serve with a side of steamed green veggies if desired.

Nutrition Facts (per serving):
Calories: 270 | Carbohydrates: 5.2g | Protein: 28g | Fat: 14g | Fiber: 0.3g

 Servings: 2　　 6 Minutes

493 Garlic Parmesan Kale Chips

Ingredients:

16 large kale leaves, washed and thick stems removed
1 tablespoon avocado oil
½ teaspoon garlic powder
1 teaspoon soy sauce or tamari
¼ cup grated Parmesan cheese

Directions:

Preheat the air fryer to 370°F.
Make a stack of kale leaves and cut them into 4 pieces. Place the kale pieces into a large bowl. Drizzle the avocado oil onto the kale and rub to coat. Add the garlic powder, soy sauce or tamari, and cheese, tossing to coat.
Pour the chips into the air fryer basket and cook for 3 minutes, shake the basket, and cook another 3 minutes, checking for crispness every minute. When done cooking, pour the kale chips onto paper towels and cool at least 5 minutes before serving.

Nutrition Facts (per serving):
Calories: 160 | Carbohydrates: 5g | Protein: 7g | Fat: 13g | Fiber: 2g

---

Servings: 4　　15 minutes

494 Loaded Egg Pepper Rings

Ingredients:

4 eggs
1 bell pepper, cut into four ¾-inch rings
5 cherry tomatoes, halved
Salt and black pepper to taste

Directions:

Preheat the air fryer to 360 F. Add the bell pepper rings to a greased baking pan and crack an egg into each one. Season with salt and black pepper. Top with the halved cherry tomatoes. Put the pan into the air fryer and AirFry for 6-9 minutes, or until the eggs are have set. Serve and enjoy!

Nutrition Facts (per serving):
Calories: 83 | Carbohydrates: 3.5g | Protein: 6.4g | Fat: 5g | Fiber: 1g

---

 Servings: 2　　 20 minutes

495 Classic Mediterranean Salmon

Ingredients:

2 salmon fillets
Salt and black pepper to taste
1 lemon, cut into wedges
8 asparagus spears, trimmed

Directions:

Preheat the air fryer to 350 F. Spritz the salmon with cooking spray. Season the fillets and asparagus with salt and pepper. Arrange the asparagus evenly in a single layer in the greased frying basket and top with the fillets. AirFry for 10-12 minutes at 350 F, turning the fish once. Serve with lemon wedges.

Nutrition Facts (per serving):
Calories: 247 | Carbohydrates: 3.5g | Protein: 26.5g | Fat: 14g | Fiber: 1.2g

---

Servings: 4　　 25 minutes

496 Spicy-Sweet Pork Chops

Ingredients:

4 thin boneless pork chops
3 tbsp brown sugar
½ tsp cayenne pepper
½ tsp ancho chili powder
½ tsp garlic powder
1 tbsp olive oil
½ cup Cholula hot sauce
Salt and black pepper to taste

Directions:

Preheat your Air Fryer to 375 F.
To make the marinade, mix brown sugar, olive oil, cayenne pepper, garlic powder, salt, and pepper in a small bowl. Dip each pork chop into the marinade, shaking off, and placing them in the frying basket in a single layer. AirFry for 7 minutes. Slide the basket out, turn the chops, and brush them with marinade. Cook for another 5 to 8 minutes until golden brown. Plate and top with hot sauce to serve.

Nutrition Facts (per serving):
Calories: 260 | Carbohydrates: 8g | Protein: 27g | Fat: 13g | Fiber: 0.5g

Servings: 4 | 5 Minutes

497 Herbed Cheese Brittle

Ingredients:
½ cup shredded Parmesan cheese
½ cup shredded white cheddar cheese
1 tablespoon fresh chopped rosemary
1 teaspoon garlic powder
1 large egg white

Directions:
Preheat the air fryer to 400°F.
In a large bowl, mix the cheeses, rosemary, and garlic powder. Mix in the egg white. Then pour the batter into a 7-inch pan. Place the pan in the air fryer basket and cook for 4 to 5 minutes, or until the cheese is melted and slightly browned.
Remove the pan from the air fryer, and let it cool for 2 minutes. Invert the pan before the cheese brittle completely cools but is semi-hardened to allow it to easily slide out of the pan.
Let the pan cool another 5 minutes. Break into pieces and serve.

Nutrition Facts (per serving):
Calories: 120 | Carbohydrates: 1g | Protein: 9g | Fat: 8g | Fiber: 0g

---

Servings: 3 | 15 minutes

498 French Toast with Vanilla Filling

Ingredients:
6 white bread slices
2 eggs
¼ cup milk
3 tbsp caramel sauce
⅓ cup cream cheese, softened
1 tsp vanilla extract
⅓ cup sugar mixed with 1 tsp ground cinnamon

Directions:
In a bowl, mix the cream cheese, caramel sauce, and vanilla. Spread three of the bread slices with the cheese mixture around the center. Place the remaining three slices on top to form three sandwiches.
Whisk the eggs and milk in a bowl. Dip the sandwiches into the egg mixture. Arrange them in the greased frying basket and AirFry for 10 minutes at 340 F, turning once. Dust with the cinnamon mixture.

Nutrition Facts (per serving):
Calories: 460 | Carbohydrates: 65g | Protein: 11g | Fat: 15.7g | Fiber: 1.3g

---

 Servings: 4 20 minutes

499 French Trout Meunière

Ingredients:
4 trout pieces
½ cup flour
Salt to taste
2 tbsp butter
1 lemon, juiced
2 tbsp chervil (French parsley), chopped

Directions:
Preheat the air fryer to 380 F. Season the trout with salt and dredge in the flour. Spritz with cooking oil and AirFry for 12-14 minutes, flipping once, until crispy. Remove and tent with foil to keep warm.
Melt the butter in a skillet over medium heat. Stir for 1-2 minutes until the butter becomes golden brown. Turn off the heat and stir in chervil and lemon juice. Pour the sauce over the fish and serve.

Nutrition Facts (per serving):
Calories: 348 | Carbohydrates: 12.1g | Protein: 31.5g | Fat: 19.6g | Fiber: 0.6g

---

 Servings: 4 25 minutes

500 Bavarian-Style Crispy Pork Schnitzel

Ingredients:
4 pork chops, center-cut
1 egg, beaten
1 tsp chili powder
2 tbsp flour
2 tbsp sour cream
Salt and black pepper to taste
½ cup breadcrumbs
2 tbsp olive oil

Directions:
Preheat the air fryer to 380 F. Using a meat tenderizer, pound the chops until ¼-inch thickness. Whisk the egg and sour cream in a bowl. Mix the breadcrumbs with chili powder, salt, and pepper in another bowl. Coat the chops with flour, then egg mixture, and finally in breadcrumbs. Brush with olive oil and arrange them on the frying basket. AirFry for 13-15 minutes, turning once until golden brown. Serve.

Nutrition Facts (per serving):
Calories: 310 | Carbohydrates: 10g | Protein: 27g | Fat: 18g | Fiber: 1g

Servings: 4   🕐 10 Minutes

501 Easy Crispy Prawns

Ingredients:
1 egg
½ pound nacho chips, crushed
18 prawns, peeled and deveined
Salt and black pepper, to taste

Directions:
Preheat the Air fryer to 355°F and grease an Air fryer basket.
Crack egg in a shallow dish and beat well.
Place the crushed nacho chips in another shallow dish.
Coat prawns into egg and then roll into nacho chips.
Place the coated prawns into the Air fryer basket and cook for about 10 minutes.
Dish out and serve warm.

Nutrition Facts (per serving):
Calories: 230 | Carbohydrates: 18g | Protein: 15g | Fat: 11g | Fiber: 2g

---

 Servings: 2   🕐 15 minutes

502 Brioche Toast with Nutella

Ingredients:
4 slices of brioche
3 eggs
4 tbsp butter
6 oz Nutella spread
½ cup heavy cream
1 tsp vanilla extract
1 tbsp icing sugar
½ cup fresh strawberries, sliced

Directions:
Preheat the air fryer to 350 F.
Beat the eggs along with heavy cream and vanilla in a small bowl. Dip the brioche slices in the egg mixture and AirFry in the greased frying basket for 7-8 minutes in total, shaking once or twice. Spread two pieces of the toast with a thin layer of Nutella and cover with the remaining toast pieces. Dust with icing sugar and top with strawberries. Serve and enjoy!

Nutrition Facts (per serving):
Calories: 1,243 | Carbohydrates: 87.5g | Protein: 21.8g | Fat: 87.5g | Fiber: 5g

---

 Servings: 4   20 minutes

503 Rosemary Catfish

Ingredients:
4 catfish fillets
¼ cup seasoned fish fry
1 tbsp olive oil
1 tbsp fresh rosemary, chopped

Directions:
Preheat the air fryer to 400 F. Add the seasoned fish fry and the fillets to a large Ziploc bag; massage to coat. Place the fillets in the greased frying basket and AirFry for 6-8 minutes. Flip the fillets and cook for 2-4 more minutes or until golden and crispy. Top with freshly chopped rosemary and serve.

Nutrition Facts (per serving):
Calories: 168 | Carbohydrates: 5.1g | Protein: 19.3g | Fat: 6.9g | Fiber: 0.3g

---

 Servings: 4   25 minutes

504 Beef Koftas in Tomato Sauce

Ingredients:
1 lb ground beef
1 medium onion, chopped
1 egg
4 tbsp breadcrumbs
1 tbsp fresh parsley, chopped
½ tbsp thyme leaves, chopped
10 oz tomato sauce
Salt and black pepper to taste

Directions:
Preheat the air fryer to 380 F. Mix all the ingredients, except for the tomato sauce, into a bowl. Shape the mixture into palm sized balls. Place the meatballs in the greased frying basket and AirFry for 12-14 minutes, shaking once. Pour the tomato sauce in a deep saucepan over medium heat and simmer for 2 minutes or until heated through. Add in the meatballs and stir with a wooden spoon to coat. Serve.

Nutrition Facts (per serving):
Calories: 310 | Carbohydrates: 10g | Protein: 25g | Fat: 20g | Fiber: 1.8g

Servings: 2   🕐 5 Minutes

505 Grilled Cheese Sandwiches

Ingredients:
4 white bread slices
½ cup melted butter, softened
½ cup sharp cheddar cheese, grated
1 tablespoon mayonnaise

Directions:
Preheat the Air fryer to 355°F and grease an Air fryer basket.
Spread the mayonnaise and melted butter over one side of each bread slice.
Sprinkle the cheddar cheese over the buttered side of the 2 slices.
Cover with the remaining slices of bread and transfer into the Air fryer basket.
Cook for about 5 minutes and dish out to serve warm.

Nutrition Facts (per serving):
Calories: 430 | Carbohydrates: 22g | Protein: 9g | Fat: 34g | Fiber: 1g

 Servings: 2   🕐 15 minutes

506 Soppressata Pizza

Ingredients:
1 pizza crust
½ tsp dried oregano
½ cup passata
½ cup mozzarella cheese, shredded
4 oz soppressata, chopped
4 basil leaves

Directions:
Preheat the air fryer to 370 F. Spread the passata over the pizza crust, sprinkle with oregano, mozzarella, and finish with soppressata. Bake in the fryer for 10 minutes. Top with basil leaves and serve.

Nutrition Facts (per serving):
Calories: 496 | Carbohydrates: 33.8g | Protein: 20.5g | Fat: 30g | Fiber: 2.6g

 Servings: 4   20 minutes

507 Jamaican Fish Fillets

Ingredients:
4 hoki fillets
1 tbsp ground Jamaican allspice
1 tsp paprika
Salt and garlic powder to taste
½ red onion, sliced
2 tomatoes, chopped
½ cup canned corn, drained
½ lemon, juiced

Directions:
In a bowl, mix the red onion, tomatoes, corn, salt, and lemon juice; toss to coat and set aside.
Preheat the air fryer to 390 F. In a bowl, mix paprika, garlic powder, and Jamaican seasoning. Rub the hoki fillets with the spices mixture. Spritz with cooking spray. Transfer to the frying basket and AirFry for 8 minutes, turn the fillets, and cook further for 5 minutes or until crispy. Serve with the corn salsa.

Nutrition Facts (per serving):
Calories: 131 | Carbohydrates: 9g | Protein: 23.8g | Fat: 1.5g | Fiber: 1.7g

 Servings: 4   25 minutes

508 Beef Meatballs with Cranberry Sauce

Ingredients:
1 small onion, chopped
1 lb grounded beef
1 tbsp fresh parsley, chopped
½ tbsp fresh thyme leaves, chopped
1 whole egg, beaten
3 tbsp breadcrumbs
Salt and black pepper to taste
1 cup cranberry sauce

Directions:
Preheat the air fryer to 390 F. In a bowl, mix all the ingredients, except for the cranberry sauce. Roll the mixture into 10-12 balls. Place the balls in the greased frying basket and Bake in the fryer for 8 minutes. Place the cranberry sauce in a saucepan over medium heat and stir for 2-3 minutes until heated through. Pour the sauce over the meatballs and serve.

Nutrition Facts (per serving):
Calories: 335 | Carbohydrates: 18g | Protein: 23g | Fat: 19g | Fiber: 1g

509 Tortilla Chips

Servings: 4 | 5 Minutes

Ingredients:
- 8 white corn tortillas
- ¼ cup olive oil
- 2 tablespoons lime juice
- ½ teaspoon salt

Directions:
Preheat the air fryer to 350°F. Cut each tortilla into fourths and brush lightly with oil. Place chips in a single layer in the air fryer basket, working in batches as necessary. Cook 5 minutes, shaking the basket halfway through cooking time. Sprinkle with lime juice and salt. Serve warm.

Nutrition Facts (per serving):
Calories: 220 | Carbohydrates: 25g | Protein: 3g | Fat: 12g | Fiber: 3g

510 Blueberry & Maple Toast

Servings: 2 | 15 minutes

Ingredients:
- 2 eggs, beaten
- 4 bread slices
- 1 tbsp maple syrup
- 1 ½ cups corn flakes
- ⅓ cup milk
- ¼ tsp ground nutmeg
- 1 cup fresh blueberries

Directions:
Preheat the air fryer to 390 F. In a bowl, mix the eggs, nutmeg, and milk. Dip the bread slices in the egg mixture, then thoroughly coat them in corn flakes. AirFry them in the greased frying basket for 8 minutes, turning once halfway through cooking. Drizzle with maple syrup and top blueberries. Serve.

Nutrition Facts (per serving):
Calories: 440 | Carbohydrates: 69.5g | Protein: 14.5g | Fat: 8.3g | Fiber: 4.3g

511 Peppery & Lemony Haddock

Servings: 4 | 20 minutes

Ingredients:
- 4 haddock fillets
- 1 cup breadcrumbs
- 2 tbsp lemon juice
- Salt and black pepper to taste
- ¼ cup potato flakes
- 2 eggs, beaten
- ¼ cup Parmesan cheese, grated
- 3 tbsp flour

Directions:
In a bowl, combine flour, salt, and pepper. In another bowl, mix breadcrumbs, Parmesan, and potato flakes. Dip fillets in the flour first, then in the eggs, and coat them in the crumbs mixture. Place them in the greased frying basket and AirFry for 14-16 minutes at 370 F, flipping once. Serve with lemon juice.

Nutrition Facts (per serving):
Calories: 293 | Carbohydrates: 27.5g | Protein: 31.9g | Fat: 6.6g | Fiber: 1.7g

512 South American Arepas with Cilantro Sauce

Servings: 4 | 25 minutes

Ingredients:
- 1 ½ lb ground beef
- 1 Fresno chili pepper, chopped
- 2 tbsp fresh cilantro, chopped
- Salt and black pepper to taste
- 4 cheese arepas (buns), halved
- ½ red onion, sliced
- 1 cup mayonnaise
- 2 tbsp fresh lime juice

Directions:
In a small bowl, mix the mayonnaise with lime juice and cilantro. Season with salt and set aside. Preheat the air fryer to 350 F. In a bowl, combine the ground beef, Fresno chili, salt, and black pepper. Mold the mixture into 4 patties. Spray them lightly on both sides with cooking spray and place in the frying basket. AirFry for 8 minutes, flip them, and cook for another 4-6 minutes or until browned and cooked through. Serve on cheese arepas with red onion and cilantro lime mayo sauce.

Nutrition Facts (per serving):
Calories: 545 | Carbohydrates: 18g | Protein: 28g | Fat: 40g | Fiber: 1.2g

513 Roasted Red Salsa

Servings: 4 | 10 Minutes

Ingredients:
- 10 medium Roma tomatoes, quartered
- 1 medium white onion, peeled and sliced
- 2 medium cloves garlic, peeled
- 2 tablespoons olive oil
- ¼ cup chopped fresh cilantro
- ½ teaspoon salt

Directions:
Preheat the air fryer to 340°F. Place tomatoes, onion, and garlic into a 6" round baking dish. Drizzle with oil and toss to coat. Place in the air fryer basket and cook 10 minutes, stirring twice during cooking, until vegetables start to turn dark brown and caramelize. In a food processor, add roasted vegetables, cilantro, and salt. Pulse five times until vegetables are mostly broken down. Serve immediately.

Nutrition Facts (per serving):
Calories: 80 | Carbohydrates: 9g | Protein: 2g | Fat: 4g | Fiber: 2g

514 Spicy Egg & Bacon Tortilla Wraps

Servings: 3 | 15 minutes

Ingredients:
- 3 flour tortillas
- 2 eggs, scrambled
- 3 slices bacon, cut into strips
- 3 tbsp salsa
- 3 tbsp cream cheese
- 1 cup Pepper Jack cheese, grated

Directions:
Preheat the air fryer to 390 F. Spread cream cheese on the tortillas. Add the eggs and bacon and top with salsa. Scatter with grated Pepper Jack cheese and roll up tightly. Place in the frying basket and AirFry for 10 minutes or until golden. Cut in half and serve warm.

Nutrition Facts (per serving):
Calories: 470 | Carbohydrates: 23g | Protein: 21.5g | Fat: 31g | Fiber: 1.3g

515 Roasted Tomatoes with Cheese Topping

Servings: 2 | 20 minutes

Ingredients:
- ½ cup cheddar cheese, shredded
- ¼ cup Parmesan cheese, grated
- 4 tomatoes, cut into ½ inch slices
- 2 tbsp fresh parsley, chopped
- Salt and black pepper to taste

Directions:
Preheat the air fryer to 380 F. Lightly salt the tomato slices and put them in the greased frying basket in a single layer. Top with cheddar and Parmesan cheeses and sprinkle with black pepper. AirFry for 5-6 minutes until the cheese is melted and bubbly. Serve topped with fresh parsley and enjoy!

Nutrition Facts (per serving):
Calories: 204 | Carbohydrates: 11g | Protein: 13g | Fat: 12.5g | Fiber: 3.2g

516 Healthy Burgers

Servings: 4 | 25 minutes

Ingredients:
- 1 ½ lb ground beef
- ½ tsp onion powder
- Salt and black pepper to taste
- ½ tsp dried oregano
- 1 tbsp Worcestershire sauce
- ½ tsp garlic powder
- 1 tsp Maggi seasoning sauce
- 1 tbsp olive oil

Directions:
Preheat the air fryer to 350 F. In a bowl, combine Worcestershire and Maggi sauces, onion and garlic powders, oregano, salt, and pepper. Add in the ground beef and mix until well combined. Divide the meat mixture into 4 equal pieces and flatten to form patties. Brush with olive oil and place the patties in the frying basket. AirFry for 14-16 minutes, turning once halfway through. Serve immediately.

Nutrition Facts (per serving):
Calories: 380 | Carbohydrates: 1.5g | Protein: 27g | Fat: 29g | Fiber: 0g

Servings: 20 | 8 Minutes

517 Spicy Cheese-stuffed Mushrooms

Ingredients:

4 ounces cream cheese, softened
6 tablespoons shredded pepper jack cheese
2 tablespoons chopped pickled jalapeños
20 medium button mushrooms, stems removed
2 tablespoons olive oil
¼ teaspoon salt
⅛ teaspoon ground black pepper

Directions:

In a large bowl, mix cream cheese, pepper jack, and jalapeños together.
Drizzle mushrooms with olive oil, then sprinkle with salt and pepper. Spoon 2 tablespoons cheese mixture into each mushroom and place in a single layer into ungreased air fryer basket. Adjust the temperature to 370°F and set the timer for 8 minutes, checking halfway through cooking to ensure even cooking, rearranging if some are darker than others. When they're golden and cheese is bubbling, mushrooms will be done. Serve warm.

Nutrition Facts (per serving):
Calories: 45 | Carbohydrates: 1g | Protein: 1g | Fat: 4g | Fiber: 0g

---

Servings: 2 | 15 minutes

518 Paprika Rarebit

Ingredients:

4 toasted bread slices
1 tsp smoked paprika
2 eggs, beaten
1 tsp Dijon mustard
4 ½ oz cheddar cheese, grated
Salt and black pepper to taste

Directions:

Preheat the fryer to 360 F. In a bowl, combine the eggs, mustard, cheddar, and paprika. Season with salt and pepper. Spread the mixture on the bread slices and AirFry them for 10 minutes or until golden.

Nutrition Facts (per serving):
Calories: 536 | Carbohydrates: 34g | Protein: 28.2g | Fat: 28.3g | Fiber: 2.3g

---

Servings: 4 | 20 minutes

519 Indian Fried Okra

Ingredients:

1 tbsp chili powder
2 tbsp garam masala
1 cup cornmeal
¼ cup flour
Salt and black pepper to taste
½ lb okra, trimmed and halved lengthwise
1 egg
1 cup Cholula hot sauce

Directions:

Preheat the air fryer to 380 F. In a bowl, mix cornmeal, flour, chili powder, garam masala, salt, and black pepper. In another bowl, whisk the egg and season with salt and pepper.
Dip the okra in the egg and then coat in the cornmeal mixture. Spray with cooking spray and place in the frying basket. AirFry for 6 minutes, shake, and cook for another 5-7 minutes or until golden brown. Serve with hot sauce.

Nutrition Facts (per serving):
Calories: 210 | Carbohydrates: 24g | Protein: 5g | Fat: 10g | Fiber: 3g

---

Servings: 4 | 25 minutes

520 Homemade Hot Beef Satay

Ingredients:

2 lb flank steaks, cut into long strips
2 tbsp fish sauce
2 tbsp soy sauce
2 tbsp sugar
1 ½ tsp garlic powder
1 ½ tsp ground ginger
2 tsp hot sauce
2 tbsp fresh cilantro, chopped
½ cup roasted peanuts, chopped

Directions:

Preheat the air fryer to 400 F. In a Ziploc bag, add the beef strips, fish sauce, sugar, garlic powder, soy sauce, ginger, and hot sauce. Seal the bag and shake thoroughly.
Open the bag, remove the beef strips, shake off the excess marinade, and place in the frying basket in a single layer. Avoid overlapping. AirFry for 6 minutes, turn the beef, and cook further for 6 minutes. Dish the meat and garnish with roasted peanuts and freshly chopped cilantro.

Nutrition Facts (per serving):
Calories: 390 | Carbohydrates: 9g | Protein: 36g | Fat: 23g | Fiber: 1.5g

Servings: 4 | 10 Minutes

521 Pita Chips

Ingredients:
- 2 rounds Pocketless pita bread
- Olive oil spray or any flavor spray you prefer, even coconut oil spray
- Up to 1 teaspoon Fine sea salt, garlic salt, onion salt, or other flavored salt

Directions:
Preheat the air fryer to 400°F. Lightly coat the pita round(s) on both sides with olive oil spray, then lightly sprinkle each side with salt. Cut each coated pita round into 8 even wedges. Lay these in the basket in as close to a single even layer as possible. Many will overlap or even be on top of each other, depending on the exact size of your machine. Air-fry for 6 minutes, shaking the basket and rearranging the wedges at the 4-minute marks, until the wedges are crisp and brown. Turn them out onto a wire rack to cool a few minutes or to room temperature before digging in.

Nutrition Facts (per serving):
Calories: 130 | Carbohydrates: 22g | Protein: 4g | Fat: 3g | Fiber: 2g

---

Servings: 4 | 15 minutes

522 Flaxseed Porridge

Ingredients:
- 1 cup steel-cut oats
- 1 tbsp flax seeds
- 1 tbsp peanut butter
- 1 tbsp butter
- 1 cup milk
- 2 tbsp honey

Directions:
Preheat the air fryer to 350 F. Combine all ingredients in an ovenproof bowl. Place the bowl in the air fryer and Bake for 10 minutes. Let cool for a few minutes before serving. Enjoy!

Nutrition Facts (per serving):
Calories: 281 | Carbohydrates: 39.3g | Protein: 10g | Fat: 11.8g | Fiber: 5g

---

 Servings: 2 20 minutes

523 Mediterranean Eggplant Burgers

Ingredients:
- 2 hamburger buns, halved
- 2 (2-inch) eggplant slices, cut along the round axis
- 2 mozzarella slices
- 1 red onion, cut into rings
- 2 lettuce leaves
- 1 tbsp tomato sauce
- 1 pickle, sliced
- Salt to taste

Directions:
Preheat the air fryer to 360 F. Season the eggplant slices with salt and place them in the greased frying basket. Bake for 6 minutes, flipping once. Top with mozzarella slices and cook for 30 more seconds. Spread the tomato sauce on the bun bottoms. Top with the cheesy eggplant slices followed by the red onion rings, sliced pickle, and lettuce leaves. Finish with the bun tops and serve immediately.

Nutrition Facts (per serving):
Calories: 300 | Carbohydrates: 30g | Protein: 10g | Fat: 15g | Fiber: 3g

---

 Servings: 4 25 minutes

524 Garlic Steak with Mexican Salsa

Ingredients:
- 2 rib-eye steaks
- 1 tbsp olive oil
- Garlic salt and black pepper to taste
- ½ cup heavy cream
- 1 avocado, roughly chopped
- 7 oz canned sweetcorn
- ½ red onion, sliced
- 10 cherry tomatoes, quartered
- 2 tbsp fresh cilantro, chopped
- 1 green chili, minced
- 1 lime, zested and juiced
- ½ cup heavy cream

Directions:
Preheat your air fryer to 390 F. In a bowl, whisk the olive oil, garlic salt, and black pepper. Massage the mixture onto the rib-eye steaks to coat on all sides. Lay the steaks in the greased frying basket and AirFry for 16-18 minutes, turning once halfway through. Remove to a plate.
In a bowl, mix the avocado, corn, cherry tomatoes, red onion, cilantro, chili, lime juice, and lime zest. Season to taste. Serve the steaks with the Mexican salsa and a dollop of heavy cream on the side.

Nutrition Facts (per serving):
Calories: 489 | Carbohydrates: 10.5g | Protein: 27.9g | Fat: 37.6g | Fiber: 3.4g

Servings: 6 | 5 Minutes

525 Sweet Chili Peanuts

Ingredients:
2 cups Shelled raw peanuts
2 tablespoons Granulated white sugar
2 teaspoons Hot red pepper sauce, such as Cholula or Tabasco (gluten-free, if a concern)

Directions:
Preheat the air fryer to 400°F. Toss the peanuts, sugar, and hot pepper sauce in a bowl until the peanuts are well coated. When the machine is at temperature, pour the peanuts into the basket, spreading them into one layer as much as you can. Air-fry undisturbed for 3 minutes. Shake the basket to rearrange the peanuts. Continue air-frying for 2 minutes more, shaking and stirring the peanuts every 30 seconds, until golden brown. Pour the peanuts onto a large lipped baking sheet. Spread them into one layer and cool for 5 minutes before serving.

Nutrition Facts (per serving):
Calories: 240 | Carbohydrates: 7g | Protein: 10g | Fat: 20g | Fiber: 3g

---

Servings: 4 | 15 minutes

526 Avocado Tempura

Ingredients:
½ cup breadcrumbs
½ tsp salt
1 avocado, pitted, peeled, and sliced
½ cup soda water (club soda)

Directions:
Preheat the air fryer to 360 F. In a bowl, add the breadcrumbs and salt and mix well. Sprinkle the avocado with soda water and then coat in the breadcrumbs. Arrange the slices in the grease frying basket in one layer and AirFry for 8-10 minutes, shaking once or twice. Serve warm.

Nutrition Facts (per serving):
Calories: 115 | Carbohydrates: 13g | Protein: 2g | Fat: 6.5g | Fiber: 2.5g

---

Servings: 4 | 20 minutes

527 Teriyaki Cauliflower

Ingredients:
1 big cauliflower head, cut into florets
½ cup soy sauce
1 tbsp brown sugar
1 tsp sesame oil
½ chili powder
2 cloves garlic, chopped
1 tsp cornstarch

Directions:
In a bowl, whisk soy sauce, brown sugar, sesame oil, ⅓ cup of water, chili powder, garlic, and cornstarch until smooth. In a bowl, add the cauliflower and pour teriyaki sauce over; toss to coat.
Place the cauliflower in the greased frying basket and AirFry for 13-15 minutes at 380 F, turning once halfway through. When ready, check if the cauliflower is cooked but not too soft. Serve warm.

Nutrition Facts (per serving):
Calories: 120 | Carbohydrates: 14g | Protein: 6g | Fat: 4g | Fiber: 4g

---

Servings: 4 | 25 minutes

528 Gorgonzola Rib Eye Steak

Ingredients:
1 ½ lb rib-eye steak
1 tsp garlic powder
1 cup heavy cream
1 cup gorgonzola cheese, crumbled
2 tbsp fresh chives, chopped
2 tbsp olive oil
Salt and black pepper to taste

Directions:
Preheat the air fryer to 400 F. In a bowl, combine olive oil, garlic powder, salt, and pepper. Rub the steak with the seasoning and place it in the frying basket. Bake for 14-16 minutes, flipping once.
Warm the heavy cream in a skillet over medium heat. Add the gorgonzola cheese and chives; stir until you obtain a smooth sauce, and the cheese is melted, 3 minutes. Drizzle the sauce over the steaks.

Nutrition Facts (per serving):
Calories: 561 | Carbohydrates: 3.5g | Protein: 29.2g | Fat: 46.7g | Fiber: 0.2g

Servings: 1 — 10 Minutes

529 Green Olive And Mushroom Tapenade

Ingredients:
¾ pound Brown or Baby Bella mushrooms, sliced 1½ cups (about ½ pound) Pitted green olives
3 tablespoons Olive oil
1½ tablespoons Fresh oregano leaves, loosely packed
¼ teaspoon Ground black pepper

Directions:
Preheat the air fryer to 400°F.
When the machine is at temperature, arrange the mushroom slices in as close to an even layer as possible in the basket. They will overlap and even stack on top of each other.
Air-fry for 10 minutes, tossing the basket and rearranging the mushrooms every 2 minutes, until shriveled but with still-noticeable moisture.
Pour the mushrooms into a food processor. Add the olives, olive oil, oregano leaves, and pepper. Cover and process until grainy, not too much, just not fully smooth for better texture, stopping the machine at least once to scrape down the inside of the canister. Scrape the tapenade into a bowl and serve warm, or cover and refrigerate for up to 4 days.

Nutrition Facts (per serving):
Calories: 430 | Carbohydrates: 9g | Protein: 5g | Fat: 42g | Fiber: 4g

---

Servings: 4 — 15 minutes

530 Quick Pickle Chips

Ingredients:
36 sweet pickle chips, drained
1 tsp cayenne pepper
1 cup flour
¼ cup cornmeal

Directions:
Preheat the air fryer to 400 F. In a bowl, mix flour, cayenne pepper, and cornmeal. Dip the pickles in the flour mixture and spritz with cooking spray. AirFry for 10 minutes until golden brown, turning once.

Nutrition Facts (per serving):
Calories: 130 | Carbohydrates: 22g | Protein: 2.5g | Fat: 3.5g | Fiber: 1.2g

---

 Servings: 4 20 minutes

531 Almond-Crusted Cauliflower Florets

Ingredients:
1 head of cauliflower, cut into florets
2 eggs
1 cup ground almonds
4 tbsp Parmesan cheese, grated
Garlic salt and black pepper to taste
2 tbsp fresh cilantro, chopped

Directions:
Preheat the air fryer to 380 F. In a bowl, mix the Parmesan cheese, ground almonds, garlic salt, and black pepper. In another bowl, whisk the eggs. Dip the florets into the eggs, then roll them up in the almond crumbs. Lay the florets in the greased frying basket and spritz with cooking spray. AirFry for 8-10 minutes, shaking once, until crispy. Serve sprinkled with fresh cilantro.

Nutrition Facts (per serving):
Calories: 220 | Carbohydrates: 8g | Protein: 11g | Fat: 17g | Fiber: 4g

---

 Servings: 2 25 minutes

532 Parsley Crumbed Beef Strips

Ingredients:
2 tbsp vegetable oil
½ tsp fresh parsley, chopped
1 cup breadcrumbs
1 whole egg, whisked
1 thin beef sirloin steak, cut into strips
1 lemon, juiced

Directions:
Preheat the air fryer to 370 F. In a bowl, add breadcrumbs, parsley, and vegetable oil and stir well to get a loose mixture. Dip the beef in the egg, then coat in the crumbs mixture. Place the strips in the greased frying basket and AirFry for 14-16 minutes, flipping once. Serve with a drizzle of lemon juice.

Nutrition Facts (per serving):
Calories: 412 | Carbohydrates: 19.7g | Protein: 25.2g | Fat: 25.8g | Fiber: 1.4g

533 Ham And Cheese Sliders

Servings: 3 | 10 Minutes

Ingredients:
6 Hawaiian sweet rolls
12 slices thinly sliced Black Forest ham
6 slices sharp Cheddar cheese
⅓ cup salted butter, melted
1 ½ teaspoons minced garlic

Directions:
Preheat the air fryer to 350°F.
For each slider, slice horizontally through the center of a roll without fully separating the two halves. Place 2 slices ham and 2 slices cheese inside roll and close. Repeat with remaining rolls, ham, and cheese.
In a small bowl, mix butter and garlic and brush over all sides of rolls.
Place in the air fryer and cook 10 minutes until rolls are golden on top and cheese is melted. Serve warm.

Nutrition Facts (per serving):
Calories: 430 | Carbohydrates: 24g | Protein: 16g | Fat: 30g | Fiber: 1g

534 Green Bean Crisps

Servings: 4 | 15 minutes

Ingredients:
1 lb green beans, trimmed
2 tbsp olive oil
½ tsp garlic powder
½ tsp onion powder
½ tsp paprika
Salt and black pepper to taste

Directions:
Preheat the air fryer to 390 F. In a bowl, mix olive oil, garlic and onion powders, paprika, salt, and black pepper. Coat the green beans in the mixture and place them in the greased frying basket. AirFry for 10-12 minutes, shaking once halfway through cooking. Serve warm.

Nutrition Facts (per serving):
Calories: 110 | Carbohydrates: 10g | Protein: 2.5g | Fat: 7.5g | Fiber: 3.6g

535 Party Crispy Nachos

Servings: 2 | 20 minutes

Ingredients:
1 cup sweet corn
1 cup all-purpose flour + some more
1 tbsp butter
½ tsp chili powder
Salt to taste
½ cup guacamole

Directions:
Add a small amount of water to the sweet corn and grind until you obtain a very fine paste. In a bowl, mix flour, salt, chili powder, and butter; stir into the corn. Knead with your palm until you obtain a stiff dough. Preheat the air fryer to 350 F. On a working surface, dust a little bit of flour and spread the dough with a rolling pin. Make it around ¼-inch thickness. Cut into triangle shapes, as many as you can. AirFry the nachos in the greased frying basket for 9-12 minutes, shaking once, until crispy. Serve with guacamole.

Nutrition Facts (per serving):
Calories: 400 | Carbohydrates: 40g | Protein: 5g | Fat: 22g | Fiber: 5g

536 Lamb Meatballs with Roasted Veggie Bake

Servings: 2 | 25 minutes

Ingredients:
½ lb ground lamb
1 shallot, chopped
½ tsp garlic powder
1 egg, beaten
1 potato, chopped
¼ red onion, sliced
1 carrot, sliced diagonally
½ small beetroot, sliced
1 cup cherry tomatoes, halved
2 tbsp olive oil
Salt and black pepper to taste
Parmesan shavings

Directions:
Preheat the air fryer to 370 F. In a bowl, mix red onion, potato, cherry tomatoes, carrot, beetroot, salt, and olive oil. Transfer to the frying basket and Bake for 10 minutes, shaking once. In another bowl, mix the ground lamb, egg, shallot, garlic powder, salt, and black pepper. Shape the mixture into balls. Place them over the vegetables in the air fryer, and AirFry for 12-14 minutes, flipping once. Remove the dish and top with Parmesan shavings to serve.

Nutrition Facts (per serving):
Calories: 458 | Carbohydrates: 20.4g | Protein: 24.7g | Fat: 31.8g | Fiber: 3.9g

Servings: 16 — 7 Minutes

537 Turkey Bacon Dates

Ingredients:
16 whole, pitted dates
16 whole almonds
6 to 8 strips turkey bacon

Directions:
Stuff each date with a whole almond. Depending on the size of your stuffed dates, cut bacon strips into halves or thirds. Each strip should be long enough to wrap completely around a date. Wrap each date in a strip of bacon with ends overlapping and secure with toothpicks. Place in air fryer basket and cook at 390°F for 7 minutes, until bacon is as crispy as you like. Drain on paper towels or wire rack. Serve hot or at room temperature.

Nutrition Facts (per serving):
Calories: 80 | Carbohydrates: 10g | Protein: 2g | Fat: 4g | Fiber: 1g

Servings: 2 — 15 minutes

538 Crispy Bacon with Butter Bean Dip

Ingredients:
1 (14-oz) can butter beans
1 tbsp scallions, chopped
½ cup feta cheese, crumbled
Black pepper to taste
3 tbsp olive oil
2 oz bacon, sliced

Directions:
Preheat the air fryer to 390 F. Arrange the bacon slices in the frying basket and AirFry for 5 minutes. Flip and cook for 5 more minutes or until crispy. Remove to a paper towel-lined plate to drain. Meanwhile, blend butter beans, olive oil, and black pepper in a blender. Add in the feta cheese and stir well. Serve the crispy bacon with the feta-bean dip and scatter fresh scallions on top.

Nutrition Facts (per serving):
Calories: 390 | Carbohydrates: 24g | Protein: 13g | Fat: 27g | Fiber: 7g

  Servings: 4 — 20 minutes

539 Air Fried Cheesy Ravioli

Ingredients:
1 package cheese ravioli
2 cup Italian breadcrumbs
¼ cup Pecorino cheese, grated
1 cup buttermilk
2 tsp olive oil
¼ tsp garlic powder

Directions:
Preheat the air fryer to 390 F. In a small bowl, combine breadcrumbs, Pecorino cheese, garlic powder, and olive oil. Dip the ravioli in the buttermilk and then coat them in the breadcrumb mixture.
Line the frying basket with parchment paper and arrange the ravioli inside. Bake for 7-9 minutes, turning once halfway through cooking, until nice and golden. Serve with marinara or carbonara sauce.

Nutrition Facts (per serving):
Calories: 350 | Carbohydrates: 38g | Protein: 12g | Fat: 16g | Fiber: 2g

  Servings: 4 — 25 minutes

540 Herby Roast Beef

Ingredients:
2 lb beef loin
Salt and black pepper to taste
½ tsp dried thyme
½ tsp dried rosemary
½ tsp dried oregano
½ tsp garlic powder
1 tsp onion powder
2 tbsp olive oil

Directions:
Preheat the air fryer to 380 F. In a bowl, combine all the ingredients, except for the beef. Rub the mixture onto the meat. Place it in the air fryer and Bake for 8-10 minutes. Turn the meat over and cook for 7-8 more minutes until well roasted. Let cool before slicing. Serve with steamed veggies if desired.

Nutrition Facts (per serving):
Calories: 412 | Carbohydrates: 0.7g | Protein: 35.6g | Fat: 28.7g | Fiber: 0.3g

 Servings: 2 7 Minutes

541 Lemon Tofu Cubes

Ingredients:
½ teaspoon ground coriander
1 tablespoon avocado oil
1 teaspoon lemon juice
½ teaspoon chili flakes
6 oz tofu

Directions:
In the shallow bowl mix up ground coriander, avocado oil, lemon juice, and chili flakes. Chop the tofu into cubes and sprinkle with coriander mixture. Shake the tofu. After this, preheat the air fryer to 400°F and put the tofu cubes in it. Cook the tofu for 4 minutes. Then flip the tofu on another side and cook for 3 minutes more.

Nutrition Facts (per serving):
Calories: 140 | Carbohydrates: 2g | Protein: 7g | Fat: 12g | Fiber: <1g

Servings: 6 15 minutes

542 Fried Sausage Ravioli

Ingredients:
2 (18-oz) packages of fresh sausage ravioli
1 cup flour
1 cup marinara sauce
4 eggs, beaten in a bowl
2 cups breadcrumbs
2 tbsp Parmesan cheese, grated

Directions:
Preheat the air fryer to 400 F. In a bowl, mix breadcrumbs with Parmesan cheese. Dip sausage ravioli into the flour, then into the eggs, and finally in the breadcrumb mixture. Arrange the coated ravioli on the greased frying basket in an even layer and spritz them with cooking spray. AirFry for 10-12 minutes, turning once halfway through cooking until nice and golden. Serve hot with the marinara sauce.

Nutrition Facts (per serving):
Calories: 430 | Carbohydrates: 42g | Protein: 18g | Fat: 20g | Fiber: 2g

 Servings: 4 20 minutes

543 Egg & Cauliflower Rice Casserole

Ingredients:
1 head cauliflower, cut into florets
2 tbsp olive oil
1 yellow bell pepper, chopped
1 cup okra, chopped
½ onion, chopped
Salt and black pepper to taste
1 tbsp soy sauce
2 eggs, beaten

Directions:
Preheat the air fryer to 380 F. Grease a baking dish with cooking spray.
Pulse cauliflower in a food processor until it resembles rice. Add the cauli rice to the baking dish and mix in bell pepper, okra, onion, soy sauce, salt, and black pepper. Pour the beaten eggs over and drizzle with olive oil. Place the dish in the air fryer and Bake for 12-14 minutes until golden. Serve.

Nutrition Facts (per serving):
Calories: 160 | Carbohydrates: 9g | Protein: 7g | Fat: 11g | Fiber: 3g

 Servings: 2 25 minutes

544 Beef Liver with Onions

Ingredients:
1 lb beef liver, sliced
2 onions, sliced
1 tbsp black truffle oil
Salt and black pepper to taste
1 garlic clove, minced
1 tbsp fresh parsley, chopped

Directions:
Preheat the air fryer to 360 F. Season the liver with salt and pepper; brush with the oil. Spread the onion slices on a greased frying basket. Bake in the fryer for 5 minutes. Arrange the liver on top of the onions and Bake further for 12-14 minutes, turning once halfway through cooking. Serve with garlic and parsley.

Nutrition Facts (per serving):
Calories: 312 | Carbohydrates: 7.8g | Protein: thirty-one.6g | Fat: 16.4g | Fiber: 1.4g

Servings: 10 | 10 Minutes

545 Bacon-wrapped Goat Cheese Poppers

Ingredients:
10 large jalapeño peppers
8 ounces goat cheese
10 slices bacon

Directions:
Preheat the air fryer to 380ºF.
Slice the jalapeños in half. Carefully remove the veins and seeds of the jalapeños with a spoon.
Fill each jalapeño half with 2 teaspoons goat cheese.
Cut the bacon in half lengthwise to make long strips.
Wrap the jalapeños with bacon, trying to cover the entire length of the jalapeño.
Place the bacon-wrapped jalapeños into the air fryer basket. Cook the stuffed jalapeños for 10 minutes or until bacon is crispy.

Nutrition Facts (per serving):
Calories: 170 | Carbohydrates: 2g | Protein: 6g | Fat: 15g | Fiber: <1g

Servings: 4 | 15 minutes

546 Roasted Coconut Carrots

Ingredients:
1 tbsp coconut oil, melted
1 lb horse carrots, sliced
Salt and black pepper to taste
½ tsp chili powder

Directions:
Preheat the air fryer to 400 F.
In a bowl, mix the carrots with coconut oil, chili powder, salt, and black pepper. Place them in the fryer and AirFry for 7 minutes. Shake the basket and cook for another 5 minutes until golden brown. Serve.

Nutrition Facts (per serving):
Calories: 100 | Carbohydrates: 12g | Protein: 1g | Fat: 6g | Fiber: 3g

Servings: 1 | 20 minutes

547 Cheesy Vegetable Quesadilla

Ingredients:
2 flour tortillas
¼ cup gouda cheese, shredded
¼ yellow bell pepper, sliced
¼ zucchini, sliced
½ green onion, sliced
1 tbsp fresh cilantro, chopped
1 tsp olive oil

Directions:
Preheat the air fryer to 390 F. Place a flour tortilla in the greased frying basket and top with gouda cheese, bell pepper, zucchini, cilantro, and green onion. Cover with the other tortilla and brush with olive oil. Bake for 10 minutes or until lightly browned. Cut into 4 wedges and serve.

Nutrition Facts (per serving):
Calories: 330 | Carbohydrates: 30g | Protein: 10g | Fat: 18g | Fiber: 3g

Servings: 4 | 25 minutes

548 Lamb Chops with Lemony Couscous

Ingredients:
4 lamb chops
2 tbsp olive oil
2 garlic cloves, minced
Salt and black pepper to taste
2 tbsp fresh thyme, chopped
1 cup couscous
1 lemon, zested and juiced

Directions:
Preheat the air fryer to 400 F. Rub the lamb chops with olive oil, garlic, salt, and black pepper. Place them in the greased frying basket. AirFry for 14-16 minutes, turning once halfway through cooking.
Meanwhile, place the couscous in a heatproof bowl and pour over 1½ cups of salted boiling water. Cover and let it sit for 8-12 minutes until all the water is absorbed. Gently stir in the lemon juice and lemon zest and fresh thyme with a fork. Serve the lamb on a bed of couscous and enjoy!

Nutrition Facts (per serving):
Calories: 412 | Carbohydrates: 18.7g | Protein: 28.3g | Fat: 25.6g | Fiber: 1.8g

 Servings: 8   7 Minutes

549 Hot Dogs

Ingredients:
8 beef hot dogs
8 hot dog buns

Directions:
Preheat the air fryer to 400°F. Place hot dogs in the air fryer basket and cook 7 minutes. Place each hot dog in a bun. Serve warm.

Nutrition Facts (per serving):
Calories: 290 | Carbohydrates: 24g | Protein: 11g | Fat: 17g | Fiber: 1g

---

Servings: 2   15 minutes + cooling time

550 Brie Cheese Croutons with Herbs

Ingredients:
2 tbsp olive oil
1 tbsp french herbs
6 oz brie cheese, chopped
2 slices bread, halved

Directions:
Preheat the air fryer to 340 F. Brush the bread slices with olive oil and sprinkle with herbs. Top with brie cheese. Place in the greased frying basket and Bake for 10-12 minutes. Let cool, then cut into cubes.

Nutrition Facts (per serving):
Calories: 410 | Carbohydrates: 22g | Protein: 10g | Fat: 33g | Fiber: 1g

---

 Servings: 4   20 minutes

551 Mexican Chile Relleno

Ingredients:
2 (8-oz) cans whole green chiles, drained
2 cups Mexican cheese, shredded
1 cup all-purpose flour
2 whole eggs
½ cup milk

Directions:
Preheat the air fryer to 380 F. Lay the green chilies on a plate, cut them open at the top and fill them with cheese. In a bowl, whisk the eggs, milk, and half of the flour. Pour the remaining flour on a flat plate. Dip the chilies in the flour first, then in the egg mixture, and arrange them in the greased frying basket. AirFry for 8-10 minutes, flipping once halfway through. Serve with slices of avocado if desired.

Nutrition Facts (per serving):
Calories: 390 | Carbohydrates: 30g | Protein: 25g | Fat: 18g | Fiber: 4g

---

Servings: 4   25 minutes

552 Easy Lamb Chop Bites

Ingredients:
1 lb lamb loin chops
1 egg
¼ cup buttermilk
1 cup corn flakes, crushed
Salt and black pepper to taste

Directions:
In a bowl, whisk the egg with buttermilk. Add in the lamb and stir to coat. On a plate, spread the corn flakes and mix them with salt and pepper. Coat the lamb chops in the cornflakes and arrange them on the greased frying basket. AirFry for 12-16 minutes at 360 F, turning once halfway through. Serve.

Nutrition Facts (per serving):
Calories: 398 | Carbohydrates: 10.6g | Protein: 27.4g | Fat: 27.2g | Fiber: 0.6g

Servings: 4   5 Minutes

553 Marinated Steak Kebabs

Ingredients:
1 pound strip steak, fat trimmed, cut into 1" cubes
½ cup soy sauce
¼ cup olive oil
1 tablespoon granular brown erythritol
½ teaspoon salt
¼ teaspoon ground black pepper
1 medium green bell pepper, seeded and chopped into 1" cubes

Directions:
Place steak into a large sealable bowl or bag and pour in soy sauce and olive oil. Add erythritol, then stir to coat steak. Marinate at room temperature 30 minutes. Remove streak from marinade and sprinkle with salt and black pepper.
Place meat and vegetables onto 6" skewer sticks, alternating between steak and bell pepper.
Place kebabs into ungreased air fryer basket. Adjust the temperature to 400°F and set the timer for 5 minutes. Steak will be done when crispy at the edges and peppers are tender. Serve warm.

Nutrition Facts (per serving):
Calories: 310 | Carbohydrates: 4g | Protein: 27g | Fat: 20g | Fiber: 1g

---

Servings: 4   15 minutes

554 French Beans with Toasted Almonds

Ingredients:
1 lb French beans, trimmed
Salt and black pepper to taste
½ tbsp onion powder
2 tbsp olive oil
½ cup toasted almonds, chopped

Directions:
Preheat air fryer to 400 F. In a bowl, drizzle the beans with olive oil. Add onion powder, salt, and pepper and toss to coat. AirFry for 10-12 minutes, shaking once. Sprinkle with almonds and serve.

Nutrition Facts (per serving):
Calories: 145 | Carbohydrates: 9g | Protein: 4g | Fat: 11g | Fiber: 4g

---

Servings: 2   20 minutes

555 Cinnamon Grilled Pineapples

Ingredients:
1 tsp cinnamon
5 pineapple slices
½ cup brown sugar
1 tbsp mint, chopped
1 tbsp honey

Directions:
Preheat air fryer to 340 F. In a small bowl, mix the sugar and cinnamon. Drizzle the sugar mixture over the pineapple slices. Place them in the greased frying basket and Bake for 5 minutes. Flip the pineapples and cook for 4 to 6 more minutes. Remove, drizzle with honey and sprinkle with fresh mint.

Nutrition Facts (per serving):
Calories: 180 | Carbohydrates: 47g | Protein: 1g | Fat: 0g | Fiber: 3g

---

Servings: 4   25 minutes

556 Lamb Taquitos

Ingredients:
1 lb lamb meat, sliced into strips
2 tbsp olive oil
2 tsp fresh cilantro, chopped
2 tsp fire-roasted green chilies
2 tbsp queso fresco, crumbled
4 corn tortillas

Directions:
Warm olive oil in a skillet over medium heat and stir-fry the lamb for 5-6 minutes. Remove and stir in green chilies. Preheat the air fryer to 400 F. Divide the mixture between tortillas and roll up them. Spritz with cooking spray and AirFry for 8 minutes, turning once. Top with queso fresco and cilantro to serve.

Nutrition Facts (per serving):
Calories: 398 | Carbohydrates: 17.2g | Protein: 26.7g | Fat: 25.8g | Fiber: 2.1g

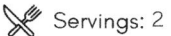 Servings: 2 8 Minutes

557 Grilled Prosciutto Wrapped Fig

Ingredients:

2 whole figs, sliced in quarters
8 prosciutto slices
Pepper and salt to taste

Directions:

Wrap a prosciutto slice around one slice of figs and then thread into skewer. Repeat process for remaining Ingredients. Place on skewer rack in air fryer. For 8 minutes, cook on 390°F. Halfway through cooking time, turnover skewers.
Serve and enjoy.

Nutrition Facts (per serving):
Calories: 150 | Carbohydrates: 8g | Protein: 9g | Fat: 9g | Fiber: 1g

Servings: 4 15 minutes

558 Spiced Almonds

Ingredients:

½ tsp ground cinnamon
½ tsp smoked paprika
1 cup almonds
1 egg white
Sea salt to taste

Directions:

Preheat the air fryer to 310 F. Grease the frying basket with cooking spray. In a bowl, whisk the egg white with cinnamon and paprika and stir in the almonds. Spread the almonds in the frying basket and AirFry for 12-14 minutes, shaking once or twice. Remove and sprinkle with sea salt to serve.

Nutrition Facts (per serving):
Calories: 200 | Carbohydrates: 7g | Protein: 7g | Fat: 17g | Fiber: 4g

 Servings: 4 20 minutes

559 Italian Pork Scallopini

Ingredients:

4 pork loin thin steaks
Salt and black pepper to taste
¼ cup Parmesan cheese, grated
2 tbsp Italian breadcrumbs

Directions:

Preheat the air fryer to 390 F. Spritz the frying basket with cooking spray.
In a bowl, mix Italian breadcrumbs and Parmesan cheese. Season the pork steaks with salt and black pepper. Roll them in the breadcrumb mixture and spray them with cooking spray. Transfer to the frying basket and AirFry for 14-16 minutes, turning once halfway through. Serve immediately.

Nutrition Facts (per serving):
Calories: 240 | Carbohydrates: 3g | Protein: 28g | Fat: 13g | Fiber: 0.3g

 Servings: 4 25 minutes

560 One-Tray Parmesan Chicken Wings

Ingredients:

8 chicken wings
1 tsp Dijon mustard
Salt and black pepper to taste
2 tbsp olive oil
4 tbsp Parmesan cheese, grated
2 tsp fresh parsley, chopped

Directions:

Preheat the air fryer to 380 F. Season the wings with salt and pepper. Brush them with mustard. Coat the chicken wings with 2 tbsp of Parmesan cheese, drizzle with olive oil, and place in the greased frying basket. AirFry for 14-16 minutes, turning once. When cooked, sprinkle with the remaining Parmesan cheese and top freshly chopped parsley.

Nutrition Facts (per serving):
Calories: 276 | Carbohydrates: 0.6g | Protein: 21.3g | Fat: 20.3g | Fiber: 0.1g

Servings: 4 | 8 Minutes

561 Corn Dogs

Ingredients:
1½ cups shredded mozzarella cheese
1 ounce cream cheese
½ cup blanched finely ground almond flour
4 beef hot dogs

Directions:
Place mozzarella, cream cheese, and flour in a large microwave-safe bowl. Microwave on high 45 seconds, then stir with a fork until a soft ball of dough forms. Press dough out into a 12" × 6" rectangle, then use a knife to separate into four smaller rectangles. Wrap each hot dog in one rectangle of dough and place into ungreased air fryer basket. Adjust the temperature to 400°F and set the timer for 8 minutes, turning corn dogs halfway through cooking. Corn dogs will be golden brown when done. Serve warm.

Nutrition Facts (per serving):
Calories: 320 | Carbohydrates: 3g | Protein: 15g | Fat: 27g | Fiber: 1g

---

Servings: 4 | 15 minutes

562 Spiced Almond

Ingredients:
½ tsp ground cinnamon
½ tsp smoked paprika
1 cup almonds
1 egg white
Sea salt to taste

Directions:
Preheat the air fryer to 310 F. Grease the frying basket with cooking spray. In a bowl, whisk the egg white with cinnamon and paprika and stir in the almonds. Spread the almonds in the frying basket and AirFry for 12-14 minutes, shaking once or twice. Remove and sprinkle with sea salt to serve.

Nutrition Facts (per serving):
Calories: 210 | Carbohydrates: 8g | Protein: 8g | Fat: 18g | Fiber: 3.5g

---

 Servings: 4   20 minutes

563 Spicy Sweet Beef with Veggie Topping

Ingredients:
2 beef steaks, sliced into thin strips
2 garlic cloves, minced
2 tsp maple syrup
1 tsp oyster sauce
1 tsp cayenne pepper
½ tsp olive oil
Juice of 1 lime
Salt and black pepper to taste
1 cauliflower, cut into florets
2 carrots, cut into chunks
1 cup green peas

Directions:
Preheat the air fryer to 400 F. In a bowl, place the beef strips, garlic, maple syrup, oyster sauce, cayenne pepper, olive oil, lime juice, salt, and black pepper; stir to combine. Transfer the mixture to the frying basket. Top with the veggies. Transfer to the fryer and Bake for 12-14 minutes, shaking once.

Nutrition Facts (per serving):
Calories: 276 | Carbohydrates: 14.2g | Protein: 22.5g | Fat: 13.5g | Fiber: 4.8g

---

 Servings: 4   25 minutes

564 Quinoa Chicken Nuggets

Ingredients:
2 chicken breasts, cut into large chunks
½ cup cooked quinoa, cooled
1 cup flour
2 eggs, beaten
½ tsp cayenne pepper
Salt and black pepper to taste

Directions:
In a bowl, beat the egg with salt and black pepper. Spread the flour on a plate and mix in the cayenne pepper. Coat the chicken in the flour, then dip in the eggs, shake off, and coat in the quinoa. Press firmly so the quinoa sticks on the chunks. Spritz with cooking spray and AirFry the nuggets in the fryer for 14-16 minutes at 360 F, turning once halfway through cooking. Serve hot.

Nutrition Facts (per serving):
Calories: 276 | Carbohydrates: 16.2g | Protein: 25.1g | Fat: 11.2g | Fiber: 1.1g

Servings: 4 — 8 Minutes

565 Steak Bites And Spicy Dipping Sauce

Ingredients:
- 2 pounds sirloin steak, cut into 2" cubes
- 2 teaspoons salt
- 1 teaspoon ground black pepper
- 1 teaspoon garlic powder
- ½ cup mayonnaise
- 2 tablespoons sriracha

Directions:
Preheat the air fryer to 400°F. Sprinkle steak with salt, pepper, and garlic powder. Place steak in the air fryer basket and cook 8 minutes, shaking the basket twice during cooking, until internal temperature reaches at least 160°F. In a small bowl, combine mayonnaise and sriracha. Serve with steak bites for dipping.

Nutrition Facts (per serving):
Calories: 540 | Carbohydrates: 1g | Protein: 47g | Fat: 38g | Fiber: 0g

---

Servings: 5 — 15 minutes

566 Sweet Mixed Nuts

Ingredients:
- ½ cup pecans
- ½ cup walnuts
- ½ cup almonds
- A pinch of cayenne pepper
- 1 tbsp sugar
- 2 tbsp egg whites
- 2 tsp ground cinnamon
- Cooking spray

Directions:
Add cayenne pepper, sugar, and cinnamon to a bowl and mix well; set aside. In another bowl, mix pecans, walnuts, almonds, and egg whites. Add in the spice mixture and stir. Grease a baking dish with cooking spray. Pour in the nuts and place the dish in the fryer. Bake for 5-7 minutes. Stir the nuts using a wooden spoon and cook for 4-5 more minutes. Pour the nuts into the bowl and let cool slightly.

Nutrition Facts (per serving):
Calories: 259 | Carbohydrates: 8g | Protein: 6g | Fat: 24g | Fiber: 2g

---

 Servings: 1 20 minutes

567 Wiener Beef Schnitzel

Ingredients:
- 1 (½ inch thick) top sirloin steak
- 1 egg, beaten
- 2 oz panko breadcrumbs
- 2 tbsp flour, sifted
- Lemon slices
- ¼ tsp garlic powder
- 1 parsley butter slice
- Salt and black pepper to taste

Directions:
Preheat the air fryer to 350 F. Combine the breadcrumbs, garlic, salt, and pepper in a bowl. Dredge the steak in the flour, then dip in the egg, and finally toss it into the crumbs mixture. Place in the greased frying basket and AirFry for 12 minutes, turning once. Top with parsley butter and lemon slices.

Nutrition Facts (per serving):
Calories: 496 | Carbohydrates: 16.8g | Protein: 36.4g | Fat: 31.8g | Fiber: 1.1g

---

 Servings: 4 25 minutes

568 San Antonio Taco Chicken Strips

Ingredients:
- 3 mixed bell peppers, cut into chunks
- 1 red onion, sliced
- 1 lb chicken tenderloins, cut into strips
- 1 tbsp olive oil
- 2 tbsp cilantro, chopped
- 1 tbsp taco seasoning

Directions:
Preheat the air fryer to 375 F. Mix the strips, bell peppers, onion, olive oil, and taco seasoning in a large bowl and stir until the strips are coated. Place the strips and veggies in the greased fryer basket and AirFry for 7 minutes. Shake the basket, and cook for 5-8 more minutes, until the chicken is thoroughly cooked, and the veggies are starting to char. Serve topped with cilantro.

Nutrition Facts (per serving):
Calories: 243 | Carbohydrates: 6.9g | Protein: 26.1g | Fat: 11.3g | Fiber: 1.8g

Servings: 2 | 7 Minutes

569 Blackened Steak Nuggets

Ingredients:
1 pound rib eye steak, cut into 1" cubes
2 tablespoons salted butter, melted
½ teaspoon paprika
½ teaspoon salt
¼ teaspoon garlic powder
¼ teaspoon onion powder
¼ teaspoon ground black pepper
⅛ teaspoon cayenne pepper

Directions:
Place steak into a large bowl and pour in butter. Toss to coat. Sprinkle with remaining ingredients.
Place bites into ungreased air fryer basket. Adjust the temperature to 400ºF and set the timer for 7 minutes, shaking the basket three times during cooking. Steak will be crispy on the outside and browned when done and internal temperature is at least 150ºF for medium and 180ºF for well-done. Serve warm.

Nutrition Facts (per serving):
Calories: 620 | Carbohydrates: 1g | Protein: 45g | Fat: 48g | Fiber: 0g

---

Servings: 4 | 15 minutes

570 Effortless Beef Short Ribs

Ingredients:
1 ½ lb bone-in beef short ribs
½ cup soy sauce
¼ cup white wine vinegar
1 brown onion, chopped
1 tbsp ginger powder
2 garlic cloves, minced
1 tbsp olive oil
2 tbsp chives, chopped
Salt and black pepper to taste

Directions:
In a shallow bowl, mix the short ribs, soy sauce, wine vinegar, onion, ginger powder, garlic, olive oil, salt, and pepper. Cover and marinate in the fridge for at least 2 hours. Preheat the air fryer to 390 F.
Arrange the ribs on the frying basket and Bake for 12 minutes. Slide the basket out, flip, and cook for another 7-8 minutes until browned and crispy. Serve sprinkled with freshly chopped chives.

Nutrition Facts (per serving):
Calories: 355 | Carbohydrates: 3g | Protein: 22g | Fat: 27g | Fiber: 0.3g

---

 Servings: 4 20 minutes

571 Sweet & Sour Lamb Strips

Ingredients:
1 cup cornflour
1 tsp garlic powder
1 tsp allspice
Salt and black pepper to taste
2 eggs
1 lb lean lamb, cut into strips
For the sauce
6 tbsp ketchup
½ lemon, juiced
1 tsp honey
2 tbsp soy sauce

Directions:
Preheat the air fryer to 350 F. In a bowl, whisk all the sauce ingredients with ½ cup of water until smooth; reserve. In another bowl, mix the garlic powder, cornflour, allspice, salt, and black pepper.
In a third bowl, beat the eggs with a pinch of salt. Coat the lamb in the cornflour mixture, then dip in the eggs, then again in the cornflour mixture. Spray with cooking spray and place in the frying basket. AirFry for 14-16 minutes, shaking once halfway through. Serve drizzled with the prepared sauce.

Nutrition Facts (per serving):
Calories: 376 | Carbohydrates: 22.3g | Protein: 27.1g | Fat: 19.3g | Fiber: 0.6g

---

 Servings: 4 25 minutes

572 Cajun Chicken Tenders

Ingredients:
1 lb chicken breasts, sliced
3 eggs
1 cup flour
2 tbsp olive oil
½ tbsp garlic powder
Salt and black pepper to taste
1 tbsp Cajun seasoning
¼ cup milk

Directions:
Sprinkle the chicken slices with garlic powder and Cajun seasoning. Pour the flour on a plate. In a bowl, whisk the eggs along with milk and olive oil. Season with salt and black pepper.
Preheat the air fryer to 370 F. Dip the chicken slices into the egg mixture, and then coat in the flour. Arrange them on the greased frying basket and AirFry for 12-14 minutes, flipping once until crispy.

Nutrition Facts (per serving):
Calories: 326 | Carbohydrates: 13.8g | Protein: 30.6g | Fat: 15.2g | Fiber: 0.5g

Servings: 1 | 10 minutes

573 Turkey & Mushroom Sandwich

Ingredients:
⅓ cup leftover turkey, shredded
⅓ cup sliced mushrooms, sauteed
½ tbsp butter, softened
2 tomato slices
½ tsp red pepper flakes
Salt and black pepper to taste
1 hamburger bun, halved

Directions:
Preheat the air fryer to 350 F. Brush the bun bottom with butter and top with shredded turkey. Arrange the mushroom slices on top of the turkey. Cover with tomato slices and sprinkle with salt, black pepper, and red flakes. Top with the bun top and AirFry for 5-8 minutes until crispy. Serve and enjoy!

Nutrition Facts (per serving):
Calories: 300 | Carbohydrates: 30g | Protein: 18g | Fat: 11g | Fiber: 3g

---

Servings: 4 | 15 minutes

574 Fiery Prawns

Ingredients:
8 prawns, cleaned
Salt and black pepper to taste
½ tsp ground cayenne pepper
½ tsp red chili flakes
½ tsp ground cumin
½ tsp garlic powder

Directions:
In a bowl, season the prawns with salt and black pepper. Sprinkle with cayenne pepper, chili flakes, cumin, and garlic, and stir to coat. Spray the frying basket with oil and lay the prawns in an even layer. AirFry for 8-10 minutes at 340 F, turning once halfway through. Serve with sweet chili sauce if desired.

Nutrition Facts (per serving):
Calories: 39 | Carbohydrates: 0.8g | Protein: 7g | Fat: 0.7g | Fiber: 0.4g

---

Servings: 6 | 20 minutes

575 Spiced Chicken Tacos

Ingredients:
1 tbsp buffalo sauce
2 cups shredded cooked chicken
6 oz cream cheese, softened
2 oz sharp cheese, grated
1 tbsp olive oil
1 tsp ground cumin
½ tsp smoked paprika
12 flour tortillas

Directions:
Preheat air fryer to 360 F. Stir the cheeses and Buffalo sauce in a bowl, then add the chicken and stir some more. On a clean workspace, lay the tortillas and spoon 2-3 tablespoons of the chicken mixture at the center of each tortilla. Sprinkle with cumin and paprika. Roll them up and put them in the air fryer, seam side down. Spray each tortilla with olive oil and AirFry for 8-10 minutes or until golden and crisp.

Nutrition Facts (per serving):
Calories: 342 | Carbohydrates: 17.6g | Protein: 21.4g | Fat: 20.8g | Fiber: 1.1g

---

Servings: 4 | 25 minutes

576 Almond-Fried Crispy Chicken

Ingredients:
4 chicken breasts, cubed
2 cups almond meal
3 whole eggs
½ cup cornstarch
Salt and black pepper to taste
½ tsp cayenne pepper

Directions:
Preheat the air fryer to 350 F. In a bowl, mix the cornstarch, salt, black pepper, and cayenne pepper and toss in the chicken. In another bowl, beat the eggs. In a third bowl, pour the almond meal. Dredge the chicken in the eggs, then in almond meal. AirFry for 14-16 minutes, shaking once or twice. Serve.

Nutrition Facts (per serving):
Calories: 386 | Carbohydrates: 10.7g | Protein: 32.4g | Fat: 23.8g | Fiber: 2.4g

Servings: 1 — 10 minutes

577 Bacon & Egg Sandwich

Ingredients:
1 egg, fried
1 slice English bacon
Salt and black pepper to taste
2 bread slices
½ tbsp butter, softened

Directions:
Preheat the air fryer to 400 F. Spread butter on one side of the bread slices. Add the fried egg on top and season with salt and black pepper. Top with the bacon and cover with the other slice of the bread. Place in the frying basket and AirFry for 4-6 minutes. Serve warm.

Nutrition Facts (per serving):
Calories: 450 | Carbohydrates: 32.5g | Protein: 19g | Fat: 24g | Fiber: 2g

Servings: 4 — 15 minutes

578 Crispy Prawns in Bacon Wraps

Ingredients:
8 bacon slices
8 jumbo prawns, peeled and deveined

Directions:
Preheat the air fryer to 400 F. Wrap each prawn from head to tail in each bacon slice. Make sure to overlap to keep the bacon in place. Secure the ends with toothpicks. Arrange the bacon-wrapped prawns in the greased frying basket and AirFry for 9-12 minutes, turning once. Serve hot.

Nutrition Facts (per serving):
Calories: 254 | Carbohydrates: 0g | Protein: 21g | Fat: 18.5g | Fiber: 0g

 Servings: 2 20 minutes

579 Rice Krispies Chicken Goujons

Ingredients:
2 chicken breasts, cut into strips
Salt and black pepper to taste
½ tsp dried tarragon
½ cup rice Krispies
1 egg, beaten
½ cup plain flour
1 tbsp butter, melted

Directions:
Preheat the air fryer to 390 F. Line the frying basket with baking paper. Season the chicken with salt and pepper. Roll the strips in flour, then dip in egg, and finally coat in the rice Krispies. Place the strips in the fryer, drizzle with butter, and AirFry for 12-14 minutes, shaking once. Top with tarragon to serve.

Nutrition Facts (per serving):
Calories: 364 | Carbohydrates: 18.7g | Protein: 33.2g | Fat: 16.4g | Fiber: 0.6g

 Servings: 2 25 minutes

580 Lemony Chicken Breast

Ingredients:
1 chicken breast
2 lemon, juiced and rind reserved
1 tbsp chicken seasoning
1 tbsp garlic puree
Salt and black pepper to taste

Directions:
Preheat the air fryer to 350 F. Place a silver foil sheet on a flat surface. Add all seasonings along with the lemon rind. Lay the chicken breast onto a chopping board and trim any fat.
Season each side with the seasoning. Place in the silver foil sheet, seal, and flatten with a rolling pin. Place the breast in the frying basket and AirFry for 14-16 minutes, flipping once halfway through.

Nutrition Facts (per serving):
Calories: 172 | Carbohydrates: 2.6g | Protein: 26.4g | Fat: 5.4g | Fiber: 0.3g

Servings: 2 — 7 minutes

581 Mediterranean Avocado Toast

Ingredients:
2 slices thick whole grain bread
4 thin tomato slices
1 ripe avocado, pitted, peeled, and sliced
1 tbsp olive oil
1 tbsp pinch of salt
½ tsp chili flakes

Directions:
Preheat the air fryer to 370 F. Arrange the bread slices in the frying basket and toast them for 3 minutes. Add the avocado to a bowl and mash it up with a fork until smooth. Season with salt.
When the toasted bread is ready, remove it to a plate. Spread the avocado and cover with thin tomato slices. Drizzle with olive oil, sprinkle the toasts with chili flakes and serve.

Nutrition Facts (per serving):
Calories: 306 | Carbohydrates: 25.5g | Protein: 6.8g | Fat: 20g | Fiber: 8.5g

---

Servings: 2 — 15 minutes

582 Cajun-Rubbed Jumbo Shrimp

Ingredients:
1 lb jumbo shrimp, deveined
Salt to taste
¼ tsp old bay seasoning
⅓ tsp smoked paprika
¼ tsp cayenne pepper
2 tbsp olive oil

Directions:
Preheat the air fryer to 390 F. In a bowl, add the shrimp, paprika, olive oil, salt, old bay seasoning, and cayenne pepper; mix well. Place the shrimp in the fryer and AirFry for 8-10 minutes, shaking once.

Nutrition Facts (per serving):
Calories: 315 | Carbohydrates: 0.5g | Protein: 40g | Fat: 16g | Fiber: 0.15g

---

Servings: 4 — 20 minutes

583 Crispy Chicken Tenders with Hot Aioli

Ingredients:
1 lb chicken breasts, cut into strips
4 tbsp olive oil
1 cup breadcrumbs
Salt and black pepper to taste
½ tbsp garlic powder
½ tsp cayenne pepper
½ cup mayonnaise
2 tbsp lemon juice
½ tbsp ground chili

Directions:
Preheat the air fryer to 390 F. Mix the crumbs, salt, black pepper, garlic powder, and cayenne pepper in a bowl. Brush the strips with some olive oil. Coat them in the crumbs mixture and arrange them in the greased frying basket in an even layer. AirFry for 12-14 minutes, turning once halfway through. To prepare the hot aioli: add the mayo, lemon juice and ground chili in a small bowl and whisk to combine. Serve with the chicken tenders and enjoy!

Nutrition Facts (per serving):
Calories: 386 | Carbohydrates: 10.6g | Protein: 28.9g | Fat: 25.4g | Fiber: 0.7g

---

Servings: 4 — 25 minutes

584 Chicken Parmigiana with Fresh Rosemary

Ingredients:
1 lb chicken breasts, halved
1 cup seasoned breadcrumbs
½ cup Parmesan cheese, grated
Salt and black pepper to taste
2 eggs
2 sprigs rosemary, chopped

Directions:
Preheat the air fryer to 380 F. Put the chicken halves on a clean flat surface and cover with a clingfilm. Gently pound them to become thinner using a rolling pin. Beat the eggs in a bowl and season them with salt and black pepper. In a separate bowl, mix breadcrumbs with Parmesan cheese.
Dip the chicken in the eggs, then in the crumbs and spray with cooking spray. AirFry them for 6 minutes, flip and cook for 5-7 more minutes or until golden and crispy. Sprinkle with rosemary to serve.

Nutrition Facts (per serving):
Calories: 362 | Carbohydrates: 11.4g | Protein: 31.8g | Fat: 20.2g | Fiber: 0.6g

Servings: 2 — 7 minutes

585 Prosciutto & Mozzarella Bruschetta

Ingredients:
½ cup tomatoes, finely chopped
3 oz mozzarella cheese, grated
3 prosciutto slices, chopped
1 tbsp olive oil
1 tsp dried basil
6 small French bread slices

Directions:
Preheat the air fryer to 350 F. Add in the bread slices and fry for 3 minutes to toast them. Remove and top the slices with tomatoes, prosciutto, and mozzarella cheese. Sprinkle basil all over and drizzle with olive oil. Return to the fryer and AirFry for 1 more minute, just to heat through. Serve warm.

Nutrition Facts (per serving):
Calories: 450 | Carbohydrates: 32.8g | Protein: 23.3g | Fat: 24.5g | Fiber: 2.1g

---

Servings: 4 — 15 minutes

586 Breaded Scallops

Ingredients:
1 lb fresh scallops
3 tbsp flour
1 egg, lightly beaten
1 cup seasoned breadcrumbs
2 tbsp olive oil
½ tsp fresh parsley, chopped

Directions:
Preheat the air fryer to 360 F. Coat the scallops in flour. Dip them in the egg, then into the crumbs. Spray with olive oil and AirFry for 6-8 minutes, flipping once until golden. Serve topped with parsley.

Nutrition Facts (per serving):
Calories: 280 | Carbohydrates: 25g | Protein: 23g | Fat: 10g | Fiber: 0.7g

---

Servings: 4 — 20 minutes

587 Greek Chicken Gyros

Ingredients:
2 chicken breasts, cut into strips
Salt and black pepper to taste
1 cup flour
1 egg, beaten
½ cup breadcrumbs
4 flatbreads
2 cups white cabbage, shredded
3 tbsp Greek yogurt dressing

Directions:
Preheat the air fryer to 380 F. Season the chicken with salt and black pepper. Pour the breadcrumbs in one bowl, the flour in another, and the egg in a third bowl. Dredge the strips in flour, then in the egg, and finally in the crumbs. Spray with cooking oil and transfer to the fryer. AirFry for 12-14 minutes, flipping once halfway through. Serve the "pitas" filled with the strips, cabbage, and yogurt dressing.

Nutrition Facts (per serving):
Calories: 376 | Carbohydrates: 29.4g | Protein: 27.2g | Fat: 15.8g | Fiber: 2.1g

---

Servings: 4 — 25 minutes

588 Spinach Loaded Chicken Breasts

Ingredients:
1 cup spinach, chopped
4 tbsp cottage cheese, crumbled
2 chicken breasts
2 tbsp Italian seasoning
2 tbsp olive oil

Directions:
Preheat the air fryer to 390 F. Grease the basket with cooking spray. Mix spinach and cottage cheese in a bowl. Halve the breasts with a knife and flatten them with a meat mallet. Season with Italian seasoning. Divide the spinach/cheese mixture between the chicken pieces.
Roll them up to form cylinders and use toothpicks to secure them. Brush with olive oil and place them in the frying basket. Bake for 7-8 minutes, turn, and cook for 6 minutes or until golden brown. Serve.

Nutrition Facts (per serving):
Calories: 264 | Carbohydrates: 2.4g | Protein: 27.8g | Fat: 15.1g | Fiber: 0.6g

Servings: 1   10 minutes

589 Toasted Herb & Garlic Bagel

Ingredients:
1 tbsp butter, softened
¼ tsp dried basil
¼ tsp dried parsley
¼ tsp garlic powder
1 tbsp Parmesan cheese, grated
Salt and black pepper to taste
1 bagel, halved

Directions:
Preheat the air fryer to 370 degrees. Place the bagel halves in the frying basket and AirFry for 3 minutes. Mix butter, Parmesan cheese, garlic, basil, and parsley in a bowl. Season with salt and pepper. Spread the mixture onto the toasted bagel and return to the fryer to AirFry for 3 more minutes.

Nutrition Facts (per serving):
Calories: 394 | Carbohydrates: 50.5g | Protein: 12.1g | Fat: 14.5g | Fiber: 2.1g

 Servings: 4   15 minutes

590 Buttered Crab Legs

Ingredients:
2 lb crab legs
2 tbsp butter, melted
1 tbsp fresh parsley

Directions:
Preheat the air fryer to 380 F. Place the legs in the greased frying basket and AirFry for 10-12 minutes, shaking once or twice. Pour the butter over crab legs, sprinkle with parsley, and serve. Work in batches.

Nutrition Facts (per serving):
Calories: 148 | Carbohydrates: 0g | Protein: 22.5g | Fat: 6g | Fiber: 0g

 Servings: 4   20 minutes

591 French-Style Sweet Chicken Breasts

Ingredients:
1 tsp yellow mustard
1 tbsp apricot jam
2 garlic cloves, minced
Salt and black pepper to taste
1 lb chicken breasts
3 tbsp butter, melted

Directions:
Preheat the air fryer to 360 F. In a bowl, mix together mustard, butter, garlic, apricot jam, black pepper, and salt. Rub the chicken with the mixture and place them in the greased frying basket. AirFry for 10 minutes, flip, and cook them for 5-6 more minutes or until golden and crispy. Slice before serving.

Nutrition Facts (per serving):
Calories: 296 | Carbohydrates: 4.6g | Protein: 27.4g | Fat: 18.2g | Fiber: 0.2g

 Servings: 4   25 minutes

592 Chicken Breasts "En Papillote"

Ingredients:
1 lb chicken breasts
2 tbsp butter, melted
Salt and black pepper to taste
½ tsp dried marjoram

Directions:
Preheat the air fryer to 380 F. Place each chicken breast on a 12x12 inches aluminum foil wrap, and season with salt and pepper. Top with marjoram and butter. Wrap the foil around the breasts in a loose way to create a flow of air. Bake the in the fryer for 15 minutes. Unwrap, let cool slightly, and serve.

Nutrition Facts (per serving):
Calories: 243 | Carbohydrates: 0.3g | Protein: 27.2g | Fat: 14.1g | Fiber: 0.1g

Servings: 1 | 10 minutes

593 Grilled Apple & Brie Sandwich

Ingredients:
2 bread slices
½ apple, thinly sliced
2 tsp butter
2 oz brie cheese, thinly sliced

Directions:
Spread butter on the outside of the bread slices and top with apple slices. Place the brie slices on top of the apple and cover with the other slice of bread. Bake in the air fryer for 5 minutes at 350 F. When ready, remove and cut diagonally to serve.

Nutrition Facts (per serving):
Calories: 500 | Carbohydrates: 44g | Protein: 16g | Fat: 26g | Fiber: 3.5g

Servings: 2 | 15 minutes

594 Soy Sauce-Glazed Cod

Ingredients:
2 cod fillets
1 tbsp olive oil
Salt and black pepper to taste
1 tbsp soy sauce
1 tbsp sesame oil
¼ tsp ginger powder
¼ tsp honey

Directions:
Preheat the air fryer to 370 F. In a bowl, combine olive oil, salt, and black pepper. Massage the fillets with the mixture. Place them on the greased frying basket and Bake in the fryer for 6 minutes.
Meanwhile, combine the soy sauce, ginger powder, honey, and sesame oil in a small bowl. Flip the fillets and brush them with the glaze. Bake for 3-5 more minutes until golden and crispy. Serve warm.

Nutrition Facts (per serving):
Calories: 232 | Carbohydrates: 1.6g | Protein: 23.5g | Fat: 14.5g | Fiber: 0.05g

 Servings: 4 20 minutes

595 French-Style Chicken Thighs

Ingredients:
1 tbsp herbs de Provence
1 lb bone-in, skinless chicken thighs
Salt and black pepper to taste
2 garlic cloves, minced
½ cup honey
¼ cup Dijon mustard
2 tbsp butter

Directions:
Preheat the air fryer to 390 F. In a bowl, mix herbs de Provence, salt, and pepper. Rub onto the chicken thighs. Transfer to the greased frying basket and Bake for 15 minutes, flipping once, until golden. Meanwhile, melt butter in a saucepan over medium heat. Stir in honey, mustard, and garlic; cook until reduced to a thick consistency, 3 minutes. Serve the chicken drizzled with the honey-mustard sauce.

Nutrition Facts (per serving):
Calories: 312 | Carbohydrates: 15.6g | Protein: 26.4g | Fat: 15.2g | Fiber: 0.3g

 Servings: 4 25 minutes

596 Ham & Cheese Chicken Breasts

Ingredients:
4 chicken breasts
4 ham slices
4 Swiss cheese slices
3 tbsp all-purpose flour
4 tbsp butter
½ tbsp paprika
1 tbsp chicken bouillon granules
¼ cup dry white wine
1 cup heavy cream

Directions:
Preheat the air fryer to 380 F. Pound the chicken and put a slice of ham and cheese onto each one. Fold the edges over the filling and seal them with toothpicks. In a bowl, combine paprika and flour, and coat in the chicken. Transfer them to the greased frying basket and Bake for 15 minutes, turning once.
In a large skillet over medium heat, melt the butter and add the bouillon granules, wine, and heavy cream. Bring to a boil, reduce the heat to low, and simmer for 5 minutes. Serve the chicken with sauce.

Nutrition Facts (per serving):
Calories: 312 | Carbohydrates: 15.6g | Protein: 26.4g | Fat: 15.2g | Fiber: 0.3g

Servings: 4   🕐 10 minutes

597 Cheddar Black Bean Burritos

Ingredients:

4 tortillas
1 cup cheddar cheese, grated
1 can (8 oz) black beans, drained
1 tsp taco seasoning

Directions:

Preheat the air fryer to 350 F. Mix the beans with the taco seasoning. Divide the bean mixture between the tortillas and top with cheddar cheese. Roll the burritos and arrange them on the greased frying basket. Place in the air fryer and Bake for 4-5 minutes, flip, and cook for 3 more minutes. Serve warm.

Nutrition Facts (per serving):
Calories: 270 | Carbohydrates: 22g | Protein: 11g | Fat: 14g | Fiber: 5g

 Servings: 4   🕐 15 minutes

598 Smoked Salmon & Cheddar Taquitos

Ingredients:

1 lb smoked salmon, chopped
Salt to taste
1 tbsp taco seasoning
1 cup cheddar cheese, shredded
1 lime, juiced
½ cup fresh cilantro, chopped
8 corn tortillas
1 cup hot salsa

Directions:

Preheat the air fryer to 390 F.
In a bowl, mix the salmon, taco seasoning, lime juice, cheddar cheese, salt, and cilantro. Divide the mixture between the tortillas. Wrap the tortillas around the filling and place them in the greased frying basket. Bake for 10-12 minutes, turning once halfway through cooking. Serve with hot salsa.

Nutrition Facts (per serving):
Calories: 410 | Carbohydrates: 26g | Protein: 32g | Fat: 18.8g | Fiber: 2.6g

 Servings: 4   🕐 20 minutes

599 Air Fried Chicken Bowl with Black Beans

Ingredients:

4 chicken breasts, cubed
1 can sweet corn
1 can black beans, rinsed and drained
1 cup red and green peppers, stripes, cooked
2 tbsp vegetable oil
1 tsp chili powder

Directions:

Preheat the air fryer to 380 F. Sprinkle the chicken with salt, black pepper, and a bit of oil. Place in the greased frying basket and AirFry for 14-16 minutes until golden and crispy. Meanwhile, in a deep skillet, pour the remaining oil and stir in chili powder, corn, peppers, and beans. Add a little bit of hot water and stir-fry for 3 minutes. Transfer the veggies to a serving platter and top with the fried chicken.

Nutrition Facts (per serving):
Calories: 328 | Carbohydrates: 18.6g | Protein: 30.2g | Fat: 13.2g | Fiber: 4.7g

 Servings: 4   25 minutes

600 Restaurant-Style Chicken with Yogurt Sauce

Ingredients:

½ cup breadcrumbs
2 whole eggs, beaten
½ cup all-purpose flour
Salt and black pepper to taste
2 tbsp olive oil
1 ¼ lb chicken tenders
1 cup Greek yogurt
1 tbsp lemon juice
1 tbsp fresh dill, chopped

Directions:

Preheat the air fryer to 380 F. Pour the crumbs, eggs, and flour into 3 separate bowls. Season the tenders with salt and pepper and dredge them first in the flour, then in eggs, and finally in the crumbs. AirFry them in the greased frying basket for 10 minutes. Flip and cook for 5 more minutes or until golden. Mix the yogurt with lemon juice, dill, salt, and pepper until smooth. Serve with the tenders.

Nutrition Facts (per serving):
Calories: 342 | Carbohydrates: 13.6g | Protein: 30.4g | Fat: 18.1g | Fiber: 0.6g

THANK YOU TO READERS & HAPPY COOKING!

Dear Reader,

Thank you from the bottom of my heart for choosing **"Time Saving Air Fryer Cookbook For Beginners: 600 Quick, Easy & Healthy Recipes for Busy People"** to be a part of your cooking journey.
Your time is valuable, and I am truly honored that you've spent it exploring these recipes, experimenting in your kitchen, and making them your own.

This book was written with one simple mission: to help busy people like you create healthy, delicious meals without the stress and time commitment of traditional cooking. Knowing that these recipes might find a place at your family table — perhaps even becoming part of your favorite mealtime memories — means the world to me.

If you enjoyed this book, I would be deeply grateful if you could take a moment to leave an honest review on Amazon. Your feedback not only helps other readers discover the book, but also inspires me to keep creating more resources to support your cooking adventures.

I hope your air fryer continues to bring you joy, flavor, and time saved for the things that truly matter.

With gratitude,

Printed in Dunstable, United Kingdom